# GEOGRAPHIC PERSONAS

# GEOGRAPHIC

# PERSONAS

*Self-Transformation and Performance in the American West*

BLAKE ALLMENDINGER

University of Nebraska Press | Lincoln

Library of Congress Cataloging-in-Publication Data
Names: Allmendinger, Blake, author.
Title: Geographic personas: self-transformation and performance in the American West / Blake Allmendinger.
Description: Lincoln: University of Nebraska Press, [2021] | Includes bibliographical references and index.
Identifiers: LCCN 2020038638
ISBN 9781496225061 (hardback)
ISBN 9781496226907 (epub)
ISBN 9781496226914 (mobi)
ISBN 9781496226921 (pdf)
Subjects: LCSH: American literature—West (U.S.)— History and criticism. | Identity (Philosophical concept) in literature. | Persona (Literature) | West (U.S.)—In literature. | West (U.S.)—Intellectual life.
Classification: LCC PS271 .A433 2021 DDC 810.9/3278—dc23
LC record available at https://lccn.loc.gov/2020038638

Set in Lyon Text by Laura Buis.

To David
*For decades of friendship*

# Contents

# GEOGRAPHIC PERSONAS

# Introduction

## *The Map and the Territory*

Perhaps no region on earth transformed as dramatically over the course of the nineteenth century as the U.S. frontier. Prior to that time, the land west of the Mississippi River had been inhabited primarily by Native Americans, Spaniards, and Mexicans. Now it became consolidated into states and territories ruled by the federal government. Over time, increasing numbers of Anglo-Saxon and European immigrants settled out West, working in such professions as farming, ranching, and mining. With the rise of the Industrial Revolution, urban centers began to appear in the region, featuring commercial businesses, factories, and manufacturing plants.

The nineteenth century was also a period of self-transformation. In "The Significance of the Frontier in American History" (1893), Frederick Jackson Turner noted: "The wilderness masters the colonist. . . . It takes him from the railroad car and puts him in the birch canoe. It strips off the garments of civilization," clothing him in the outfit of an intrepid frontiersman. After taming the land, the historian argued, the white man once again donned his gentleman's garb and headed to the next frontier, where the process of reinvention repeated itself.[1]

Turner argued that people transformed like actors changing costumes, performing their new roles like participants in the metaphorical parade of westward expansion. "Stand at Cumberland Gap and watch the procession of civilization, marching single file—the buffalo following the trail to the salt springs, the Indian, the fur-trader and hunter, the cattle-raiser, the pioneer farmer."[2] The historian alluded to an artistic rendering of Manifest Destiny depicted in George Caleb Bingham's painting, "Daniel Boone Escorting Settlers through the Cumberland Gap" (1851–52). The painting portrays the famous explorer leading a group of emblematic figures through a pass in the Cumberland Mountains. The characters include a livestock herder, a forester with an axe, and a woman on horseback, symbolizing the domestication of the western territories.

Many of these participants in Manifest Destiny kept records of their journeys, although they did not consider themselves professional writers. They were military leaders and Indian scouts, educated members of New England society and backwoods adventurers. They were fur trappers, traders, and translators; geologists, surveyors, and mapmakers; botanists, zoologists, and cultural ethnographers. Meriwether Lewis and William Clark wrote journals during their western expedition. But they referred to President Thomas Jefferson as "the author" of their "literary" enterprise.[3] The purpose of their mission was to map the territory acquired by the Louisiana Purchase. In the process Lewis and Clark were instructed by Jefferson to find a trade route linking the Missouri River to the Pacific Ocean and to establish economic relations with the region's indigenous peoples. They considered the composition process the least important aspect of their expedition, as reflected by Clark's final entry on September 26, 1806: "we commenced wrighting &c."[4]

Like *The Journals of Lewis and Clark* (1804–6), later exploration narratives read less like great works of literature and more like unimaginative factual documents. In his preface to *The Expeditions of Zebulon Montgomery Pike* (1810), the author wrote that he spent every night at camp taking notes and "plot[ting]" the course of the next day's journey. Yet he was unable to transform the account of his enterprise into a story with a compelling plot.[5] In his preface to the 1895 edition Elliott Coues complained about the difficulty in turning Pike's episodic and ungrammatical journals into a book. "The author, like many another gallant soldier, versed in the arts of war, was quite innocent of literary strategy, though capable of heading an impetuous assault upon the parts of speech."[6]

In addition to being authors, skilled or otherwise, these explorers were performers in the sense that they wrote for an audience. They were also representatives of the U.S. government. Coues described Pike as "the brilliant young soldier who impersonated the authority of the United States" during his travels.[7] The word "impersonated" suggests that Pike embodied the absent president who sponsored the enterprise and that Pike was empowered to "act" on his—and the nation's—behalf. Other explorers were also considered government actors or agents and were sometimes compared to fictional characters in recognition of their heroic service. After leading five western expeditions between 1842 and 1854, John C. Frémont became known as the Pathfinder. Named after James Fenimore Cooper's popular protagonist, Frémont achieved fame as a result of his exploits. He capitalized on his celebrity by getting elected as a senator from California in 1850 and by running (unsuccessfully) for president six years later.

Authors who followed in the footsteps of these early American writers were more aware of the self-transformative aspects of the western experience and the performative nature of their craft. Three factors explain this heightened awareness. First, as the population in the region continued to grow, writers began to feel less geographically isolated from the rest of the nation. This awareness contributed to a shift in perception, as they began to realize that westerners had both personal identities and public selves. Louise Clappe lived for two years with her husband in a California mining camp. She documented her experience in *The Shirley Letters* (1851–52), creating an alter ego, "Dame Shirley," for the amusement of her audience. Writing in character, the author humorously portrayed herself as a stereotypical New England gentlewoman roughing it on the western frontier. In one letter, the *"mineress"* asks her sister Molly: "Did I not martyrize myself into a human mule by descending to the bottom of a dreadful pit (suffering mortal terror all the time, lest it should cave in upon me), actuated by a virtuous desire to see with my own two eyes the process of underground mining, thus enabling myself to be stupidly correct in all my statements thereupon? . . . Yea, verily, this have I done for the express edification of yourself and the rest of your curious tribe."[8]

James Beckwourth was an ex-slave from Virginia who passed as white in his autobiography, fooling readers in the states who did not know the mountain man, fur trapper, and Indian fighter. Although Beckwourth never denied his African ancestry, he boasted that the white leader of the

Rocky Mountain Fur Company expedition treated him like a "brother." The author complained about living with Indians while trapping beaver but rationalized that "civilized man can accustom himself to any mode of life when pelf is the governing principle." He added that "the Crows had never shed the blood of the white man during my stay in their camp." They were "uniformly faithful in their obligations to my race."[9] Whites who knew Beckwourth while he lived out West dismissed him as a liar and speculated regarding his racial origins. In *The Oregon Trail* (1849), Francis Parkman Jr. described Beckwourth as a "mongrel of French, American, and negro blood."[10] In his copy of *The Life and Adventures of James P. Beckwourth*, Parkman wrote that Beckwourth was mulatto, "though he represents otherwise."[11]

The most famous example of a westerner with dual identities was Samuel Clemens, better known as Mark Twain. His western travelogue, *Roughing It* (1872), features con men, hoaxers, and western stereotypes like the gunslinger Slade, whom the eastern narrator claims to have met in person. "Here, right by my side was the actual ogre who, in fights and brawls and various ways, *had taken the lives of twenty-six human beings*, or all men lied about him!"[12] The author contrasts the legendary Slade with the unprepossessing specimen whom he encounters out West. Twain loved to expose fraudsters and myth-makers. But he was a first-class liar as well, acknowledging the roles exaggeration and artifice played in people's daily lives. In his essay, "On the Decay of the Art of Lying," Twain proclaimed: "Lying is universal—we *all* do it."[13] On the lecture circuit, however, Twain adopted a "natural" style of storytelling. He made even the most preposterous anecdotes seem plausible, taking his cues from other contemporary forms of popular entertainment, including "minstrel shows, melodeons, theatrical burlesques, amateur tavern performances, and street theater." His comic method was as unique as the white suits he typically wore, and as recognizable as the words "Mark Twain"—not "a pen name but . . . a trademark (as it always appear[ed] on the copyright page of his books), a brand name for the various enterprises of lecturing, door-to-door subscription sales of novels or travel books, printing investments, and public appearances."[14]

A second factor contributing to the transformation of the frontier was technology. By the late nineteenth century the stagecoach that brought Twain out West had been replaced by the railroad. This new means of transportation enabled people to travel across prairies, mountains, and other natural barriers to human progress more quickly and comfortably. It also changed the ways in which travelers experienced time and place. The window—which thinly separated a train's inhabitants from the passing terrain—simultaneously created a greater imaginative distance, making "our memories speak" and drawing "out of the shadows the dreams of our secrets"; the "unknown landscapes and the strange fables of our private stories."[15] Willa Cather's *My Ántonia* (1918) begins on a train, as an unnamed female narrator meets Jim Burden passing through Iowa. Both of them were raised in rural Nebraska and now live in New York City. As they sit in "the observation car," they watch wheat fields flashing by and recall their childhood friend, Ántonia. Feeling nostalgic for his childhood, Burden decides to write a memoir about the girl who represented "the country, the conditions, the whole adventure" of the early frontier. He satisfies his yearning for the past by transforming Ántonia into a symbol, by recasting himself as a child, and by turning his female traveling companion—who agrees to read the finished manuscript—into his audience.[16]

As immigration continued throughout the nineteenth century and new modes of transportation became available, the region transformed into an object of transnational desire, attracting people from around the world. The Polish actress Helena Modjeska left her homeland after it was partitioned by its European neighbors and stripped of its political autonomy. Modjeska came to California and established a commune where she and other artists could express themselves, free from censorship. Japanese poet Yone Noguchi also flourished as a writer in the West, though he later returned home to support the Japanese nationalist movement. His conquest of the U.S. literary marketplace anticipated the international role he imagined Japan would play in the twentieth century. His German counterpart, Karl May, wrote westerns set on the U.S. frontier, featuring Germans who drank imported beer and sang native folksongs.[17] May became a bestselling writer because he tapped into his nation's nostalgia for its Teutonic heritage at a time when nationalist sentiment was on the rise. He later became Adolf Hitler's favorite writer, inspiring the National Socialist Party, which argued for the supremacy of the Aryan race. May's characters conquered the western frontier, as the United States had done decades earlier. For politicians such as Theodore Roosevelt, the West was "a Darwinian region in which 'races' representing different phases or principles of social organization" contended for mastery. Like the "Teutonic barbarians" who emerged "from their northern forests to invade the Roman Empire," the U.S. government claimed a "racial or *volkish* basis for an American nationality." (May depicted the West as a forested region, reminiscent of Germany's early frontier.) This evolutionary process culminated in the "expansion of the English-speaking peoples" over the "waste spaces" occupied by the so-called primitive North American races.[18] The U.S. frontier transformed into a cosmopolitan region, no longer inhabited primarily by Hispanics and Native Americans, but colonized instead by European immigrants from various nations.

A third factor contributing to the transformation of the region—and the writers and artists associated with it—was the rise of literary realism. During the Enlightenment period explorers focused on the acquisition of empirical knowledge. Accounts of early fact-finding missions initially concentrated on the land's geographical and topographical features, its flora and fauna, the customs of its native inhabitants, and other observational and quantifiable data. As the movement of literary realism gained momentum over the course of the nineteenth century, writers sought to achieve a similar degree of verisimilitude in their fiction, rivaling the authenticity of earlier scientific, historical, and anthropological narratives. In his performances on the lecture circuit and in his published work, Twain told tall tales about his western adventures, "mimicking and travestying other authors, genres, and texts." Before publishing *Roughing It*, the author "steeped himself in other travel books," producing a picaresque autobiographical narrative set in the continental West and Hawai'i that was part fact, part fancy.[19] Twain's fondness for tall tales was supposedly balanced by his objectivity as a roving reporter, just as Clarence King's romantic travelogue—*Mountaineering in the Sierra Nevada* (1872)— was complemented by his scientific study of the region's natural history, *Systematic Geology* (1878). In a similar fashion, Willa Cather challenged her narrator's "nostalgic memory" in the first edition of *My Ántonia* by contrasting Jim Burden's subjective impressions with illustrator W. T. Benda's "stark black-and-white drawings" of the Nebraska prairie.[20]

As writers began to create simulated versions of the "real" West, the line between truth and fiction started to blur. The Industrial Revolution led to the invention of machines creating consumer objects that "mimicked handcrafted things."[21] In the publishing industry, serial fiction—featuring historical figures such as Buffalo Bill and Calamity Jane—replaced factual accounts of the western frontier written by earlier explorers and settlers. In the nation's collective consciousness, the West became "both an actual place with a real history" and "a mythic space populated by projective fantasies."[22] During this period of literary realism, western dime novels presented fictionalized versions of history. The West became synonymous with "the western," as the "real" became associated with the fake, the undetectable fraud, or the performance that substituted for authentic experience.

If Twain was the most popular writer associated with the western frontier, Theodore Roosevelt was the most famous politician—"a showman of his own personality," a performer who "created a character and lived up to it with winning consistency."[23] Originally Roosevelt went out West to improve his health, undergoing a metamorphosis that transformed "the sickly, scrawny boy" into a "masterful man." In the process he became so closely identified with the West that "for the remainder of his life, the public thought of him as a rough-riding cowboy rather than a New York dude." But Roosevelt was "a *ranchman* who employed cowboys," a performer playing a role. Even his Rough Riders dressed in costume. The cavalry troupe that Roosevelt commanded during the Spanish-American War sported "flannel shirts with loosely knotted blue polka-dot handkerchiefs around their necks" and "canvas trousers . . . stuffed into their boots," presenting a uniformly picturesque appearance.[24]

The West was a theatrical space filled with dramatis personae drawn from Roosevelt's imagination. The Dakota Badlands reminded him of Edgar Allan Poe's gothic fiction. Other landscapes recalled scenes from novels by Captain Mayne Reid, which Roosevelt had read as a boy. The Rough Riders resembled characters in Bret Harte's "The Luck of Roaring Camp" (1868). Each one had a nickname that belied his appearance. Harte wrote that "the greatest scamp had a Raphael face, with a profusion of blond hair; Oakhurst, a gambler, had the melancholy air and intellectual abstraction of a Hamlet; the coolest and most courageous man was scarcely over five feet in height, with a soft voice and an embarrassed, timid manner."[25] Harte's characters resembled the Rough Riders, as described by one of Roosevelt's biographers. "An eastern clubman was known as 'Tough Ike'; his tentmate, a rough cowboy, was christened 'The Dude.' One cowpuncher was called 'Metropolitan Bill'; a young Jew accepted with equanimity the name 'Pork Chop,' while a huge red-haired Irishman became 'Sheeny Solomon.'"[26] Roosevelt viewed the West through a literary lens and preferred to be seen in a similar fashion. His books about the region—including *Ranch Life and the Hunting-Trail* (1888) and the historical trilogy *The Winning of the West* (1889–94)—were praised by reviewers for capturing the author's "masculine and vascular" personality. Like Buffalo Bill and Calamity Jane, the larger-than-life politician eventually became a quasi-fictional dime novel hero, starring in *From the Ranch to the White House: The Life of Theodore Roosevelt*, published by Edward S. Ellis in 1906.

All three of these transformational factors—population growth, technology, and literary realism—play roles in Stephen Crane's "The Bride Comes to Yellow Sky" (1898). The story begins as a small town sheriff returns from San Antonio with his new bride on a Pullman sleeper car. Railroads now crisscross the continent, linking the residents of rural areas and small towns with larger cities throughout the country, blurring the distinction between East and West; between the industrialized states and the rapidly developing territories. When the sheriff and his wife look out of the window of their moving carriage, the plains appear to be "pouring eastward," as if reversing the course of Manifest Destiny.[27] At the same time the passengers on the speeding train seem immobilized. The window frames the landscape as it rushes past, transforming the husband and wife into observers who witness the spectacle from the comfort of their plush compartment.[28]

The spectators are also performers, self-conscious in their roles as husband and wife. The sheriff in "his new black clothes" appears nervous on his honeymoon, his hands "constantly performing in a most conscious fashion." The bride, dressed in finery befitting her married state, continually twists "her head to regard her puff sleeves, very stiff, straight, and high." She blushes under the other passengers' "scrutiny," then composes herself, concealing her feelings beneath an "almost emotionless" mask of indifference (Crane 151). Other passengers stare at the couple with "derisive enjoyment," as does the Black Pullman porter, who surveys them "from afar with an amused and superior grin" (152). The audience of fellow travelers witnesses the couple's discomfort and enacts their response, as if they were performers as well. One man, observing their "clumsy coquetry," becomes "excessively sardonic" and winks "at himself in one of the [train's] numerous mirrors" (153).

The region—formerly inhabited by cowboys, ranchers, and members of other predominantly male professions—has been transformed by a growing population that includes Black people, women, and heterosexual couples. The bride and groom arrive at Yellow Sky, a homosocial community represented by a saloonkeeper, sheepherders, and itinerant tradesmen. The town seems like a theatrical construct, the yards of its residents resembling "the grass mats used to represent lawns on the stage." The townspeople play parts in a script that seldom varies from day to day. Every time Scratchy, the town drunk, becomes inebriated, he wanders the streets with a loaded gun, forcing everyone else to take shelter in the saloon. When a newcomer asks what happens next, one of the other men replies that the sheriff typically comes to the rescue, protecting people from the town bully (158). On this occasion, however, the gunslinger encounters Joe Potter—"his ancient antagonist" (161)—walking "sheepishly" up the street from the train station (163), accompanied by his wife, the first harbinger of civilization in this frontier outpost. A single man in a community of bachelors, Scratchy is startled to witness the couple in "the environment of [their] new estate" (164). In "the presence of this foreign condition he [becomes] a simple child of the earlier plains" (165). Once known as the town menace, Scratchy morphs into a symbol of a Wild West that no longer exists; into a harmless child playing shoot-'em-up. Crane notes that his character wears "a maroon-colored flannel shirt, which had been purchased for purposes of decoration, and made principally by some Jewish women on the East Side of New York." His boots have "red tops with gilded imprints, of the kind beloved in winter by little sledding boys on the hillsides of New England" (160). There is no longer any difference between the East and the West. Scratchy's cowboy outfit is merely a costume, and his role as the town's disturber of the peace is nullified when the bride comes to Yellow Sky, signifying the end of an era.

*Geographic Personas: Self-Transformation and Performance in the American West* features men and women who played pivotal roles in the region from the mid-nineteenth through the early twentieth century. Each writer, dancer, actor, imposter, and con artist was influenced by one or more of these three transformative factors, which contributed to their personal reinvention during a transitional period in the American West.

Chapter 1 examines the various roles played by geologist and nature writer Clarence King. By the time he began his career the region's development had already led to a blurring of the boundary between "civilization" and "savagery."[29] King commuted back and forth across the country, "spending part of [his] life in the wilderness only to return for a while to the city."[30] In California he worked as a scientist, while dressing like an eastern dandy. In his spare time he played the role of a tourist, ultimately writing an account of his adventures in the Sierra Nevada. Ironically, King began surveying the developing region at the same time New York City was transforming into an urban jungle; into an industrial landscape inhabited by a growing number of immigrants, Black Americans from the South, and a new class of low-paid factory workers. Eastern gentlemen's clubs were "island[s] of homogeneity in an ever-diversifying urban ocean,"[31] places where white men from wealthy and powerful families could gather. King belonged to one of these clubs, while secretly living with a Black woman in a segregated neighborhood in New York City.[32] In the West King alternated between different personas. In the East he performed the same juggling act. He appeared as a gentleman of privilege in white society, while passing as a light-skinned Black man, telling his common-law wife he was a Pullman porter whose travels forced him to leave home for extended periods of time.

Chapter 1 also considers another role played by technology in representing King to a national audience. Although the camera was invented in the seventeenth century, the first photographic images were not created until 1814, using a camera obscura. Because these images faded over time, they were later replaced by daguerreotypes and more sophisticated forms of still photography. Initially, self-portraits (now called "selfies") were easier to take than portraits of other people, who had to appear and pose in a photographer's studio. But King preferred to pose in various guises: as a mountain climber, an eastern gentleman, and a scientist holding a theodolite—a rotating telescope used for measuring angles. King was an observer of nature. In *Mountaineering in the Sierra Nevada* he wrote that he merely recorded his impressions, like a "sensitized photographic plate."[33] Yet he also submitted to the reader's gaze, influencing how people perceived him. Other subjects featured in *Geographic Personas* dressed in costumes, presenting themselves as cowboys, Indians, aristocratic land grant claimants, dancers, and actors, captured on film while performing in character. As one historian has noted, nineteenth-century photography did not change the way Americans viewed the western frontier. Instead, the way people imagined the region influenced the images they chose to create.[34] On a few occasions, the camera caught them off-guard, exposing the private lives of these public figures. James had to pose for a mug shot after he was arrested in Nevada for cattle rustling. The photograph presents a different image of the author and artist, who later romanticized his career as a cowboy. A picture of Reavis, taken in prison, shows him in a convict's striped uniform, appearing terrified, looking away from the cameras. The fact that King led a double life did not become public knowledge until after his death, when photographers caught his widow going to court to contest having been omitted from his will, along with their four surviving children.

King contributed to the settlement of the U.S. frontier by participating in the Geological Survey of the Fortieth Parallel, exploring Yosemite, and advocating for the creation of national parks. Over the course of the nineteenth century the region became defined—and confined—by barbed wire fences built by property owners as well as by invisible boundaries established by government agencies. At the same time the West remained elusive, a conceptual space as well as a symbol of freedom and opportunity for immigrants from around the globe. Chapter 2 investigates a little-known event that resulted from Spain's colonization of the American Southwest in the sixteenth century. During this period the country began issuing "floating" land grants to aristocrats and high-ranking members of the military.[35] Most recipients resided in Spain and were offered unspecified parcels of land, the boundaries of which had yet to be determined. Before the fencing of the range in the 1880s cattle had moved freely across the land, distinguished from each other only by the brands ranchers placed on their hides. Rustlers could steal this mobile property simply by altering the brands cattlemen inscribed on the animals' bodies. The con man James Reavis attempted a similar feat, forging documents to suggest he had legally inherited a floating grant from the descendant of a Spanish aristocrat. Since the grant did not specify where the property was located, Reavis sought to appropriate an 18,600-square-mile parcel of land spanning the New Mexico and Arizona Territories. In the process he posed as a respectable gentleman who had married the long-lost heir to the nobleman's estate. In reality she was a Mexican woman whom Reavis had met on a train and coaxed into performing as his accomplice. Reavis was a scam artist who resembled many of the characters in Twain's *Roughing It*. His ingenious attempt to swindle the U.S. government out of its territorial holdings by forging a preexisting claim finds its corollary in "The Great Landslide Case." In chapter 34 of Twain's western travelogue, a farmer stands his ground after his property slides down a hill, covering his neighbor's land. "And when I reminded him . . . that it was on top of my ranch and that he was trespassing," the neighbor complains, "he had the infernal meanness to ask me why didn't I *stay* on it, the blathering lunatic."[36]

In addition to railroads the invention of barbed wire contributed to the disappearance of the open range and the settlement of the region as a whole. Cowboys began losing their jobs as ranchers started fencing their land and shipping their stock by rail to meat-packing plants in Chicago, thus eliminating the need for employees to patrol and herd their cattle. Chapter 3 considers how these changes impacted the artist and writer known as Will James. In 1914 a young Canadian named Ernest Dufault immigrated to the U.S. West, changing his name and becoming a cowboy, at a time when the nation's nostalgia for its mythic past led Hollywood to produce films idealizing the conquest and settlement of the western frontier. When James was unable to achieve fame as a movie star, he decided to write and illustrate children's books, which allegedly drew on his own experience as one of the country's last real cowboys. Claiming to be an orphan raised by a fur trapper, as well as a self-trained horseman and convicted cattle rustler (this last part of the story was true), James published an "autobiography" and numerous works of juvenile fiction, including the Newberry Award-winning novel, *Smoky the Cowhorse* (1926).

Ironically, the fencing of the range transformed cowboys from manual laborers into mythic symbols of a bygone time. Chapter 4 examines another aspect of frontier settlement—the killing or displacement of indigenous peoples—and the consequent romanticization of Native Americans as representatives of a vanishing wilderness. The mixed-race son of a North Carolina janitor, Sylvester Long exploited this myth by pretending to be an Indian chief—a "noble savage," in the parlance of white society. The transformation process began when Long applied to the Carlisle Indian School in 1909, claiming to be a full-blooded Cherokee. After fighting in World War I he emigrated to Canada, seeking to avoid friends and family who might expose him as a fraud. He reinvented himself as Chief Buffalo Child Long Lance, a leader of the Blackfoot tribe. In the guise of his new persona, Long published a fictional autobiography in 1928. Two years later he starred in a silent movie, playing a character supposedly based on the "real" Blackfoot chief—in fact, another character created by Long.[37] Like James, Long feared he would one day be exposed as a fraud. The "cowboy" and the "Indian" were two sides of the same buffalo nickel: opportunists who capitalized on the public's desire to commemorate a past that only existed in the collective imagination.

Movies—another new form of technology—revolutionized the entertainment industry, replacing dime novels as the most popular purveyor of formula westerns. They also constituted a visual version of realism, featuring celluloid stars who were more charismatic than the people on whom they were based. Long enjoyed a brief career in show business, starring in *The Silent Enemy* (1930), a quasi-documentary film about the threatened extinction of a group of indigenous people. (Ironically, James failed to become a movie star because he was told he didn't "look" like a cowboy.)[38] Hollywood captured the spectacle of Manifest Destiny, a rapidly progressing westward movement that had accelerated over the course of the nineteenth century. Major events such as the Gold *Rush* and the Oklahoma Land *Rush* were defined by the speed with which they occurred. "These rushes began as new technologies of communication spread news [of these events] internationally."[39] Changes in the entertainment industry happened just as rapidly. By the 1890s vaudeville had adapted to the needs of the nation's growing urban population, presenting "an assortment of brief, fast-paced acts" with "machine-like efficiency."[40] "Movies" moved even more quickly, serving as a perfect vehicle for depictions of the "iron horse."[41] *The Great Train Robbery* (1903), a short silent film about an express car held up by bandits, was so successful that it spawned a series of similar entertainments, including *The Little Train Robbery* (1905) and *The Hold-Up of the Rocky Mountain Express* (1906).

As the industry evolved, movies strove to appear more realistic, while becoming increasingly adept at mimesis. Actors struggled during the silent era to appear natural on camera. Charles Darwin believed humans shared certain characteristics with their prehistoric ancestors and other species of mammals. In *The Expression of the Emotions in Man and Animals* (1872), Darwin argued that certain reactions, "such as the bristling of the hair under the influence of extreme terror, or the uncovering of the teeth under that of furious rage, can hardly be understood, except on the belief that man once existed in a much lower and animal-like condition." These instinctive reactions resembled the stock expressions displayed by actors in silent films, so melodramatically exaggerated did they appear in Darwin's experiments. Darwin preferred to study races "who have associated but little with Europeans" because their expressions were "innate or instinctive."[42] Sylvester Long benefited from this belief, exploiting racial stereotypes for personal gain. At a time when Native Americans were believed to be in danger of extinction, it was necessary to cast an actor in *The Silent Enemy* who was unmistakably "Indian."

Like Long, Willa Cather also played with notions of regional and ethnic identity. Chapter 5 contrasts the Bohemian immigrants who came to the American prairie with artistic "bohemians" who were cultural signifiers of cosmopolitanism at the turn of the previous century. As an adult Cather moved back East, writing about the frontier from a geographical distance and altered temporal perspective. In such works as "The Bohemian Girl" (1912), *O Pioneers!* (1913), and *My Ántonia* (1918), the author bridged the gap between the nineteenth-century frontier and the twentieth-century urban West by comparing the immigrants who lived in Nebraska during her childhood with the artists whom she later knew in Greenwich Village. While her Bohemian characters adapted to their new environment, her literary colleagues were social nonconformists who appealed to the author's subversive nature. Cather briefly cross-dressed as a man in Nebraska. She adopted a more feminine appearance once she became a writer, using her Bohemian characters as fictional alter egos to express her own unconventional tendencies.

The increasing number of international immigrants coming from places such as Bohemia, combined with the establishment of cities and towns in the once rural region, led to the eventual appearance of cosmopolitan cultural sites, such as San Francisco's Bohemian Club. Yone Noguchi was welcomed by its members because of his "exotic" background and gender-nonconforming behavior. Chapter 6 reveals how the poet benefited from Japonism, the late nineteenth-century craze by people in the Western Hemisphere for Japanese culture and art. Noguchi curried favor by transforming into a stereotypical Japanese male, becoming Joaquin Miller's house servant. By playing a role designed to ingratiate himself to his patron, Noguchi became a poser, not unlike members of the Bohemian Club. Earlier, Miller had fabricated a literary persona based on his fictitious western heritage. At a time when San Francisco was evolving from a mining town into a modern metropolis, Cincinnatus Hiner Miller capitalized on the public's nostalgia for the early frontier by choosing the pen name "Joaquin" (an allusion to the legendary Mexican bandit Joaquin Murieta) and inventing a past for his character. Claiming he had lived with an Indian tribe, while participating in various escapades that could be neither verified nor disproven by critics, Miller became his own best advertisement, publishing works that were allegedly based on his own experiences, such as *Life Amongst the Modocs* (1873), and *The Danites* (1878), about a band of vigilante Mormons.

Other members of San Francisco's literary circle sought to conceal certain facts pertaining to their personal lives, desiring social respectability instead of publicity. Ina Coolbrith never acknowledged she was related to the founder of the Mormon Church, Joseph Smith, while the homosexual Charles Warren Stoddard posed as a "gentleman bachelor." Periodically, he escaped to the South Seas, where he formed romantic friendships with native islanders. On the early frontier, men living in mining camps, on ranches, and in other homosocial communities had been able to engage in same-sex relations without fear of condemnation.[43] However, by the late nineteenth century homosexuality had been classified as abnormal behavior, and San Francisco had become a city in which eccentrics such as Miller were celebrated but "deviants" such as Stoddard were not. The Pacific Islands were the new frontier; a place where the writer was free to explore his sexuality.

While homosexuality was frowned upon, male romantic friendships were encouraged among local artists. Thus Noguchi was doubly attractive to San Francisco's bohemians, who perceived Japanese men as "artfully feminine."[44] Miller befriended the aspiring poet by introducing him to local publishers and editors. While pursuing his literary career, Noguchi also engaged in a flirtatious correspondence with Stoddard. Although homosexuality and "interracial intimacies hardly met with full approval" at the turn of the century, "in cities such as San Francisco, alternatives to heterosexuality and antimiscegenation seemed tolerated if not wholly embraced, especially within bohemian circles."[45]

San Francisco also welcomed Polish immigrant and acclaimed actress Helena Modjeska. Instead of seeking to ingratiate herself with the city's cultural elite, Modjeska initially founded an experimental utopian commune in central California for artists and other national exiles. She returned to acting once the experiment ended, commencing her American tour in San Francisco. Like Noguchi, the eastern European diva was an ardent nationalist who escaped to the United States during the political partitioning of Poland in the late nineteenth century. Chapter 7 argues that Modjeska became popular with western audiences during a period of regional transformation because she was a theatrical chameleon. She was also a symbol of cultural sophistication at a time when western audiences craved more than the crude forms of entertainment that had been available on the earlier Gold Rush frontier.

By contrast, chapter 8 contends that Karl May appealed to readers who were nostalgic for a German frontier that no longer existed. The author created a fictional character nicknamed "Old Shatterhand," a German immigrant version of Natty Bumppo. Later he claimed his protagonist was an autobiographical version of May, even though the writer had never visited the U.S. frontier. Will James, Sylvester Long, and Yone Noguchi played occupational, ethnic, and racial stereotypes, creating professional personas based on the public's perception of a cowboy, an Indian, and a "feminine" Japanese male. Modjeska played a variety of roles on stage, while never pretending to be anything other than an "artist"—a vague term that acquired more specific connotations with the rise of bohemianism in the late nineteenth century. May created a fictional character and then *became* the creature of his own imagination, turning the pages of his novel into a real-life public arena, where he enacted his new identity.

Modjeska personified the art of acting. May was a shape-shifting writer. By contrast, Isadora Duncan was the inventor of modern American dance. Chapter 9 analyzes Duncan's free-flowing and seemingly spontaneous performances, which differed from earlier choreographed forms of dance, such as classical ballet. The innovator displayed "natural" moves in the same way as the public speaker Twain perfected a kind of "gestural expression" that seemed instinctive rather than studied.[46] Duncan's performances were contained on the stage and presented within a theatrical frame. Like passengers looking through a train window at the passing landscape, audiences were presented with an illusion of movement while remaining stationed in their seats.[47] Born in California at the end of the Gold Rush, Duncan represented a frontier that no longer existed. The performer she most closely resembled was Will Rogers, the vaudeville cowboy who twirled a lariat alone on stage, telling jokes instead of roping horses.[48]

The three factors that facilitated a process of self-transformation became less influential over time. First, continued growth in the region led to the rise of a new urban frontier. Western writers who successfully transitioned into the twentieth century acknowledged this fact. For authors such as Raymond Chandler and Dashiell Hammett, the West was an asphalt landscape, the modern equivalent of a wilderness filled with gangsters and detectives, instead of cowboys and Indians. In "The Simple Art of Murder" (1944), Chandler praised Hammett for "debunking" the traditional language of fiction by writing in a contemporary American colloquial style,[49] in accordance with modernist writers who elevated "the vernacular into the realm of high culture."[50] Chandler wrote cynically as well as romantically about the modern metropolis, transforming Philip Marlowe into a twentieth-century Arthurian knight whose quest for justice forces him to travel the "mean streets" of modern Los Angeles.[51]

Second, writers and artists became less concerned about the authenticity of their work with the decline of realism and the rise of modernism in the early twentieth century. Authors took "an inward turn," exploring the psychological and emotional states of their characters. As a consequence, western writers "began to question the power of place," focusing less on their connection to the external environment and on their credentials as westerners, qualified to represent the "real" place by virtue of their association with the region.[52] In addition, industrialization gradually transformed the West into an extension of "civilization," until it no longer seemed like "a separate regional entity."[53] Much of the western literature published during the modernist period continued to depict the early frontier, rather than the present-day West, and to offer realistic portrayals of the historical past, suggesting writers were sometimes slow to adapt to changing trends.[54] The formula western was merely a refinement on the earlier dime novel, rather than a break with the regional genre.[55] Although Isadora Duncan was considered the founder of modern American dance, she represented human movement more realistically and less abstractly than her modernist successor, Martha Graham. Willa Cather also published during the modernist era but was less experimental in her approach to literature than many of her contemporaries. By contrast, Mark Twain's use of irony and pastiche made him "nearly unique" among late nineteenth- and early twentieth-century western writers.[56]

Third, modernists responded to technology with ambivalence, unlike previous generations of performers and writers. They blamed industrialization for the increasing sense of alienation people experienced living in urban areas, while acknowledging recent technological inventions offering "an aesthetic excitement and a variety of popular forms that energized the vocabulary of the arts."[57] In A Cool Million (1934) Nathanael West mocked American industry, which no longer "mimicked handcrafted things," producing consumer goods with purposes that belied their appearance. "Paper had been made to look like wood, wood like rubber, rubber like steel, steel like cheese, cheese like glass, and, finally, glass like paper."[58] In The Day of the Locust (1939), the cowboy Earle is unable to find work in Hollywood. He spends his days standing outside an establishment on Sunset Boulevard like a cigar store Indian, holding "a sack of tobacco and a sheaf of papers," rolling a cigarette "twice every hour."[59] By now such ironies had become familiar to readers and moviegoers, who accepted fictional and cinematic characters as substitutes for the "real" thing.

Jean Baudrillard has defined the postmodern world as a place in which simulacra replace the things to which they once referred. "The territory no longer precedes the map" because there is no longer any difference between "the 'true' and the 'false.'"[60] In the U.S. West, however, the imaginary preceded the real. Cartographers began making maps of the New World long before it was encountered by European explorers.[61] Later, people who had no knowledge of the region were offered forms of entertainment that represented the frontier in ways which were not always factually accurate. One critic suggests that the entire body of western literature "may be understood as a series of simulacra."[62] Yet early writers and artists lacked the postmodern sensibility required to view the West as nothing more than a verbal construct or pliable conceit.

Baudrillard refers to the territory as a metaphorical desert. Contending that the map or simulacrum is more fruitful than the "real," he compares it to an arid domain, devoid of life and unworthy of intellectual study. According to Baudrillard, the simulacrum "engenders the territory whose shreds slowly rot across the extent of the map. It is the real, and not the map, whose vestiges persist here and there in the deserts that are no longer those of the Empire, but ours. *The desert of the real itself.*"[63] However, the territory mapped by *Geographic Personas* includes a diverse international group of writers and artists, con men and charlatans, performers and posers. These women and men experimented with notions of reality and representation during a period of regional development and creative self-transformation in the American West. As the southwestern writer Mary Austin noted in *The Land of Little Rain* (1903): "Desert is a loose term to indicate land that supports no man." But in the actual American desert, readers who look closely may discover "essays in miniature."[64]

# 1

## Geographic Personas

### *The Passing of Clarence King*

No one understood the difference between the map and the territory better than Clarence King. King led the exploration of the nation's Fortieth Parallel, mapping many of the territories west of the Mississippi River. A century after King published his findings in *Systematic Geology* (1878), Jean Baudrillard ridiculed the belief that maps faithfully mirror reality.[1] King's *Mountaineering in the Sierra Nevada* (1872) made no such authoritative claims. It was more "vivid and graphic" than King's empirical maps and dry geological data.[2] Intermixed with the author's subjective impressions of the California mountains, however, were learned passages explaining the region's subterranean history. King was a romantic as well as a scientist. This dichotomy became apparent when he exposed the Great Diamond Hoax in 1872, revealing that investors had salted a diamond mine in order to lure prospectors to the northwest Colorado Territory. The news cemented King's reputation as a trusted public guardian and zealous fraud-buster. The story broke the same year King published his somewhat fanciful travelogue.

If there are questions concerning the reliability of King's autobiographical work, there are also doubts pertaining to who was the "real" Clarence King. Was it the California geologist and well-known nature writer or the man named James Todd, who passed as a Black man living in New York City?[3] In 1888 King entered into a common law marriage with Ada Copeland, an African American immigrant from the deep South. Identifying as a light-skinned Black man, Todd explained his absences from home by telling his wife he was a Pullman porter.[4] He kept his personal life a secret from white friends and colleagues, maintaining a separate residence in one of the city's upper-class neighborhoods and joining an exclusive gentlemen's club where members included other eastern frontiersmen, such as Theodore Roosevelt.[5] As already noted, in 1872 King exposed the Great Diamond Hoax, revealing that land in the northwest Colorado Territory had been salted with gems in order to scam potential investors.[6] Thus it might be fair to ask: which was the territory and which was the map? Who was the original and who was the copy: King or his eastern counterpart?

With the settlement of the West and the rise of the Industrial Revolution, places such as New York City became the new American wilderness, filled with European immigrants, rural Black southerners, and other low-income laborers, who sought employment in factories and manufacturing plants.[7] On the western frontier, white men had frequently engaged in sexual relations with indigenous women of color.[8] Now, in New York City, King was able to live with his common law wife in an unofficially restricted neighborhood while avoiding encounters with whites, who remained on the opposite side of the color line. King viewed the city as a "new frontier," a place where he was not "governed by rules and values so different from those of his comfortable professional life."[9] Like the frontier line, which separated "civilization" from "savagery," the invisible boundary that segregated minorities from their white counterparts enabled King to maintain his double life. Turn-of-the-century New York City was "a collection of neighborhoods, many defined by the residents' class or race or national origin." As one of King's biographers notes: people "lived largely within the bounds of their immediate neighborhoods, rarely venturing into worlds where their social class or physical appearance might make them conspicuous."[10]

King passed in a different sense during his career out West, presenting himself as a white college-educated scientist. While one might argue that this was the "real" Clarence King, it was also a pose: a deliberately constructed identity. In California King played a second role when he was not working for the government. As an amateur nature enthusiast, who wrote *Mountaineering in the Sierra Nevada* (1872), King viewed the West as a playground for tourists, a site where privileged male members of the eastern upper classes could test their manhood by engaging in adventurous and athletic endeavors. Although King worked as a geological surveyor, most photographs taken in the 1870s show him dressed like a prospector or mountain climber, posing for the camera. Consistent with his race and social class, King maintains the persona of a privileged white easterner in his nature writing, depicting California's Indians in a disparaging manner. Whether these opinions reflected the author's true beliefs or whether they concealed his actual feelings—serving as a literary façade, behind which the man who privately lived with a woman of color could hide—is impossible to determine. The only thing one can declare with certainty is that there were two "Clarence Kings": the Black East Coast working-class porter and the white author and scientist known for his exploration of the American West.

King was the son of a prosperous merchant who died when King was six years old. His mother continued to receive income from the family business until it dissolved in 1857, leaving King and his mother financially destitute. After his mother remarried, his stepfather paid for King to go to the Sheffield Scientific School, where he studied geology. When his stepfather died in 1866, King and his mother adjusted to their new misfortune while struggling to maintain social appearances. These traumatic childhood events haunted King throughout his life. In *Mountaineering in the Sierra Nevada*, the author notes the success of certain immigrants and the failure of others. Some pioneers establish farms and ranches in the central valley, while others barely scratch a living from the soil. "There is about [their homes], these specimens of modern decay, an air of social decomposition not pleasant to perceive. Freshly built houses, still untinted by time, left in rickety disorder, half-finished windows, gates broken down or unhinged, and a kind of sullen neglect staring everywhere."[11] As a cautionary lesson, King cites the Newty family, whose members have degenerated into "weak-minded restlessness." They are "perpetual emigrants who roam as dreary waifs" across the western frontier (123). To a scientist such as King, the Newtys seem to disprove Charles Darwin's theory of evolution.

King struggled to reconcile Darwinism with his Christian faith. In California he discovered fossils and other evidence of prehistoric life that challenged the account in Genesis of the earth's creation. Although King believed in the adaptability of the human race, he also compared the Newtys to the children of Cain, who were doomed to wander the earth in the aftermath of original sin. King adapted to his western environment by climbing mountains and surveying rugged terrain, proving that science was a "manly pursuit and a worthy career."[12] He boasts about "the amount of muscular force" required to tackle Mount Tyndall (105) and describes his escape on horseback from a band of Mexican highwaymen (137). In conversation he also liked to regale friends with recollections of his western adventures.[13] Later writers, in their biographies of the western explorer, repeated King's stories about his encounter with a grizzly bear and his confrontation with a herd of stampeding buffalo, transforming King into a heroic literary figure.[14]

For King, mountain climbing was the ultimate test because it symbolized aspiration and failure. One critic notes that the "courtship of disaster" recurs in *Mountaineering in the Sierra Nevada* as "a curiously obsessive pattern."[15] King compares Mount Tyndall to a "sharp granite needle." During their ascent King and his climbing partner find their course impeded by a series of "fantastic pinnacles." The author uses his lasso to lower their knapsacks, then "pioneer[s]" down the precipitous slope (76). In the process of climbing Mount Shasta, King navigates his way through craters strewn with boulders. He threads his way with "extreme caution" around the edges of "these horrible traps," occasionally dislodging rocks, which roll down the mountainside, disappearing "out of sight" (264). A photograph taken by Andrew J. Russell captures the dangerous nature of this pursuit. Entitled "Clarence King on Rope, Uinta Mountains, Utah, 1869," the picture shows King posing while holding a rope as he leans against a granite wall, his right leg extended forward, with his foot in a crevice, his left leg dangling in the air.[16]

King also took risks in his personal life. The exposure of his common law marriage with a Black woman would have scandalized his eastern friends and professional colleagues, who "considered racial mixing to be nothing short of evolutionary catastrophe."[17] King's racial passing coincided with contemporary debates among geologists about the role that "catastrophe" played in evolution.[18] Uniformitarianism was based on the theory that the earth had steadily evolved over the eons, according to set principles and natural laws. In contrast, catastrophism posited the notion that the evolutionary process had been periodically interrupted over the centuries by catastrophic events, such as earthquakes, floods, and volcanic eruptions. King suggested a compromise between these competing theories, contending that the rate "of biological adaptation, rather than always proceeding at a uniform pace, could [occasionally] occur with greater rapidity in response to abrupt climatological change."[19]

This compromise explains King's seemingly contradictory representations of nature in *Mountaineering in the Sierra Nevada*. In his catastrophic imagination, the eastern slope appears "stark and glaring," while the barren foothills resemble the "emaciated corpses of once noble ranges." The inhospitable landscape reminds King of the pioneers who died before reaching California. Those who succeed in crossing the mountains encounter a blooming oasis on the other side; a western slope "flanked by rolling hills covered with a fresh vernal carpet of grass" and ripening crops (41-42).

In an article entitled "Catastrophism and Evolution" (1887), King explained that he had come to believe in a modified version of catastrophism after observing marine fossils "entombed in rocky beds far removed from present seas,—beds which compel the natural inference that they are sea bottoms upheaved." He concluded: "Beneath our America lies buried another distinct continent,—an archaean America."[20] As a U.S. surveyor, King participated in the future-oriented enterprise of westward expansion, while simultaneously working backward in time to reconstruct the frontier's geological history. The notion of a hidden world was also an apt metaphor for King's personal life. Commenting on his secret lifelong attraction to women of color, one biographer writes: "His loves, it seems, were all subterranean."[21]

King kept his career separate from his private domestic affairs. As a public figure, he was also known for pursuing different—seemingly incompatible—interests. *Systematic Geology* was the product of his exploration and research as a geological surveyor, while *Mountaineering in the*

*Sierra Nevada* was the work of an amateur nature enthusiast. As carto-graphic scholars have noted, surveys and maps indicate "how the land is controlled or spatialized," while literature "questions how landscape is perceived or experienced." Maps "value the land for its pathways and resources," while literature creates "interior landscape[s]" filled with "emotional richness."[22] King is more subjective and effusive in responding to nature. His reactions are typical of nineteenth-century U.S. writers, who romanticized the western landscape. King employs the same aesthetic vocabulary, describing the "grandeur" of a mountain canyon (70) and calling Mount Tyndal a "sublime white giant" covered in snow (85). It is unclear whether his phrase making was a sign of his lack of originality or was intended to suggest that he was a conventional writer, an appearance that the public figure with an unorthodox personal life strove to maintain.

It is also difficult to assess whether his prejudice against Native Americans was a sign of racism or merely a pose to disguise the fact that he was attracted to women of color. King refers to an Indian "squaw" as a "fat girl" and is surprised to learn her husband finds her attractive (60). When "an obese Digger squaw" flirts with the author, he is repulsed by her "picturesque squalor" (269). After King's death, however, Henry Adams revealed his friend's preference for women of other races and ethnicities. He speculated that King liked nonwhite women because he did not associate them with the intellectual life from which he secretly sought to escape. According to Adams, King "loved the Spaniard as he loved the negro and the Indian and all the primitives because they were not academic."[23] One critic claims that King was not attracted to "tradition-bound, seemingly affected and artificial, Victorian women.... His liaisons with Indian maidens, and with young working women in Cuba, Hawaii, Central America, and Mexico, were legion."[24] One biographer suggests that Ada Copeland's "'chocolate hue' aroused the compulsions of his color fetishism."[25] Another one states that King was drawn to people of color, as well as to racial causes throughout his life, noting that he had a "colored nurse" during childhood and that he later became an abolitionist, traveling out West with a Black valet who was "close to his employer in ways that elude easy categorization. . . . He was at once a friend and servant, confidant and social inferior, a man who surely knew much about King's personal affairs but kept his counsel close."[26]

If the man who was known for his western exploration and nature writing was a complex individual, so was his East Coast counterpart. King divided his time in New York City between his home with Ada Copeland and their five children in a racially restricted neighborhood and the privileged realm of white society. He belonged to a gentlemen's club where members included educated professionals and members of the upper class, among them fellow westerners Theodore Roosevelt and Owen Wister.[27] These elite institutions were "island[s] of homogeneity in an ever-diversifying urban ocean."[28] King oscillated between the two worlds, just as he traveled between East and West, crossing the frontier line as well as the color line. Ironically, as a surveyor he established boundary lines that determined the parameters of government land, while posing as a Black man and transgressing the invisible borders that separated the races in New York City.

King was aware of this contradiction, as passages in his writing subtly indicate. Regarding the government's decision to create a national park system, King claims in *Mountaineering in the Sierra Nevada*: "By an Act of Congress the Yosemite Valley had been segregated from the public domain, and given—'donated,' as they call it—to the State of California, to be held inalienable for all time as a public pleasure-ground" (151). King refers to the congressional mandate as an act of segregation. He questions what right "they" have to "donate" the land, suggesting that the property does not belong to the government and mocking the notion of a "public pleasure-ground," designed for the enjoyment of a privileged few. Fellow nature writer John Muir also advocated for the creation of national parks, seemingly unaware that his words had a double meaning when he celebrated the country's "forest reservations," praying "may their tribe increase."[29] At a time when Indians were being forcibly removed from their tribal lands, Muir suggested that containment was a means of preservation, a way of saving an endangered natural resource or vanishing race. By contrast, King implies that boundaries both include and exclude, contain and imprison.

Like King, Timothy H. O'Sullivan believed in a modified version of catastrophism. O'Sullivan was a geophotographer who visually documented the U.S. exploration of the Fortieth Parallel.[30] Many of O'Sullivan's photographs suggest the negative effect the passage of time had on the western landscape. "Witches' Rock, Echo Canyon, Utah, 1869" features weathered pinnacles of stone, standing in stark contrast to the surrounding desert. "Limestone, near Ruby Valley, East Humboldt Mountains, Nevada, 1868" displays craggy mountains devoid of vegetation.[31] In order to illustrate the theory of catastrophism more dramatically, O'Sullivan sometimes manipulated his camera "to create the effect of a landscape seemingly set on edge," filming rocky outcroppings and cliffs at an angle to make them appear more precipitous.[32] He also photographed areas that had been affected by earthquakes and other natural catastrophes, as illustrated by "Fissure, Steamboat Springs, Nevada, 1868."[33]

The Survey of the Fortieth Parallel was sponsored by the U.S. Department of War. Not surprisingly, photographs from the expedition tend to portray indigenous peoples in the West as conquered subjects. Two of O'Sullivan's photographs feature Native Americans. These "group portraits of friendly tribes" were taken at reservations near Pyramid Lake (ca. 1867–68) and in the East Humboldt Mountains in northeastern Nevada (1868).[34] Other photographs suggest that tribes opposing westward expansion have been defeated or removed from the region. These "documents" present abandoned dwellings ("Characteristic Ruin of the Pueblo San Juan, New Mexico, 1874")[35] and extinct civilizations ("Ancient Ruins in the Cañon de Chelle, New Mexico Territory, 1873").[36] The dates in these captions serve "to situate the colonized in historical time," transforming Native Americans into relics from an earlier era.[37]

King's surveys of the Fortieth Parallel also effectively erase the indigenous presence. The area surrounding Pyramid Lake had once been inhabited by Paiute Indians. After their defeat by the U.S. military, the land became a reservation for surviving members of the tribe, some of whom appeared in O'Sullivan's photograph. A map of the area, based on King's survey and published in 1876, shows the lake as well as other topographic features. No signs of habitation appear on the map.[38] The lake's name is also a white toponym, chosen in 1844 by John C. Frémont. The explorer named the body of water after a rock formation on the eastern shore. By comparing the region to ancient Egypt, Frémont disavowed the relationship between Native Americans and their surrounding environment.

Maps can be read as "a series of erasures and overwritings."[39] Created by teams of researchers—including scientists, surveyors, mathematicians, and technical artists—maps seem to present facts that resist interpretation. However, the removal of Indians from maps and photographs related to the Survey of the Fortieth Parallel constitutes a series of acts of erasure. Pictorial representations of the Great Basin region overwrite the frontier, transforming maps into palimpsests that conceal the existence of earlier human societies.

King denigrates natives on the rare occasions when he acknowledges their existence in *Mountaineering in the Sierra Nevada*. Like other nineteenth-century naturalists, the geologist seemed to assume a relationship between race and geography. Naturalists identified groups of people based on the region in which they lived, referring to them as "geographical races," while arguing that "major races of humans constituted different species."[40] Thus the Five Civilized Tribes were believed to be more evolved than other Native Americans because they resided east of the Mississippi River and adopted certain white customs—learning English, converting to Christianity, becoming farmers, and creating tribal governments modeled on the nation's bicameral legislature. Western tribes were isolated from white society and were considered more primitive than their eastern counterparts.

King seems to subscribe to this theory. But in *Mountaineering in the Sierra Nevada*, the man who fathered five biracial children also notes how different species of flora mix within the same geographical region and documents how different ecosystems historically coexisted in earlier geological eras. The foothills are covered with orange and purple blossoms, "cloudings of green and white, [and] reaches of violet." King compares the California scenery to a Moorish or Arabic work of art, describing how "natural patterns" form an "arabesque" design in the landscape (43). He discovers the fossils of "savage fishes" and "Asiatic" mollusks in the same canyon wall as well as the bones of horses, elk, deer, camels, and elephants (200). In *Systematic Geology* he divides the Great Basin region into "five equal areas," observing the diversity of plants and wildlife contained in each one.[41]

King proved that different species could coexist in the same location, during the same geological era. In his own life he explored the equally complex relationship between race and geography. Moving back and forth, between the East and the West, was another form of passing: a means of changing identity by literally traveling through space. Telling his wife that he was a Pullman porter was a further example of the same phenomenon. King told his wife this lie in order to explain his absences from home. But working as a servant on a luxury passenger train in the late nineteenth century was also one of the few opportunities for Black men to achieve upward mobility; to pass into the ranks of the middle class.[42] Exchanging a series of personas—as a white man working in a western state that was still inhabited by various Native American tribes, and as a non-Black resident in a segregated New York City neighborhood— King demonstrated there was no inherent correlation between race and geography.

The most noteworthy events in King's career have been amply documented. His exploration and mapping of the U.S. frontier contributed to the settlement of the western states and territories, while his most popular book, *Mountaineering in the Sierra Nevada*, remains a classic in the field of American nature writing. Yet the most remarkable chapter in his personal life remains partially unwritten. As the West transformed into an extension of white civilization, King became increasingly visible; celebrated for his work as a surveyor and memorialized as a subject in his creative nonfiction. Conversely, as New York City devolved into a wilderness, King found it relatively easy to disappear. After his death the discovery that King had passed as a Black man led to his temporary banishment from the literary canon and the erasure of his presence in white society. One biographer questions whether racism led "to his tumble from the highest peaks of renown," noting that King's gentlemen's club "refused to hang his portrait" in the aftermath of the scandalous revelation.[43] Mabel Dodge—who later formed an artists' colony in Taos, New Mexico, and married a Native American—may have suspected King's attraction to women of color when she described his apartment on lower Fifth Avenue, which he rented in 1865, while writing *Systematic Geology*. According to Dodge, the building had "a black look like a face that hides its thoughts."[44]

King was posthumously exiled from white society.[45] His wife remains a mystery to scholars for different reasons. Believed to have been born into enslavement, Ada Copeland apparently moved from Georgia to New York City in the mid-1880s, like thousands of other rural Black southerners, allegedly working as a nursemaid before meeting King. The scarcity of information concerning Copeland becomes apparent when reading the definitive work on King's common law marriage, *Passing Strange: A Gilded Age Tale of Love and Deception across the Color Line* (2009). While researching her book Martha Sandweiss excavated census records and other archival data that had languished in government repositories for decades. When pieced together, these shards of information present an incomplete portrait of a woman who was never able to tell her own story. Did Copeland believe the blond, blue-eyed King was a light-skinned mulatto? Did she accept this lie for her husband's sake? Or did the two conspire to fool people while presenting a united front? King cryptically told a friend once that "Negroes seemed more wise about human relationships."[46]

Copeland's absence from the historical record can be partially explained by the fact that she was Black. Like most women in the late nineteenth century, and like other people from rural and impoverished backgrounds, Copeland did not have the education or the kind of career that would have enabled her to become a distinguished public figure. But living in a racially restricted neighborhood also meant that she was surrounded by invisible barriers, separating her from non-Black residents in New York City. Like Native Americans, whom cartographers erased from maps of the American West, Black Americans in eastern urban areas were seldom acknowledged, except in census records and other obscure historical documents.

As Toni Morrison has demonstrated, there is a similar "silence and evasion" about the Africanist presence in American literature. By refusing to acknowledge Copeland, King essentially reinvented himself, appearing in public and in *Mountaineering in the Sierra Nevada* as a white, college-educated, gentleman bachelor; as a scientist who was free to explore the western frontier, using his leisure time to expound on the beauties of nature. According to Morrison, whites typically define themselves in contrast to Blacks. To be white means to be "free," not "enslaved"; "not helpless, but licensed and powerful."[47] King used that power to deny his wife and children, even after his death. To understand how he wrote his family out of his life, one need only consider King's last will and testament. Before dying of tuberculosis in Arizona in 1902, King wrote a letter to Copeland, revealing his true identity. Yet he left his entire estate to his mother, who never knew about her son's other family. Although Copeland believed that King had set aside a trust fund for her and her children, to be managed by one of his friends, she later learned that it was hush money, which she was offered in exchange for her silence.[48]

Referring to her study of blackness in the American literary imagination, Morrison employs a metaphor that reminds one of King's career as a surveyor, though her project is more liberating in its analysis of race and representation. "I want to draw a map, so to speak, of a critical geography and use that map to open as much space for discovery, intellectual adventure, and close exploration as did the original charting of the New World—without the mandate for conquest."[49]

# 2

# Lord of the Limber Tongue

### *The Great Spanish Land Grant Fraud*
### *and the Barony of Arizona*

Clarence King refused to acknowledge his family during his lifetime and after his death. In doing so, he also denied the part of himself known as James Todd. As one critic has poetically noted, King "evaded into space" when his spirit left his body. He pulled off "a vanishing act—of the soul."[1] King evaded detection by leaving the East and the West, where he had established separate existences, escaping into an unspecified realm where no one could follow him. By contrast, James Addison Reavis created two families. He invented an eighteenth-century Spanish aristocrat, giving him a spouse, children, and imaginary descendants, who had allegedly inherited a land grant that Reavis claimed to have purchased. In addition, fearing that investigators might discover his ruse, Reavis hedged his bets by marrying a Mexican woman, contending she was the aforementioned heir. He added flesh to his earlier lie by "producing" the actual claimant in person.

According to Jean Baudrillard, "To dissimulate is to feign not to have what one has. To simulate is to feign to have what one hasn't."[2] King pretended his African American family did not exist, while Reavis created both families for the purpose of defrauding the government. Forgery experts consider documents or works of art in relation to "personhood" (legally acknowledged or otherwise).[3] "Genuine" items are classified by classical scholars as *gnesioi*, the same term applied to legitimate children, while "spurious ones" are deemed *nothoi* or bastards.[4] The noun *forgery* derives from the verb "to forge" or "to make."[5] A forged work has no antecedents, no provenance or history of previous ownership. It is an orphan, created by a self-made person such as Reavis, an imposter with his own invented families or fake genealogical trees.

The nineteenth-century U.S. frontier was a rapidly developing region, especially conducive to such creative inventions or self-transformations; a place where imposters, the illegitimate, minorities, and marginal people could escape from the law, discrimination, and established social conventions. Previously Arizona had been governed by a succession of political entities. Originally inhabited by Native Americans, the land was first explored by the Franciscan friar Marcos de Niza in 1539. After Mexico achieved independence from Spain in the early nineteenth century, it became part of the territory of Alta California. Mexico ceded the northern part of Arizona to the United States after the Mexican-American War in 1848. The U.S. acquired the remaining portion of the area through the Gadsden Purchase five years later. During the Civil War, the South briefly annexed Arizona as a Confederate state. It was reclaimed by the Union in 1863, and remained a U.S. territory until declaring statehood in 1912.

After entering the Union, the territories of California, New Mexico, and Arizona became mired in political turmoil when the owners of Spanish and Mexican land grants defended their right to properties now contained within U.S. borders. Most of these estates were located in California, where the climate and geography were more favorable to ranching and farming. In desert territories such as Arizona, indigenous tribes waged war on settlers until they were forced onto reservations in the 1870s. Afterward, individuals seeking to purchase land in Arizona had to compete with wealthy and powerful corporations such as the Southern Pacific Railroad, which was charting a route from California through Arizona on its way to New Orleans, and the Silver King Mining Company, which had recently discovered ore in the region.[6]

In the late nineteenth century James Addison Reavis attempted to perpetrate one of the greatest frauds in U.S. history by claiming he had purchased a land grant that had originally been awarded to a Spanish nobleman by King Ferdinand VI in 1748. Reavis visited government archives in Spain and Mexico, learning how to read Spanish and write in the style of legal scriveners. In addition he stole blank sheets of paper from files that contained actual eighteenth-and nineteenth-century documents, forging a grant—as well as a series of wills, codicils, deeds and transfers—to prove that the property had passed from the original fictitious recipient to one of the owner's imaginary American descendants, from whom Reavis had allegedly purchased the grant. Along with this manufactured evidence, Reavis included a family coat of arms, a genealogical tree featuring members of the mythical Peralta family, as well as portraits of those individuals, which he found at a flea market in Madrid. When the U.S. courts identified the documents as forgeries, Reavis concocted another scheme to legitimate his claim. After meeting a young Hispanic woman on a train and persuading her that she was the granddaughter of the original claimant, Reavis married her and placed her in a Catholic convent, where she was taught to speak and behave like a member of the Spanish aristocracy. Shortly afterward, Reavis appeared with his wife in Arizona, dressed in splendid finery, once again staking his claim to the "barony" that his wife had supposedly inherited.[7]

Reavis was born in rural Missouri in 1843. Although he had little formal education, he developed a "great facility with words and a rather grandiose style of writing" in childhood. While fighting for the Confederate Army during the Civil War, he learned how to imitate his commanding officer's signature. Forging a furlough pass granting him leave from duty, he surrendered to Union forces. After the war he traveled to Brazil, where one biographer claims Reavis "gained a fair knowledge of Portuguese which may have been the basis for his later fluent but faulty Spanish." Eventually he returned to St. Louis, drifting from job to job, investing his meager earnings in local real estate ventures. On at least one occasion he altered the title to a piece of property, transferring it to himself.[8]

In 1871 Reavis met George Willing, who claimed he had purchased a land grant from a man named Miguel Peralta at a mining camp in Arizona. Willing showed Reavis an *expediente*—a "copy of legal proceedings in relation to the Peralta Grant"—accompanied by a letter from Mexican President Santa Anna, certifying that the documents were housed in the national government archives. The letter, dated prior to the Gadsden Purchase, granted the recipient twelve million acres, covering most of Arizona and part of western New Mexico.[9]

Reavis agreed to help Willing prove the grant's authenticity. At the county courthouse in Prescott, Arizona, in 1874, Willing recorded a deed that conveyed the grant from the fictitious Peralta to himself. Then he went to a local hotel, where he was discovered the next morning dead in bed.[10] Reavis canceled his trip to Arizona after learning of his cohort's mysterious passing. Six years later, he suddenly appeared in Prescott with a letter allegedly written by Willing's widow, granting Reavis custody of the papers that had been found in the deceased's possession. In 1881 he visited government archives in Mexico City and Guadalajara, posing as a journalist and cultivating friendships with employees who gave him access to the institutions' materials. Then he returned to the United States with photographs and copies of papers supposedly pertaining to the grant. Reavis contended that in recognition of service to his majesty, a lieutenant in the king's army named Don Miguel Nemecio Silva de Peralta de la Córdoba had been awarded a land grant by Philip V. Sixteen years later, according to Reavis, Ferdinand VI had designated a specific parcel of land to bestow on Don Miguel. The nobleman had subsequently traveled to North America to survey the boundaries of the Peralta grant, choosing a rock called the Inicial Monument to represent the center of the estate's western boundary line. Because the presence of hostile Apaches had made it impossible for him to settle on his land, the don had bequeathed the estate to his son, reaffirming his decision in a later codicil. He had also created a *cedula*—or official document—including paperwork related to the grant, before dying in 1824 at the age of 116.[11]

Reavis returned to Arizona, informing owners who lived on the land that he had a legal right to confiscate their property. A few of them purchased quitclaim deeds from the new American baron to secure their titles, while the rest fought their eviction. When local newspapers called for government action, surveyor Royal A. Johnson agreed to examine Reavis's documents. In 1890 he published the *Adverse Report of the Surveyor General of Arizona, Royal A. Johnson, upon the Alleged Peralta Grant. A Complete Expose* [sic] *of Its Fraudulent Character*.[12] In his report Johnson noted that the Spanish king's name had been signed with a "steel pen," instead of a quill. Comparing the print on other documents with that "done in Mexico during the same century by the Inquisition," the surveyor declared them "altogether different [in] appearance" (12). In addition, "neither on the title page [of the grant] nor on the last page where the king's signature is alleged to be signed does the name of Miguel Peralta appear or anything in connection with a grant to him; which founds a very reasonable suspicion that these pages might have been used originally for some other purpose" (23).

Fearing the surveyor might reject his claim, Reavis concocted a backup plan. During a train trip to California he met a young, uneducated Hispanic woman who bore a strong resemblance to one of the fake family portraits he had submitted as evidence to the Arizona court. Reavis convinced her that she was the last surviving member of the Peralta dynasty and thus the legal heir to one of the largest land grants in North America. Having abandoned his first wife shortly after their marriage in 1874, Reavis wed this stranger and sent her to a Catholic convent, where the nuns taught her to speak proper Spanish and dress like a lady. After honeymooning in Europe, Reavis returned to California with his bride, the newly christened Doña Sophia Micaela Maso Reavis y Peralta de la Córdoba, the self-proclaimed "Baroness of Arizona." In 1886 he convinced a man named Alfred Sherwood to sign an affidavit stating that Sophia's husband was also her adoptive father. Reavis claimed he had raised Sophia after the deaths of her fictitious parents and twin brother, before taking her hand in marriage. He reappeared in Arizona the following year. Calling himself James Addison Peralta-Reavis, he filed a new claim on behalf of Sophia, the original grant recipient's alleged granddaughter.[13]

After Johnson submitted his surveyor's report, the respondent filed a suit in the U.S. Court of Claims, contending that the government had illegally sold his land to settlers and demanding eleven million dollars in damages. It took the government eight years to test Reavis's case. Spanish, Mexican, and U.S. lawyers, forgery experts, and archival historians examined boxes of supposed evidence, tracing Reavis's trail across Europe and North America.[14] The con man got lucky in 1893 when his wife gave birth to sons Carlos and Miguel, thus "proving" that twins ran in the family. After the U.S. Court of Claims rejected his suit in 1895, Reavis was arrested and charged with forty-two counts of forgery and conspiracy to defraud the U.S. government. The twins came to court during the trial, dressed in "regal velvet," creating "great sympathy" for the defendant.[15] Nevertheless, Reavis was found guilty and sentenced in 1896 to two years in prison. (Sophia had sued him for desertion four years earlier.) After his release Reavis unsuccessfully resumed his quest to establish his claim. He died in Denver, Colorado, in 1914 and was buried in a pauper's grave.[16]

Over the course of several decades, Reavis created a chain of documents, collected portraits, and drew a genealogical diagram that showed property passing from one member of the Peralta family to another, proving his ownership of an imaginary land grant based on his marriage to the alleged legal heir. Like other documents and recorded court proceedings, these forgeries can be read as chapters in a fictional narrative. As scholars in the fields of literature and law have noted, even authentic documents and testimonies can yield various and sometimes conflicting interpretations.[17] Conservatives interpret the U.S. Constitution in light of what they believe its framers intended, while liberals view it as a living document and apply it to the needs of present-day society. A prosecuting attorney tells one version of a story, while a defense lawyer presents another. A witness may be seen by a judge and jury as credible or not. One critic states: "Law stories are narrative in structure, adversarial in spirit, inherently rhetorical in aim, and justifiably open to suspicion."[18] In Reavis's case, the U.S. government had reason to suspect fraud. But although the plaintiff attempted to steal land while pretending to assert his legal rights, the court also sought to verify Reavis's claim while simultaneously pursuing its own agenda. Even if Reavis's documents had been authentic, the government would have been reluctant to rule in the plaintiff's favor, preferring to seize his property as a national asset.

The courts had a history of ruling in favor of the federal government. After the Mexican-American War both countries had signed The Treaty of Guadalupe Hidalgo. According to Article 8, Mexicans who had owned land in California before the war were allowed to retain "the property which they possess,"[19] a promise the U.S. courts repeatedly failed to honor. In 1853 the Gadsden Purchase had made similar promises to owners of Spanish land grants in the New Mexico and Arizona territories. Most of these claims were later renounced by the courts. Some historians believe the U.S. judicial system found the foreign practice of assigning land grants "confusing" and did not know how to adjudicate claims brought by Mexican landowners in accordance with "Hispanic civil law."[20] Apaches in Arizona also had a "complex network of understandings, obligations, and privileges governing their relation to the land and one another. . . . The U.S. government's difficulty with incorporating and respecting these prior [Hispanic and Apache] regimes" was based partly on the different ways in which these cultural and legal systems operated.[21] Other historians contend that the government deliberately stripped landowners of their rights in order to benefit U.S. citizens and corporations. "Rather than respecting treaty obligations, federal officials stood by, and sometimes joined in, as a vast land grab dispossessed hundreds of communities of their rightful property."[22]

Reavis prepared his first claim in the early 1880s, at the same time that the Southern Pacific Railroad sought to purchase land in Arizona. The Silver King Mine had also been operating since the 1870s, while fighting the Apaches for control of the region. John C. Frémont was another formidable foe who tried to use his political position as Arizona's territorial governor for personal gain. After the war Frémont became the first U.S. custodian of the Mexican archives in California. He showed "an appalling neglect" of important records, "losing" documents that made the forging of "fraudulent land grants possible." During the Gold Rush Frémont purchased a Mexican grant of "questionable origin" and became wealthy when ore was found on his property. As the governor of Arizona, he associated with railroad barons and mine owners, who profited from their ties to the territory's most influential political figure.[23]

Although Reavis and the government opposed each other, they both sought to eradicate the Hispanic presence. A film based on Reavis's life, *The Baron of Arizona* (1950), portrays the charlatan as a regional white folk hero. The opening scene takes place in the home of the first state governor, Jonathan Hale, on the day Arizona is admitted to the Union. The governor celebrates statehood by offering a toast to "a real lover of Arizona, my friend, James Addison Reavis." Hale says, "It infuriated [Reavis] that ignorant people inherited land because the United States recognized Spanish grants," acknowledging that Reavis and the state of Arizona shared a common enemy. The introductory credits appear in antique lettering on an aged tattered scroll, making no distinction between the documents that Reavis forged in Spanish script on eighteenth-century paper and the film that glorifies its subject as a part of "Arizona legend."[24]

Reavis transformed himself from a poor man in rural Missouri into the alleged owner of the largest land grant in the U.S. Southwest. Then he reinvented himself as "James Addison Peralta-Reavis," the husband of the fictional Peralta's granddaughter, who was now supposedly the sole legitimate heir to his fortune. Reavis's forged documents were textual fabrications as well as performative acts that helped him maintain a series of public and legal postures. Much of his written "evidence" can be read as performative speech. In one of Reavis's forgeries King Ferdinand VI *grants* Don Miguel a parcel of land by creating a *grant* consisting of written authorization and a drawing that identifies where the gift is located. (The word *grant* is used as both a verb and a noun, indicating a relationship between the word and the thing to which it refers.) Lawyers *certify* the legality of Reavis's documents by providing *certifications* in writing. Elsewhere Don Miguel asserts his *will* to bequeath his estate to his son by writing a *will* making his intentions clear, then affixing his signature. The Spanish word for *signature* is replaced in English translations of these documents with the word *flourish*, a noun that transforms the writing of one's name into a theatrical gesture. The scribe who allegedly executes the handwritten documents in the original Spanish is referred to as a *scrivener*, a term that can mean both *writer* and *copyist*. The scrivener—who is also a notary—certifies that certain materials are copies of original documents, as evidenced by the notary's seal, engraved or embossed in wax and stamped on documents in a final performance that legitimizes the forged yet seemingly authentic decree.[25]

Because these documents had to pass visual inspection, they can also be considered artistic forgeries. Authorities who sought to determine the authenticity of these materials analyzed the type of ink used; the age of the parchment; the Spanish diction and grammar, which had to conform to eighteenth- and nineteenth-century custom and style; and the writings of royal court and legal scriveners, who tended to enlarge, elongate, and add flourishes to certain words and letters. A forger such as Reavis "must give his text the appearance—the linguistic appearance as a text and the physical appearance as a document—of something from a period dramatically earlier than and different from his own. . . . Two forms of imagination should lead to two different, complementary acts of falsification: he must produce a text that seems distant from the present day and an object that seems distant from its purported time of design. . . . Imagination and corroboration, the creation of the forgery and the provision of its pedigree."[26]

A person's identity is constituted in performative acts that express information about that individual. Thus to impersonate someone else is to assume "the pose of a pose."[27] When "Peralta-Reavis" and his wife appeared in Arizona in 1887, they gave a performance that involved impersonation, the creation of forged documents, and the publication of an additional fictional narrative. They entered Tucson dressed in Spanish regalia, accompanied by servants, and proceeded to the most expensive hotel in town, where Reavis "signed the hotel register with a flourish." While he prepared his documents, Reavis's wife gave an interview with a local reporter that reads like fairy tale, rehearsed in advance. "My life's history opens in a cloud of mystery," she claimed. "From the earliest period of my recollection I was aware that in some way my antecedents were a mystery which it was the interest of certain persons to weave into an impenetrable web." She described her orphaned childhood and her later job working for a dressmaker in California. One day on a train she met a stranger who "was struck with my resemblance to a family whose history was interwoven with his own." Learning her true identity, she married Reavis, "and the secret which had so long been kept was open to the world."[28]

Reavis added an additional role to his repertoire. His mother was half Spanish and claimed to have been seduced by a frontiersman who left her "soon after their marriage." According to one biographer, Maria Reavis was proud of her ancestry. "From the few tales her mother had told her, she had created over the years for her children a picture of an illustrious and romantic background, a family of prestige and wealth, perhaps of nobility, which had contributed to the glory of Spain." Maria loved to read novels "recounting the exploits of Spanish conquistadors, stories that were based on historical reports and memoirs of Spanish monks and royal officials." She retold those adventures to her son, translating the purple prose into English. As a result, Reavis acquired "a distinct gift for expressing himself on paper in a fluent, if flowery, manner."[29] Later, Arizona residents referred to Reavis as "Lord of the Limber Tongue" because he could talk his way out of any situation.[30]

Reavis appeared to be a white man claiming land that had once belonged to Spain. But he could also be described as a light-skinned man of Spanish heritage, attempting to reclaim an estate that had once belonged to his fictional ancestors. His second wife was a lower-class Hispanic woman passing as a Spanish aristocrat. *The Baron of Arizona* presents yet another passing narrative. In the film Sophia is a light-skinned Native American woman posing as white.

The Reavis case was complicated by differences between Spanish and American law as well as questions concerning national, racial, and ethnic identity. (Before the invention of DNA testing, the birth of Reavis's sons seemed to support the theory that his wife was related to the fictional Peralta family, whose women had a supposed history of producing twins.) It was also a case about class, pitting the entitled European aristocrat against the American self-made man. Reavis and his wife based their claim on the assumption that whoever held Don Miguel's grant would prevail in court. They competed against small U.S. landowners who had come to Arizona to pursue the American dream. In turn, those landowners were competing against corporate monopolies and wealthy private industries for control of the region.

The Reavis case was also a contest between religious and secular governmental powers. The forged documents reveal the relationship between Catholicism and Spanish law. In the royal decree, or original grant, Ferdinand VI is referred to as "the King our Lord." At the end of Don Miguel's will, leaving the land to his son, the notary certifies the owner's wishes represent his last will and testament. He quotes the don: "having now done my duty, be it as God may will."[31] The people working on the U.S. government's side were participating in a secular judicial investigation that concluded in favor of Manifest Destiny. The court's findings can be viewed a defeat for Catholicism and as a victory for the Protestant notion that U.S. westward expansion was a result of God's will. (Reavis was motivated by personal greed, not religion or politics. One of his most influential supporters was the religious skeptic and noted agnostic Robert G. Ingersoll.[32])

The Reavis case is a chapter in the history of frontier colonization, involving the dispossession of indigenous peoples and foreign empires. The notion of a divinely entitled Anglo-Saxon race was formulated during earlier skirmishes with Hispanics during the Texas Revolution, culminating in the Mexican-American War and the subsequent secession of lands comprising the California, New Mexico, and Arizona territories.[33] But the case can also read as a romance heralding the return of the Spanish military and social aristocracy, signifying the restoration of a European civilization in a savage North American colonial outpost. The twin motif runs throughout these contrasting narratives, involving sets of real and imaginary twins; fake and authentic documents; Reavis and Peralta-Reavis, both of whom are a mixture of white and Spanish; two races, each with its own claim to shared territory.

Reavis represented whites who immigrated to the West after the war, displacing Spaniards, Mexicans, and Native Americans—people whose plight was depicted in Helen Hunt Jackson's sentimental romance, *Ramona* (1884). But Reavis was also a romancer in his own right, raised on the popular Spanish fiction of an earlier era. He was a cousin to Mark

Twain's protagonist in *The American Claimant* (1892), Colonel Mulberry Sellers, who is proud of his English lineage, and who imagines he is the heir to an earl's estate. The novel features twins, characters who die in order to reappear as someone else, cases of mistaken identity, and discussions about death and resurrection. It debates issues such as authenticity and subjectivity, legitimacy and imposture, and biological and socially constructed forms of identity.[34]

During the period of U.S. settlement, western historians were unable to imagine a future Anglo-Saxon empire comparable to the glories of New Spain. In *Memoir of the Proposed Territory of Arizona* (1857), Sylvester Mowry claimed that by the time of the Gadsden Purchase, Apaches "had gradually extirpated every trace of civilization, and roamed uninterrupted and unmolested, sole possessor of what was once a thriving and populous Spanish province." The missions and settlements had been "destroyed" by the natives, and the priests and settlers "massacred or driven off." A "superior" society had disappeared, "and today there is scarcely a trace of it left."[35] Mowry's "memoir" was a history of the region as well as a personal exercise in nostalgia.

In his first attempt to steal land in Arizona Reavis represented himself as a white man, seeking to usurp territory that had once been part of New Spain. In his second attempt Reavis tried to reinstate the Spanish presence in the U.S. Southwest by using forged evidence to establish his wife's claim to the Peralta estate. As one art critic notes, early Greek and Roman forgeries were designed to fill gaps in classical historical narratives. "National histories not fully covered in canonical texts were now filled out by the discovery of coherent documents not in the classical languages; full blown romantic emotions not mirrored by the classics were provided with ancient inspiration of a novel sort."[36] Reavis's second claim was also based on forged documents, inserted into historical archives, contributing to the historical record of Spanish conquest and empire by establishing a fictional military explorer's claim to a portion of the U.S. Southwest. But the government's exposure of Reavis can also be construed as a U.S. victory. "Narratives of literary forgery tend to be triumphalist, because the 'crime' is always identified and usually solved."[37] Like the U.S. conquest of Spanish and Mexican territories, the legal verdict in favor of the U.S. government concludes the court's triumphalist narrative.

A forgery implies its opposite: a genuine document on which the fraud has been based. However, as the history of forgery reveals, a genuine document can be as mythical as the notion of a perfect society. People tend to share a "commonsense conviction that because the structure of temporality is unilinear, the genuine always precedes the spurious." In fact, "the genuine may not be the origin from which spuriosity deviates or lapses. Instead, it may be a wholly imaginary state, like utopia, produced by the mechanism known to lexicographers as 'back-formation': that is, the genuine may be something extrapolated from the spurious as its imagined opposite, and then retrojected as its equally imagined antecedent."[38] One can only posit a Hispanic utopia (New Spain) by ignoring the prior existence of "uncivilized" Apache tribes in the region. Similarly, one can only imagine an edenic New World by ignoring the U.S. government's refusal to honor Spanish and Mexican land grants, legalizing the dispossession of the region's earlier nonwhite inhabitants.[39]

The case of James Addison Reavis illustrates the difficulty in using documents to authenticate identity and transfer property. The nineteenth-century U.S. West was a site of contestation, where rival nations and different legal systems competed for jurisdiction, as well as a place that attracted people seeking economic opportunities or refuge from the law.[40] More property was conveyed by land grants on the western frontier than anywhere else in the nation during this period. Yet these contracts and other agreements, such as the Gadsden Purchase and Treaty of Guadalupe Hidalgo, were not always authentic or binding. They could be forged by individuals and undermined by courts that refused to enforce their nation's laws or those of another country. Reavis's initial forgery was issued to a nonexistent Spanish nobleman in recognition for his service to King Ferdinand VI. It was a reward for his political loyalty rather than a boon to his fortune, since the land was located in a desert occupied by hostile indigenous tribes. Realizing the region was worthless as "real" estate, Reavis hoped to make a profit by offering quitclaim deeds to the few existing white settlers willing to defend their titles, selling the remaining land rights to railroad and mining corporations, for which the desert had no value as livable space.

Reavis inserted subsequent records in international archives, creating a chain of evidence or history of documentation to substantiate his claim. One scholar defines archives as official storehouses of public memory, as institutions containing "documents, maps," and other items "supposedly resistant to change." Such repositories become agents of "expansionism" when they seek to preserve a nation's claims to sovereignty or its citizens' property rights. Reavis undermined such attempts, as well as the U.S. government's desire to claim the disputed territory, tampering with these seemingly inviolable archives for personal gain. In addition to infiltrating the institutions of foreign governments, Reavis offered a series of impersonations—a "repertoire" of performances—as the lawful beneficiary of the original grant and as the husband of the last remaining heir, involving costumes, gestures, and speech, "all those acts usually thought of as ephemeral, nonreproducible knowledge."[41] Along with the narrative created by these "official" documents, Reavis enacted "scenarios" incorporating textual props and other forms of misinformation. Earlier, while scouting the Arizona desert to determine where he might locate his grant, Reavis had discovered a prominent rock carved with Indian petroglyphs that marked the center of the western boundary of the Peralta estate. In a report allegedly written by an eyewitness during an expedition to prove the grant's validity, a Mexican priest supposedly confirmed the existence of this landmark. Visible "on said rock [was] the *diseño* (layout) of the said Barony of Arizona." The priest performed a ceremony to consecrate the spot, naming the rock "Inicial Monument."[42] In Spanish and English, *inicial* (initial) means first or original. It also refers to a letter, abbreviation, or sign. Reavis tampered with the inscription, carving a map on the rock which purportedly outlined the parameters of his personal property.[43]

In a study of Spanish land grants, one scholar notes that "the American West was not an exceptional place. Rather, it was a region that reflected the broader trends of nineteenth-century imperialism and colonial endeavors throughout the rest of the world."[44] Such conflicts often occurred in the Southwest and California, a battleground for international colonial powers. It was also "a playground for negotiations of identity," a place where "historical, cultural, and social power relations" led to "the invention of new selves for personal gain, whether social or monetary." In addition to the American myth of the self-made man, "the encounter of white settlers with Native Americans, and class divisions induced by capitalism created the oppression and disenfranchisement of certain groups. Racial passing, going Native, or faking white upper-class identity became a backdoor for escaping underprivileged social strata."[45] All these factors came into play in the case of Reavis, a lower-middle-class, biracial imposter and forger who operated within the legal conventions established by various colonial powers, while seeking to subvert those systems for financial gain by forging Spanish documents and defacing Indian markers, alternately passing as a white frontier gentleman and as the husband of a Spanish aristocrat: a self-made man fighting national forces at home and abroad. After serving a prison sentence for conspiracy to defraud the U.S. government, Reavis published a magazine article in 1900, admitting: "I was playing a game which to win meant greater wealth than that of a Gould or a Vanderbilt."[46] Afterward, Reavis disappeared. Records indicate that he lived for a month at the Los Angeles County Poor Farm in 1913. Homeless, broke, and forgotten by the public, he died a year later in Denver, Colorado.

# 3

# A French Canadian Cowboy

*Branding Will James*

James Reavis's legal documents were forgeries, like fake works of art. Will James's paintings and sketches, as well as his publications, were both inauthentic and genuine. James was a writer and illustrator of children's literature. His best known novel, *Smoky the Cowhorse*, won the Newberry Medal in 1926. Although James considered himself a serious artist, he never received the same acclaim as Frederic Remington and Charlie Russell, whose representations of the American West were praised by critics for their realism—especially their later works, which depicted negative aspects of white frontier settlement, including the forced removal of Indians from their native lands. By contrast, James's stories and pictures appealed to children because they typically focused on the personal relationship between a boy and his horse, ignoring social, political, and environmental changes that were occurring in the region in the early twentieth century.

In *Lone Cowboy: My Life Story* (1930) the author recalled his own childhood, writing about the death of his parents, being raised by a French-Canadian trapper, and learning to survive on the U.S. frontier. The autobiography was a work of fiction. James's real name was Joseph Ernest Nephtali Dufault. Born in Quebec, Canada, in 1892, Dufault moved to Saskatchewan in 1910. Four years later he immigrated to the United States, where he changed his name and became a cowboy. After serving a prison sentence for cattle rustling, James went to Hollywood, where he performed as a stunt man in early westerns. Later he found success as an artist and writer, creating works that reinforced the myth of "Will James," self-made American cowboy. Like James Addison Reavis, Ernest Dufault was a gifted imposter whose greatest creation was his own alter ego; a fictitious character whom he played for the rest of his life.

The celebrated American artist known as Will James was born and raised in Quebec. Established as a province of New France in 1534, Quebec became a central outpost in the North American fur-trading industry by the early seventeenth century. During this period King Louis XII restricted immigration to French-speaking Catholics, a policy that remained in force for the next several centuries. In accordance with the Treaty of Paris in 1759, France ceded its territories to Great Britain. Afterward Quebec entered into a confederation with its neighboring English-speaking provinces, becoming part of the Dominion of Canada. During this period of political reformation and cultural change the majority of Quebec's population continued to speak French and practice Catholicism, insisting on its unique status among the country's provinces and its independence from Europe.[1] Quebec's colonists "neither lived in a French manner nor thought of themselves as French." Although the majority of residents were descendants of European immigrants, they believed their settlement in North America had resulted in the creation of "a unique cultural product." Quebec's culture was "the end product of the transformation that an originally European way of life underwent upon contact with a new environment."[2]

Afraid of losing their majority at home, Quebec's French-speaking inhabitants were statistically less likely than other Canadians to immigrate to western provinces and foreign countries. French Canadians were also more "family-minded" than their Anglo counterparts.[3] Most of those who left Quebec moved to nearby New England, where the textile mills employed men, women, and children as cheap sources of labor.[4] Unlike his peers, however, Dufault moved to Saskatchewan, where he worked on ranches, herding cattle and wrangling horses. As the Industrial Revolution spread throughout the United States and Canada, transforming cities into centers of commerce and manufacturing, Dufault relocated to one of his country's most rurally isolated regions to pursue his dream of becoming a cowboy.

Dufault began drawing as a child, sketching animals on scraps of wrapping paper while lying on the floor in his parents' kitchen. His father owned a boarding house in Montreal where the tenants read pulp magazines filled with adventure stories set on the U.S. frontier. Although Dufault could not read English, he copied the illustrations, basing his notion of a cowboy on the colorful characters who appeared in these fictional tales.[5] During adolescence he decided to become a cowboy in order to work with horses. But the cowboys whom he sought to emulate were romantic figments of the imagination who resembled the pictures he had seen as a child.

Dufault could have remained in Saskatchewan if he had wanted to work in the same profession as his childhood heroes. There were cowboys in Canada, not only on the prairie but in the mountains on the border between western Saskatchewan and eastern Alberta.[6] Nevertheless, Dufault believed that a man could never be "a top hand" unless he was "born in the West."[7] Like the illustrations in popular magazines, novels by authors such as B. M. Bower contributed to this misconception. Unbeknownst to James, his favorite writer (the creator of the Hopalong Cassidy series) was a housewife originally from Minnesota named Bertha Sinclair.

Dufault's immigration to the United States made little sense from a historical perspective. By the time he came to Montana in 1914, cowboys were already a dying breed. In the late nineteenth century the invention of barbed wire had led to the end of the open range and the need for cowboys to tend their employers' stock. Railroads also enabled ranchers to ship their cattle to market, making trail drives unnecessary.[8] Writing under an assumed name in his autobiography, Default ignores these realities, portraying the U.S. frontier as unfenced territory. He claims to remember rounding up cattle on an open range and sorting them based on the brands that distinguished them from other ranchers' stock. He also describes stealing cattle that roamed free on the prairie, while "drifting" on horseback throughout the region.[9] The pseudo-autobiographer transformed the West into a fictional space bearing little resemblance to the settled territory.

French Canadians viewed Quebec as a nation within a nation. Its citizens had a different language and religion as well as French-based laws and cultural institutions. But Dufault was not nationalistic, unlike other Quebecers. He had a disregard for territorial boundaries, state lines, and political and geographic borders. Dufault successfully transitioned from the Canadian to the U.S. frontier, drifting within his adopted homeland from place to place, unencumbered by a sense of patriotism and cultural loyalty. Unlike other transnational subjects, who developed a cosmopolitan sensibility—feeling "at home in the world," while simultaneously straddling the U.S.-Canadian border[10]—"Will James" seemed to live in a void. To prevent readers from fact-checking his autobiography, the author never identified the places he visited, the ranches where he worked, or other people he encountered. The American West became a liminal space, a site of transition where Dufault transformed into his fictional alter ego.

In addition to changing his name, the immigrant created a new family and childhood narrative, while acquiring skills that enabled the son of a Montreal merchant to pass as an American cowboy. Although he became fluent in English, he retained a foreign accent, which he accounted for by telling readers that he had been raised by a French Canadian trapper. Unlike cosmopolitan travelers and multilingual speakers who code-switch as they move back and forth between various languages, combining standard and colloquial forms of expression,[11] James never reverted to French once he changed his birth name, except in letters he wrote to his brother Auguste, begging his sibling not to reveal "his true identity."[12]

The self-christened James was careful never to jeopardize the new life and career he had deliberately chosen. Yet he also acted aimlessly, drifting from job to job. Cowboys were seasonal, itinerant workers. Most of them were young, unmarried men who traveled on horseback, maintaining no fixed address or permanent place of employment. Cowboys were defined by their mobility, independence, and undomesticated nature. James performed this aspect of his new identity, "drifting" through the West in his autobiography as well as in his short story collection *The Drifting Cowboy* (1925). "In this book," he promised readers, "you'll find the cowboy still very much alive . . . as he drifts and hunts for new cow countries."[13]

James played a cowboy, though not in the same way that people "played Indian" at the turn of the century by wearing costumes and reenacting native rituals.[14] Playing cowboy did not require racial cross-identification. Cowboys were racially diverse members of an occupational group. Becoming a cowboy meant learning to ride horses, build fence, and brand and castrate cattle. "Will James" was an imaginary person, but his skills were genuine. While living in Nevada the artist learned to break horses, a ritual that transformed greenhorns into expert riders. In short story collections such as *Horses I've Known* (1940) and *The American Cowboy* (1942), James celebrated the relationship between a cowboy and his mount. His fictional characters resembled the author and participated in various stages of the horse-taming process: lassoing a mustang, saddling a skittish mare, leaping through the air on a bucking bronc, hobbling a wild stallion, fording a river, or chasing a herd of runaway cattle. The act of "breaking" a wild animal symbolized the complex relationship between a horse and its rider. Both were nomadic by nature. Like a drifting cowboy, a mustang refused to be captured, tamed, haltered, and saddled. But a cowboy was also an agent of westward expansion, someone who conquered the wilderness. Once broken, a horse became almost human. A cowboy cared for his mount, who became his trusted companion—unlike cattle, which were merely bred to be killed. Cattle were easily controlled and confined in closed spaces: herded, corralled, roped and tied, squeezed through branding chutes, packed into railroad cars, and sent to slaughterhouses. As James states in his autobiography, a cow "was just beef, an animal to raise and ship to market and set up on the table in a big platter" (59). Horses were friends, yet inferior to their masters. They symbolized a cowboy's mobility, independence, and ability to conquer nature.

James drifted until he was imprisoned for cattle rustling in 1914. He does not explain why he turned to crime in his autobiography. James could not admit that the open range no longer existed and that cowboys sometimes rustled cattle from their former employers rather than train for new professions. James used his time at the state penitentiary in Carson City, Nevada, to continue sketching, inspired by the horses he saw through the bars of his window. A three-part drawing entitled "The Turning Point" (1915) shows the artist roping the cow he was arrested for stealing; then sitting in his cell; and finally standing at an easel, recreating his crime on canvas. The picture is subtitled "Have Had Ample Time for Serious Thought and It Is My Ambition to Follow up on My Art."[15]

Instead of pursuing this plan, James went to Hollywood after being released from prison. Dreaming of stardom may have been his reason for leaving Saskatchewan, since the one thing Canada lacked was a national film industry. Before going to California, James spent several years in the West, using this time to rehearse the skills necessary for becoming a cowboy. Other men had gone to Hollywood after the open range closed in the late nineteenth century, working as stunt doubles and horse wranglers in silent westerns. None of them became successful film stars. As the urban West displaced the rural frontier, symbolized by the rise of Hollywood, cowboys were replaced by their celluloid doubles, who were deemed to be more believable than their real-life inspirations. In his autobiography James recalls how the star of a western behaved condescendingly toward the actual cowboys who worked on the film as extras (363–63). In a story entitled "Filling the Cracks" another character tells the protagonist he has no future in Hollywood because he can't "act" like a cowboy. "Your expression is just the same wether you're eating a plate of 'frioles' or riding a bronc; fact is you aint got no such thing as expression."[16]

World War I put an end to James's acting career. The "lone" cowboy resented seeing men being treated by the military like cattle. "About a thousand head of us rookies was loaded on a train" and taken to boot camp, where he complains that he was neither "independent nor free." James calls his commanding officers "pointmen," a name for cowboys who led trail drives, determining the route taken by a herd. (The term was also used in combat to refer to the person heading a military expedition.) James states, "I wasn't used to regular hours . . . nor to take orders from anybody. A cowboy, if he knows his work, never gets no orders on the range. He's pretty well his own boss" (378–79). After the war James sought to distinguish himself from the "herd." Having failed as an actor, he reinvented himself as an artist and writer. Though he identified as a cowboy for the rest of his life, James stressed his alleged origins less frequently as he became increasingly successful. In 1920 he sold his first sketches to *Sunset* magazine. The periodical was owned by the Southern Pacific Railroad, which had contributed to the demise of the open range at the turn of the century.[17]

Although James lacked "expression" as an actor, he had a knack for self-invention. His education as an artist-performer began in Nevada. Ranchers branded their stock to prevent them from being stolen by rustlers. Thieves altered these brands, transferring stock from their legal owners to rustlers or "brand artists."[18] James allegedly became interested in brands as a child. According to his autobiography, when the orphan became bored he would "pick up things and want to make marks, tracing something in the dirt with a stick, or, with a hunk of charcoal [he'd] pick up from the last fire at the branding pen" (9). This incident was a product of the author's imagination. Yet it suggests a connection between branding and drawing. Later in the book James refers to his childhood doodles as "markings" (30).

In *Lone Cowboy* the author claims he was taught the art of branding by the fur trapper who was his surrogate father. "In picking out cattle, he warned me never to take a 'marker' (an animal that could easy be recognized by odd markings). When he changed a brand he didn't use no knife, no hot iron, no wet blanket. . . . By dipping a twig in [a bottle of acid] he could work over the old brand and spread out with the new one. In a few hours the new brand would show up in a scaly ridge and look as old as the first one it blended with. There'd even be gray hairs showing and that brand would stand inspection from the outside of the hide as well as from the inside, in case trouble come and the animal would have to be killed and skinned to show evidence" (184). Later James develops his own technique as a rustler. After altering a brand, he writes: "I plastered some mud over the whole thing and I brushed it off again when it got dry. I left just enough on so the brand was hard to read and so it wouldn't look disguised" (255). James transforms a new mark into one that seems older and thus more likely genuine. At the same time a brand is a signature, usually an encrypted version of the name of an owner's ranch. Thus a rustler's alteration is an act of forgery.

Brands have visual and semantic components, including letters, numbers, geometric shapes, and symbols. James understood that brands were visual "markings" as well as a literate means of communication. In the autobiography he makes his first "marks" as an artist by branding a piece of wood (9). In order to read he also learns how to interpret the "marks" he sees in a newspaper (33). Here brands become a textual metaphor—an encrypted language or a code that must be deciphered so that the author can write his autobiography. Unable to remember his early childhood, James uses "the tally of what [Bopy the fur trapper] told me" (3). The author refers to books brand readers used during roundups to tally the number of cattle that belonged to ranchers. Livestock associations kept similar records, listing the brands that had been legally registered by cattlemen in each state or territory. James transforms the brand book or tallied compilation of animal marks into a metaphor for his autobiographical narrative, like fellow cowboy-turned-author Andy Adams, who alluded to the relationship between brands and books by titling his collection of short fiction *Cattle Brands: A Collection of Western Camp-Fire Stories* (1906).

James incorporates brands into sentences, making them carry the same semantic weight as words. In the story "Borrowed Horses" a prison official says to a pair of convicted rustlers: "I suppose you boys can prove you've been riding for the [here James draws a square with a vertical line crossing the middle of the lower horizontal border] until a couple of days or so ago, that you never laid eyes on the [stock] until yesterday."[19] In another story the narrator describes his "job breaking a string of fine three and four year old colts for the Kant-Hook [here James inserts a lazy capital Y, tilting to the right] horse outfit."[20] In the first instance James substitutes the brand for the name of the ranch; in the second example he follows the name with the brand, translating English into another language familiar to western readers. In "Borrowed Horses," as well as in "Regular Folks," the brand is not translated for the sake of a general audience, emphasizing the fact that branding is a foreign language for non-westerners. "Being the [here James inserts a capital H, with a short vertical bar on the right, tilting upward] was a much disliked outfit from many miles around, most everybody felt free with their stock which scattered a hundred miles and much more off their range."[21]

Other marks also signify animal ownership. An earmark is a notch made by a knife, while a wattle is a "mark of ownership made on the neck or the jaw of an animal by pinching up a quantity of skin and cutting it down but not entirely off."[22] Branding is a more complex sign system, requiring the practitioner to master the grammar and syntax of bodily signification. A vertical brand reads from top to bottom; a horizontal brand, from left to right; an enclosed brand, from the outside in.[23] A "lazy" brand features a sign lying on its side. A "flying" brand has wings attached to it. A "walking" brand has marks that look like feet, while a "running" brand includes a straight line with a curve at the end. A "drag" brand has a projected line at the bottom, which angles downward. A "rafter" brand features two lines meeting at a point, like the roof on a house. An upside-down brand is considered "crazy."[24] In addition the English language includes technical terms to describe these marking methods. A "maverick" is an unbranded animal. More specifically, a "slick" is an unbranded horse. A "sleeper" is a calf that has been earmarked by a rustler who intends to claim it at a later date.[25]

James's characters boast about their brand-reading skills, claiming that "cow language" is more difficult to learn than English. A character says in "On the Middle": "I'd like to see the teacher who can read different brands at a glance thru the hair, tell the earmarks, wattles and vents."[26] In his autobiography James demonstrates such skills when he applies for a job at a ranch. The cattleman "took me in the house, drawed a long line and made earmarks 'facing me' on both sides, then he gave me his tally book and asked me to read it" (178). Western writers use the term "cow language" to refer to branding as well as to a workplace vernacular spoken by cowboys and ranchers that features ungrammatical English mixed with regional slang. James spoke a similar form of French when he lived in Quebec. Turn-of-the-century French Canadians distinguished themselves from people who spoke and wrote standardized French by using a modified version of the language called *joual* (a corruption of *cheval*, meaning "horse").[27] In his autobiography James blames the French Canadian trapper for his stylistic *faux pas*. In fact the author's writing reflected his imperfect command of English as a second language as well as a self-conscious attempt to inflect his prose with a western twang. As a rustler James altered the brands on livestock. As an author he played with the "marks" in books, tinkering with the orthography of printed words. The author intentionally uses ungrammatical and misspelled words, creating a cowboy character who appears authentic—"wether [he's] eating a plate of 'frioles' or riding a bronc." At times the artist applies this vernacular with a heavy brush. Although he notes in the autobiography that his "edducation" consisted mostly of drawing, roping, and riding (63), he maintains that he seldom "misspelt" words (38). Yet he did so deliberately, using his semi-literacy to suggest his western authenticity.[28]

Like a brand, which has visual and semantic components, James was an artist as well as a writer. "I always liked to draw something with a little story in it," he admits in the autobiography (63). Although he wrote on paper with ruled lines, he preferred to sketch on blank canvases (27)— not surprisingly for a cowboy who objected to fences, effectively erasing them from his autobiography. Having learned to draw before becoming a writer, James rebelled against grammatical rules and conventional standards of literary excellence. He seldom signed his sketches before becoming a professional artist, leaving them tacked to the bunkhouse wall when he left a ranch or giving them to friends as parting souvenirs.[29] "[A] feller can't keep much while knocking around the country with only two horses, one to pack you and the other to pack your gatherings. I scattered them drawings around as I went," he observes in *Lone Cowboy* (273). James uses the same word to describe the "scattered" herds of unfenced cattle that are stolen by rustlers (186).

The cowboy began signing his work when he became a professional artist. The subtitle in "The Turning Point" (1915) professes his determination to quit rustling and "Follow up on [His] Art." His signature represents his promise to become a productive member of society. James elongates the W and the J in "Will James" and places three short horizontal bars on top of the J. He transforms the letter into a branding iron, reinforcing the connection between brands and names, while playfully alluding to the reason for his incarceration (changing the brands on stolen stock). Ten years later, in *The Drifting Cowboy*, James replaced his exaggerated initials with capital letters of equal size. In his signature at the end of the preface and on the illustrations in this collection of short stories, the author removes the bars from the J and places them vertically beneath his name. Ten years later, in *Horses I've Known*, the bars disappear from the signature in the preface, though not from the stories' illustrations. These changes reflect James's desire to (re)brand himself as an artist in the marketplace as well as his ongoing efforts to refine his public persona.

Brands tell stories. In the advertising industry, marketers transform products into brands by associating them with "compelling" narratives. According to one executive: "Stories are how we give meaning to what happens to us. . . . When an archetype is embodied in the narrative, in the visuals, and in the artifacts, it becomes instantly recognizable."[30] According to marketers, Will James embodied not one but three mythic archetypes: the explorer, the hero, and the outlaw. The explorer represents the desire to discover oneself by "exploring the world." His greatest fear is "getting trapped" or being forced to conform. The explorer fulfills his need to keep moving by seeking adventures—though at times he appears to wander aimlessly. By contrast, the hero proves his worth by undertaking a difficult task or mastering his surroundings, while the outlaw operates outside society, committing crimes in his search for "radical freedom."[31]

James was a drifter, a rustler, and the heroic subject of his fictional autobiography: an orphan who overcame adversity on the western frontier, becoming a celebrated author and artist. Over time the personality rather than the work became "the product."[32] Every story and illustration repeated a variation on the same theme—a lone cowboy taming a horse, then becoming a successful artist. James sold himself to the public, becoming a cowboy, a commodity, a signature brand. In order to strengthen that brand, he tried to eradicate every trace of Ernest Dufault. Initially he refused to acknowledge in his autobiography that he was married, believing that the truth "detracted from the idea of his being a 'lone cowboy.'" For the same reason he objected to having children—though he eventually adopted a boy, paralleling the "fact" that he had been raised by a trapper.[33] Once he became successful, he returned to Montana and built a ranch called the Rocking R (an allusion to the rocking horse the orphan rode in *Lone Cowboy*). The pseudo-rustic abode featured an outhouse instead of an indoor bathroom. The celebrity served guests franks and beans for dinner, and when he visited New York City, he dressed like "the second coming" of Buffalo Bill.[34]

At the end of his autobiography James claimed: "What I write is built around facts" (431). Years earlier he had begun drinking to cope with his fear of being exposed as a fraud. He composed *Lone Cowboy* on a typewriter because his shaking hands prevented him from "writing legible longhand." As time went by he disappeared at irregular intervals. On one occasion his wife found him in Tucson, Arizona, living with an alcoholic girlfriend in a cheap apartment. In 1942 he returned to Hollywood, cohabiting with a mistress while revising his final book, *The American Cowboy*. A friend said "he had been living on liquor. He wouldn't eat. It was difficult to communicate with him." A few months later, James died in a local hospital due to "alcoholic complications." A plane scattered his ashes over his home in Montana, while "his last two horses, Pecos and Cortez," grazed in attendance.[35]

James became a cowboy at a time when the rural West was transforming into an urban region, dominated by a film industry that commemorated the past by producing westerns for mass consumption. Although James was a fictional character, the man who played him was more "real" than the actors who starred in these films. Ernest Dufault came from a Canadian province whose motto—*Je me souviens*—reminded Quebecers to remember their history and preserve their customs. Eventually his alter ego moved to Los Angeles, a city that had a "history of forgetting." By the early twentieth century, business people, real estate investors, and tourist industry executives had succeeded in erasing the city's Hispanic past, transforming Los Angeles into a modern metropolis that welcomed white immigrants and entrepreneurs.[36]

The National Film Board of Canada produced a documentary entitled *Alias Will James* in 1988. The film reveals its subject's true identity, while showing that modern Canadian cowboys still dream of going to Hollywood. The men who are interviewed make no distinction between being a cowboy and acting like one. "It's all showbiz," says a rodeo performer who went to Los Angeles to take guitar lessons, hoping to work in westerns. The filmmakers illustrate the interviewees' comments by including clips from films starring John Wayne and Gregory Peck. One man boasts about his Texas accent, which he learned in the states. He performs for the camera, reading a selection from James's autobiography, sounding like a Texas or French Canadian actor as he recites the author's "cow language," which was the product of James's imagination. The speaker vouches for the authenticity of the author's vernacular, noting the number of times James uses the word "ain't." The comment provides a fitting summary for the career of a man who once claimed: "When I published *Lone Cowboy* people believed I was sincere. And I guess I was."[37]

# Making an Indian

*The Case of Sylvester Long*

Like Will James, Sylvester Long identified with a culture that was quickly disappearing. In a foreword to the first edition of Long's autobiography, a reporter for the *New York World* claimed the author depicted "graphic phases of . . . a race which is rapidly vanishing." The writer congratulated Long for recording his tribe's history and cultural traditions.[1] In reality, Native Americans were not on the verge of extinction and Long was not the person he claimed to be. He was one of the greatest impostors of the early twentieth century. The son of a janitor, Long was born in Winston-Salem, North Carolina in 1890. Although his parents claimed to be of mixed Indian heritage, they were considered "colored" and were forced to live in a segregated neighborhood inhabited primarily by African Americans. In 1904 Long joined a Wild West show that was touring the South.[2] During his employment the boy with high cheek bones, long black hair, and copper-colored skin was frequently mistaken for a full-blooded Indian. While working behind the scenes he became friends with a Cherokee actor who taught the boy his native language. Later Long capitalized on this acquired knowledge, applying to the Carlisle Indian Industrial School as a member of the Cherokee tribe. His parents supported their son's application, hoping an education would enable Long to have a better life. Thus began the first chapter in his notorious career as an ethnic impersonator.[3]

Long was born the same year Frederick Jackson Turner claimed the frontier had "closed," thus fostering the impression among white Americans that Indians were in danger of becoming extinct.[4] The publication of Turner's influential essay coincided with the growing popularity of western dime novels, which reproduced the frontier—or a romanticized and sensationalized version of it—for readers who had become nostalgic for the nation's preindustrial past. Previously "the image of the Indian" in popular culture, although "confused and fictional," had been based on actual encounters between whites and Native Americans. That image "radically shifted," as "real" Indians were gradually replaced by figures of "urban fantasy."[5] The mass-manufacturing of cheaply priced serial fiction made the West accessible to consumers in cities throughout the United States, many of whom had never encountered actual Native Americans.[6] Earlier, Wild West shows had blurred the distinction between Indians and their theatrical counterparts.[7] In the 1890s, films began to sell their own version of the western frontier. Short silent films—sometimes called "peep shows"—were followed by feature-length productions that offered "flickering ghosts of invented as well as real Native people."[8]

Long reinvented himself, first as a member of the Cherokee tribe, then as a Blackfoot chief, and finally as an actor playing an Ojibwe character in a silent film. Adopting a series of racial personas, he exploited the dominant culture's fascination with the "noble savage" at a time when there were limited opportunities for people of color.

Founded in 1879, the Carlisle school was a federally funded institution that sought to assimilate Indian children by teaching them English and marketable vocational skills. Upon entering the school, students were forced to cut their hair and exchange their clothes for uniforms. Afterward they posed for before-and-after pictures, their skin "photographically enhanced to look whiter" in order to emphasize their transformation into "civilized" members of society.[9]

Long may have been the only student in the history of the Carlisle school who hoped to become more Indian by the time he graduated. During his stay, from 1909 until 1913, he was listed in student files under such various names as Sylvester Long, Sylvester Clark Long, Sylvester Chahuska Long, and Sylvester Long Lance.[10] He associated with Cherokee students, absorbing "their stories, seeking to become all that they were taught to deny." In 1910 Long wrote a series of essays for the *Carlisle Arrow* describing the customs and traditions of his adopted tribe.[11] In his

"Valedictory Address," printed in the school newspaper in 1912, he identified as a newly assimilated graduate, proclaiming that he and his classmates did "not wish to be designated as Cherokees, Sioux, or Pawnees." Rather, "we wish to be known as Carlisle Indians, belonging to that great universal tribe of North American Indians, speaking the same language and having the same chief—the Great White Father at Washington."[12]

Other graduates described the former army barracks as a "prisonlike environment, run in a strict, military manner."[13] Some students used their education to subvert the assimilation process, returning to their tribes after graduation to reaffirm "their identities as Native Americans."[14] However, Long remembered his alma mater fondly. In 1924 the author—now known as Chief Buffalo Child Long Lance—published "The Story of Carlisle Indian Military School." Recalling the school's founder, U.S. General Henry Richard Pratt, he wrote: "A perpetual smile of kindly satisfaction would play over his rugged, red, clean-shaven features as he made his way about the campus. . . . Though Indians seldom tip their hats to anyone, I never saw a student pass General Pratt without touching the brim of his cap."[15]

The complicated relationship between the institution and its residents extended beyond the classroom. Carlisle's football team became famous in the early 1900s with the arrival of Jim Thorpe, the future two-time All American running back and track and field Olympic gold medalist. Pratt introduced the sport of football at Carlisle, believing it offered Indians an opportunity to compete with whites in an acceptable social setting. At the same time, football was "a contest for yardage, a bone-crunching struggle for the control of territory." It ritualized "the moving frontier, and the teamwork, cooperation, and individual heroism" necessary to withstand one's opponent.[16] This analogy struck many sports writers and spectators who watched the Indian team play white opponents across the country. One commentator compared the gridiron to a "frontier" battlefield.[17] Football presented Indians with "an entrée into American society." But it also appealed to them as a version of the "warrior tradition," one that gave Indians the chance to beat "whites at their own [game]."[18]

Although Long was not talented enough to play with Thorpe on the varsity team, he thrived in the school's militaristic environment.[19] After graduating in 1913 he spent the next two years at St. John's Military Academy, then considered applying to West Point, where he would have become the first Indian cadet. Realizing the academy might attempt to verify his alleged Cherokee heritage, Long moved to Montreal instead, enlisting in the Canadian Expeditionary Force and eventually becoming part of the 237th Battalion of the American Legion. Long was shipped to a training camp in England in 1916 and sent to France early the following year. After being wounded in battle, he was discharged from the military in 1919.[20]

Instead of going home, where he risked being exposed as an imposter, Long moved to Alberta, Canada, where he worked as a journalist throughout the following decade. He relinquished his identity as a Cherokee Indian (as a member of one of the Five Civilized Tribes living east of the Mississippi River) and reinvented himself as a Blackfoot chief (as the leader of an allegedly more primitive group of indigenous people living on the western American plains). In the process Long transformed from a "civilized" Indian into a twentieth-century "savage," the romantic survivor of an earlier era. It was a pattern Long continued to follow the rest of his life: identifying with tribes from different nations and geographical regions, disregarding national and international borders as he moved back and forth between the United States and Canada.

As a journalist working for the *Calgary Herald* in the early 1920s, Long interviewed Indians on the Blackfoot Reserve, observing their customs and learning their tribal history. This information became useful when he published his purported autobiography, *Chief Buffalo Long Lance* (1928), in which he represented himself as a member of the reserve. Long also wrote articles condemning the Canadian government's treatment of indigenous tribes. Moving to British Columbia in 1922, he criticized the Department of Indian Affairs and local missionaries who insisted that natives "work, dress, and play like Euro-Canadians."[21] He also denounced the Methodist Church, which sought to stop Pacific Coast

Indians from conducting potlatch ceremonies. In Regina, Saskatchewan, he complained about the government's broken treaty promises and inadequate education and medical care for minorities.[22]

Before leaving Regina "Chief Long Lance" posed for photographs, dressed in "tribal regalia." During the 1920s the writer increasingly began to fancy his role as an advocate for native rights. While working for the Winnipeg *Tribune* in 1923, Long participated in a publicity stunt, along with other "Blackfoot, Stoney, and Saracee warriors." Mounted on ponies, wearing war paint and feather headdresses, the band of Indians attacked City Hall, kidnapping the mayor and installing a fellow conspirator named Running Rabbit in his place.[23] By 1926 Long's lies were becoming even "more compulsive" and "outrageous." At the same time, his fame was beginning to spread beyond the Canadian border. That year the *Minneapolis Sunday Tribune* published an article entitled "To the Plains Indians, Chief Long Lance is 'Big Boss.'" Some observers were skeptical. After participating in a "trail ride of the Canadian Rockies," an English journalist described a series of Indian dances performed by the alleged Blackfoot chief. "One was a kind of sex dance after the manner of the prairie chicken and the other a very exhausting and almost horrible war dance. This, he told us, was danced by a war party just before they went out for scalps. I do not know how they preserved enough energy to lift a wig from a barber's block if they kept it up all night as he said they did."[24]

Long's most daring performance was his publication of a fictional autobiography—a literary publicity stunt that chronicled his childhood as a Blackfoot born in northern Montana and raised in northwest Canada. The book begins with the author's recollection of an incident that supposedly occurred during infancy: a fight with the Crow tribe which resulted in his uncle's death. Years later, when he shares this story with his aunt, she is astounded by the "remarkable awakening" of his memory.[25] Her testimonial suggests to the reader that Long is a trustworthy narrator. "Long Lance" reinforces that impression by claiming Blackfoot boys were taught not to lie, writing that deception was considered a dishonorable "characteristic" in an Indian brave (38).

The author displays his knowledge of Blackfoot customs, vividly bringing those traditions to life in his autobiography. He describes a war dance in which the performers thanked "the Great Spirit for allowing us to survive the winter and to steel our tempers for any trouble or fights that we might encounter during the turbulent summer season." He begins by reproducing the sounds of drums. "'*Boom, boom, boom, boom!*' Four thundering beats on the big war-drum would announce that the dance was to start." Then "our fathers would come prancing into the crowded lodge, stripped to their breech-cloths, painted all over, and uttering short, gruff grunts as they stamped their feet—thump-*thump*, thump-*thump*." In the next paragraph, the author shifts to the present tense, creating a sense of immediacy as he "reconstructs" the fictitious scene from his childhood. "At first [the warriors] dance mildly, with much dignity and grace of movement. Then, as the chanting and beating grows louder and wilder, they start to work themselves up into a warlike frenzy, shouting, 'Ee-h-whoop, hy-yuh,' and gradually jumping higher and higher as they circle the booming tom-toms" (19). Long uses a similar technique in the "Snow Dance," entering into the minds of his characters, who pray for a storm to conceal them from their enemies during a horse raid. "There is not much noise to this dance, but it sometimes lasts for several hours, everyone concentrating his thoughts on rain or snow with each beat of the drum. 'Ta-plum, ta-plum, ta-plum'—goes the drum. 'Give rain, give rain, give rain'—go our thoughts" (68).

Long uses italicized words, recreated sound effects, and the rhythmic repetition of a brave's unspoken chant to dramatize the performative nature of Blackfoot ceremonies. In one dance "the most renowned warriors of the tribe [traditionally] relate their most famous exploits on the warpath," then "dance and reenact the fight as it actually happened" (82). Elsewhere in the autobiography the narrator imagines himself in the midst of the action, even though he has earlier told the reader that the tribe's women and children had been safely removed from the battleground beforehand. As the men "assailed the Crows from their left, White Dog and our chief raced around the edge of the cut-bank and struck them on their right. The Crows were willing to fight it out, but their horses were not. They became frightened at the gun-fire, and their riders having no bridles to hold them, they began to buck" (74).

The author occasionally disappears from the text, assuming the role of an omniscient narrator. Long would have the reader believe this trait is also a characteristic of Blackfoot warriors. According to Long, nomadic tribes had to be resourceful in order to hide from their enemies on the barren plains. The flat landscape enabled Indians to "see as far as the human eye could reach" (4). But his tribe was also visible—and therefore vulnerable—in this open environment. In the winter, the men "cover[ed] the buffalo-hide teepees with tree bark to conceal them from the view of prowlers and possible enemies" (5). At other times they painted their bodies "the color of the local landscape so that [they] could not be easily seen" (30). The Crows used similar tactics, disguising themselves as "wolves, buffalo and antelope" in order to spy on the author and his fellow tribe members (67). However, the chief of another tribe acknowledges the superior skills of Blackfoot warriors, claiming, "you see everything, but nobody ever sees you" (146).

Long also disappears from the text when he writes about Blackfoot customs and tribal legends. Like most Native American autobiographies, his fictitious memoir focuses primarily on the history of the tribe rather than on the author's personal story.[26] Long devotes entire chapters to accounts of dances and other ritual ceremonies, to the relationship between the Blackfoot medicine man and the spiritual world, and to oral folk stories about native mythological figures. The most dramatic scenes recall hunting for "the vanishing buffalo" (4), as the tribe faces starvation and the fear of extinction (25, 106, 198). The book concludes with the arrival of "the white man" and the end of the tribe's nomadic existence. Long serves as a spokesperson for the tribe's few remaining members when he writes: "Our job is to try to fit ourselves into the new scheme of life which the Great Spirit has decreed for North America. And we will do that, keeping always before us the old Blackfoot proverb: *Mokokit-ki-ackamimat*—Be wise and persevere" (276-78).

Long does not mention his education at the Carlisle Indian School, his service during World War I, or his subsequent career in journalism.

Two years after publishing the book Long starred in *The Silent Enemy* (1930), a film about a Canadian tribe of Ojibwe Indians. Coincidentally, the plot paralleled Long's fictional history, adding an element of realism to a film in which the author-turned-actor reinvented himself once again. Like the Blackfoot tribe, the Ojibwes face starvation ("the silent enemy"). Instead of hunting buffalo, they search for caribou, led by Baluk, an expert tracker. The producers cast Long as the hunter after seeing his "arresting portrait" on the cover of his autobiography.[27] Wanting to achieve the same ethnic verisimilitude as in the earlier Inuit film, *Nanook of the North* (1922), they hired the self-proclaimed Blackfoot chief instead of a Hollywood actor, believing Long's tribal affiliation was less important than the color of his skin.

Long became more "primitive" each time he assumed a new identity. The man whose mother had been born a slave during the final months of the Civil War became a Native American when he applied to Carlisle.[28] When he moved to Canada, Long exchanged his fabricated membership in one of the Five Civilized Tribes for a more "authentic" native persona, becoming a Blackfoot Indian, born before the conquest of North America. *The Silent Enemy* is set even further in the past, during the pre-Columbian era. Baluk's only antagonist is nature and his only rival is the tribe's medicine man, who competes with him for the affections of the chief's daughter.

As westerns became less popular in the 1920s, Hollywood stopped making cowboy-and-Indian films and began producing movies that depicted Native Americans living peacefully in nature, prior to the arrival of Anglo-European civilization. Although it was filmed in Canada, *The Silent Enemy* followed the same cinematic trend.[29] In a spoken introduction Chief Chauncey Yellow Robe assures viewers that the wikiups, bows and arrows, and other Ojibwe artifacts used by the actors are genuine. In addition to the main plot, chronicling the tribe's pursuit of a caribou herd, *The Silent Enemy* features a boy in a canoe spearing a fish, the chief's daughter using a stick with a loop to catch a bird, and Long's character killing a bear. Like his fellow actor, Chief Yellow Robe was a Carlisle graduate, a former Wild West show performer, and a non-Ojibwe Indian. Yet the chief testifies to the film's authenticity, claiming the white man's cinematic "magic" will preserve the legacy of the endangered tribe depicted on screen.[30]

Although the film received critical praise, it failed at the box office, an indication that the "Indian's screen image was inextricably tied to the Western."[31] Instead of solidifying his status as a bona fide Indian and silent movie star, the film signaled the end of Long's career. Yellow Robe was a Lakota chief and founding member of the Society of American Indians. He raised questions about Long's identity during filming, prompting the studio's legal advisor to launch an investigation that led to the discovery of the actor's actual origins. After *The Silent Enemy* premiered, rumors continued to circulate, causing many of Long's wealthy white friends to banish him from New York City high society. Socialite Anita Baldwin remained loyal to the disgraced impostor, hiring him as her bodyguard. In 1932 Long committed suicide in her Los Angeles home, bringing his infamous career to a tragic conclusion.

Long's lies led to his undoing. But his success as a performer cannot be overemphasized. The author writes in his autobiography that "a [white] man may be one thing and appear to be another. But this is not possible in the social structure of the Indian" (41). It was arguably more difficult to pass as an Indian in the early twentieth century than it was to impersonate a member of any other race or ethnic group, simply because there was no such thing as an "Indian." There were Cherokees, Blackfeet, Crows, and Ojibwes as well as hundreds of other tribes spread across the North American continent. Each one had its own geographic homeland, rituals and traditions, language, history, and manner of dress. In order to pass as a member of a particular tribe it was necessary to do more than look like white society's notion of a stereotypical Indian. One had to "perform" in multiple ways, mastering another language, learning a tribe's history, and becoming familiar with the region in which it lived.

One of Long's shrewdest decisions was to highlight the performative aspects of Blackfoot culture in his autobiography. The author describes how boys in the tribe mimicked their fathers' actions. "While our elders raced their horses, ran long-distance races, and pitted their strength against one another in wrestling, weight-lifting and weight-throwing, we youngsters were given the freedom of the entire prairies on which to carry out our little games and 'fights.' . . . We knew the game of Indian warfare almost as well as our fathers; for it was the Indian custom for noted warriors to relate and reenact all of their famous battles at the Sun Dance—and we boys had memorized most of our tribal conflicts in every detail" (29). Later the boys in the Blackfoot and Crow tribes compete with each other in similar "games and mimic battles" (242). The childhood version of the narrator performs like an adult Blackfoot brave, recalling earlier times in Long's actual life when he interviewed tribe members, studiously preparing for the role he would eventually perform.

Long began acting as an adolescent, when his parents signed a false application attesting to his Native American heritage. During his interview with Carlisle's admissions board he also passed a language test, speaking in fluent Cherokee. Long sustained this ethnic masquerade until 1920, when he moved to Canada, reinventing himself as a Blackfoot chief. Although the author may not have become completely conversant in his new "native" language, he stressed the necessity of perfecting that language in his autobiography. "Our mothers spent about two hours every day teaching us how to speak our tribal language correctly. This is a very important point with the Indian . . . as his social status in later years depends on his ability to handle his grammar properly. Any Indian allowed to grow up without being able to speak his language with absolute correctness is relegated to the rank of an outcast in the tribe; and he is never allowed to speak in public, lest his linguistic defects should be passed on to others." In this passage, and throughout the rest of the paragraph, Long gives a double performance. First, he claims to have mastered the Blackfoot language, noting that his tribe had no books or written alphabet, thus forcing children to memorize a complex grammatical system that included "nine conjugations, four genders and eighty forms." Stressing the need to speak the Blackfoot language correctly, the author also demonstrates his perfect command of English, writing in a formal style, using pompous diction—"lest his linguistic defects should be passed on to others . . . thus defil[ing] the tribal tongue" (6-7).

Long's ethnic transformations were acts of translation that involved learning to speak and write in different languages. Long also mastered sign language, a communication system used by North American tribes, especially Plains Indians, which enabled them to overcome their linguistic differences.[32] All forms of language are performative. But sign language dramatizes the act of communication more explicitly than speech or writing. It requires the performer to assume a series of poses and to execute various physical gestures involving the actor's arms and hands. Taking advantage of the white man's desire to "play" Indian,[33] Long's alter ego, Chief Buffalo Child Long Lance, published *How to Talk in the Indian Sign Language* (1930). The book taught readers how to sign certain basic words and phrases. A photograph of the author—wearing a loincloth, pigtails, and a feathered headdress—appeared next to each entry. For the term "sign language," Long illustrated the following instructions: "Bring left hand in front of chest, fingers extending, touching, and pointing to right, palm facing downward. Bring right hand, similarly fixed, over to left and touch the backs of the left fingers with the lower surface of the right fingers. Then bring left hand out from under right hand, and similarly touch backs of right fingers."[34] Appearing the same year as the film *The Silent Enemy*, the book was published by the B. F. Goodrich Tire Company, which used the instruction manual to promote a new rubber-soled athletic shoe designed by its fleet-footed star for the benefit of American consumers who wanted to run like an Indian.

Long's performances did not always impress his critics or members of the Blackfoot tribe, with whom he claimed to be affiliated. For a photograph taken in the 1920s Long wore "a Blackfoot vest, a Blood tobacco pouch, Crow Indian pants—worn backwards—and a headdress used in the Chicken Dance," a variation of which was performed by numerous Plains tribes. In another picture he also sported "a wig with two long braids to cover his cropped hair."[35] One critic notes that by "racially" cross-dressing, Long made his "color performative." A second one refers to Long's impersonation as "ethnic transvestism."[36] It was also a clumsy pastiche of various indigenous modes of dress, which must have looked "ridiculous" to Blackfoot Indians.[37]

Long was more convincing when he performed in a state of undress. His muscular physique was seen as proof of his ethnic identity. In his autobiography the author emphasizes the importance of becoming a Blackfoot man. "Our fathers looked after our physical training. . . . The Indian's only profession was that of a warrior and hunter. Hence, outside of our linguistic and moral teaching, our sole training was to make us brave and stoical, and good and courageous fighters." According to Long, the warriors whipped their sons with fir branches, raising welts on their bodies, which the boys displayed "with great pride" (7). The author also claims he and his friends burned themselves to "see who could stand the most pain" (10) and used their mothers' sewing needles to rip "each other's legs until they bled" (11).

During Long's lifetime white anthropologists studied Native American men, looking for perfect "primitive" specimens of "physical manhood." At a facility in St. Augustine, Florida, where Indians were incarcerated in the 1880s, a sculptor made "plaster cast busts" of Indian prisoners, and in one instance a mold of a man's "entire body," which were sent to the Smithsonian Institute.[38] Carlisle founder General Pratt believed his students' "manly" abilities enabled them to excel at football.[39] In the "Editor's Introduction" to Long's sign language manual, Kenneth Williams also acknowledged that the Indian's superior running skills made him the perfect prototype for a new athletic shoe. Influenced by Long's "'barefoot tread' theory of design," the rubber company's experts manufactured a product that enabled the consumer to compete with his native counterpart. "I watched [Long] walking, running, shadowboxing in these experimental shoes," Williams stated, adding, "every single muscle in his body seemed a delicate instrument ready to detect the smallest flaw in the design. To me he is the perfect experimental laboratory of ways and means of adapting our primitive bodies to modern conditions."[40]

In *The Silent Enemy* Long wears a loincloth that reveals his smooth bare torso and muscular limbs. During the course of the movie he paddles a canoe through the rapids, commandeers a dog sled, climbs mountains, escapes from a pack of wolves, and rescues members of the tribe from other animal predators. The silent film is a perfect vehicle for a performer who could not speak his "native" language fluently but who looked like an "Indian." Although Long was forty years old when the film premiered, he convincingly performed his own stunts in an action vehicle that required physical strength and stamina. At the same time Long avoided becoming a negative caricature of the Native American male—the "lustful" savage, a bogeyman who first appeared in eighteenth-century Indian captivity narratives.[41] In the absence of white women his character falls in love with the daughter of the Ojibwe chief. After the hunter saves his tribe from starvation, the film concludes with a scene set in the near future, showing Baluk and his wife looking at pictographs illustrating the hero's exploits.

Long makes his character appear non-threatening to white viewers, while at the same time subverting stereotypes about Native Americans. In an article entitled "The Hollywooden Indian" (1936), western historian Stanley Vestal criticized the typical Native American actor. "When he is half-naked, his inability to act the Indian becomes pitifully apparent. Indians are not muscled like white men; their limbs are smooth and boyish. They are ephebic."[42] By comparing an actor to an *ephebus* (an adolescent male in ancient Greece who had not yet been initiated into manhood or trained by the military), Vestal denigrated the Indian's masculinity and his role as a warrior, while linking the supposedly vanishing Native American to an extinct civilization. Long defied this stereotype by giving an athletic performance as a Blackfoot chief and soldier who had fought during World War I, the most famous Carlisle graduate since Olympian Jim Thorpe.

Another film critic argued that to "act as an Indian is the easiest thing possible, for the Redskin is practically motionless."[43] Generic Indians were static and "inarticulate" characters. During the silent era they "stood flat-footed with their arms folded high on their chests, said very little but could be seen grunting, and had an almost perpetual scowl on their faces."[44] Silent film reinforced this stereotype, as did sign language (the typical means of Indian communication in early westerns), transforming these characters into mute primitives. However, Long took advantage of this new kinetic medium, giving an energetic performance as he moved across the screen, executing feats of prowess.

Long engaged in a practice called "redfacing," playing white society's version of an Indian. His performance—in *The Silent Enemy*, in his auto-biography, and in his life as a reputed member of several tribes—"reified negative stereotypes" about Native Americans, while liberating him at the same time.[45] Long achieved social respectability, "geographic mobility, [and] financial security," unlike other minorities who were confined to segregated neighborhoods and reservations, who suffered from legal inequality, and who had limited economic resources and opportunities. He was a con man as well as an inspirational figure. His suicide was an admission of guilt, as well as a final act of heroism, performed on the private battlefield where Long had fought throughout his life.

# L'Ouest Bohème

## *Willa Cather's Transnational Prairie*

With the transformation of the U.S. frontier, movement became synonymous with change. It symbolized white society's rapid development of the region, while accounting for the quickly disappearing preindustrial cultures of the West's indigenous peoples. Sylvester Long's movements were consistent with his changing personas. The mixed-race impersonator moved from the United States to Canada, from England to France, and then back to Canada, escaping detection by avoiding those who had known him since childhood, while portraying members of various nomadic tribes that had been displaced by white civilization.

Unlike Long, many immigrants settled permanently on the western frontier. Some of them were actual members of displaced ethnic communities such as Bohemia. Originally an independent principality ruled by a succession of monarchs, the central European region was later incorporated into the Holy Roman Empire, the Hapsburg Monarchy, and finally the Austrian Empire. After World War I it became part of Czechoslovakia.[1] Over time Bohemians who had lost their regional autonomy migrated to other countries or became permanent nomads. Hence their association with "gypsies," with foreigners generally, and with people who were "judged to be morally and legally suspect"—social outcasts doomed to wander the earth.[2] During the Romantic period the French began using the term "bohemian" to refer to "penniless and carefree" individuals who identified with "the vagabond vocation of the bohemian artist" and who "dissented from the prevailing values of middle-class society," such as the cross-dressing writer George Sand.[3] In the nineteenth century "bohemian" communities started appearing in Paris and other European capitals. They were "floating" territories with numerous international outposts. "Bohemia" became a signifier of marginality; a term that referred to a geographic location, as well as to a mobile, conceptual realm inhabited by impoverished artists of various backgrounds, who were united by their contempt for the bourgeoisie.[4]

Ethnic Bohemians first arrived in the United States in the mid-nineteenth century. By 1880 Central and Eastern Europeans comprised 80 percent of American immigrants.[5] Some Bohemians settled in Nebraska, where Willa Cather and her family moved in 1883.[6] During her childhood Cather explored the immigrant prairie communities surrounding her parents' ranch, becoming friendly with her Danish, Norwegian, and Bohemian neighbors. Cather played with "the little herd girls, who wore men's hats" and heard "a great many stories" about distant lands.[7] Cather's early fiction—including "The Bohemian Girl" (1912), *O Pioneers!* (1913), and *My Ántonia* (1918)—features Bohemian women in especially prominent roles, perhaps because strong female characters appear frequently in Bohemian folklore—most notably Libuša, the oldest and wisest daughter of the mythical Czech ruler Krok, who inherited the crown after her father's death and who allegedly founded the city of Prague.[8]

Like her female playmates who wore "men's hats," Cather began experimenting with her appearance during adolescence, cutting her hair, wearing masculine apparel, and signing her name William, instead of Willa. While some scholars view this behavior as evidence of Cather's lesbianism, others disagree.[9] One critic claims Cather was simply determined to obey "her individual nature," while another contends she was rebelling against her mother, who "frequently objected to Willa's way of dressing."[10] Yet another critic argues that Cather cross-dressed in order to taunt "male authority."[11] Sharon O'Brien believes the young woman's "metamorphosis into William signified her attempt to fashion an independent, autonomous, and powerful [non-gendered] self."[12] However, one of her college classmates shrugged off the controversy, saying that "Willa was just plain Billy to all of us."[13]

During the period in which Cather dressed unconventionally—from 1886 until 1892—the term "Bohemian" became increasingly associated with artists and social nonconformists. While she was an undergraduate at the University of Nebraska, Cather contributed to the campus news-paper, the *Hesperian*, reviewing student plays as well as professional productions of dramas and musicals. Cather's passion for theater began during this process of self-transformation, leading to the construction of a public self differing from that of other women. Cather developed a "bohemian" sensibility, showing a preference for George Sand and other French writers, while becoming involved in the local arts scene at a time when Nebraska was developing into a rural American version of cosmopolitan Bohemia, replete with European transplants.[14] Yet Cather also criticized the tendency to romanticize Bohemian life and condemned its members' worst excesses. Reviewing Henri Murger's *Scènes de la vie de Bohème* (1847-49), a novel that popularized the notion of starving artists living in Parisian garrets, Cather described the charac-ters as "defiant young disciples of art who hated all orthodox power, all recognized authority, and who called themselves Bohemians because they did not care to call themselves outcasts."[15] She also deplored Oscar Wilde's "infamy," despite her enthusiasm for "1890s decadence."[16]

Critics have noted many conflicts and inconsistencies in Cather's life and work. One biographer claims that as a lesbian, Cather "often felt alienated from society," arguing that she explored "this sense of divi-sion" in her writing.[17] Marilee Lindeman notes the "tension between conformity and nonconformity that is evident in her life story and in her contradictory sense of the West." That conflict recurs in her fiction, "as characters struggle to create a sense of self as well as relationships to family, community, and region."[18] Susan J. Rosowski identifies a similar pattern, stating that "Cather wrote of two worlds . . . and of two selves in each person . . . an artistic self and a common one."[19]

Cather welcomed Bohemian immigrants and celebrated the diversity of Nebraska's rural population. Before the rise of nativism in the second decade of the twentieth century she imagined "a multinational America in which different cultures coexisted."[20] After college, however, she left Nebraska to pursue her writing career. Although she continued to depict the West in her fiction, she returned home with decreasing frequency, distancing herself from her former Bohemian neighbors while becoming an artist; embracing aspects of literary bohemia while rejecting full-fledged membership in its nontraditional society.

After graduating from college Cather moved to Pittsburgh, where she worked for a women's magazine called *Home Monthly*. A year later, in 1897, she became a drama critic for the *Pittsburgh Leader*, as well as a contributor to the *Library*, a fiction and poetry journal. When her friend Isabelle McClung invited Cather to live with her family, the writer exchanged "the quasi-bohemian, hard-driving life of a newspaper woman living in a boarding house on a plebeian street" for a place in the home of one of Pittsburgh's most prominent residents.[21] Cather considered McClung's father—a judge and member of the Presbyterian Church—"rigorously and comically puritan."[22] Although she concealed this opinion from her host, she continued to identify publicly in writing as a bohemian. In an article published in *Home Journal*, Cather wrote: "All Pittsburgh is divided into two parts. Presbyteria and Bohemia, and the former is much the larger and the more influential of the two." By Presbyteria, Cather meant "the fusion of religious and commercial values that ruled the city, the mutually reinforcing Protestant ethic and spirit of capitalism that denigrated emotion and art."[23]

Yet a letter to her friend Marie Gere suggests Cather's "growing desire to acquire dual citizenship in [both] conventional and unconventional realms." Being in a puritanical atmosphere "reinforced her sense of herself as a romantic rebel" while allowing her to don playfully "the disguise of propriety." According to O'Brien, Cather was "deeply conservative" but also radical in her departure from gender norms: "a professional woman, a lesbian, and an artist."[24] After moving to Pittsburgh Cather started dressing in a more feminine style, wearing brocade jackets, chunky jewelry, and skirts that "some believed exposed too much of her ankle."[25] In articles for *Home Monthly* she dispensed "wholesome domestic advice" for middle-class housewives. In reviews, however, she expressed more idiosyncratic views, using a variety of male and female pseudonyms, partly because she delighted "in disguise for its own sake."[26] In another letter to Gere, Cather quoted from Shakespeare's

*A Winter's Tale*, acknowledging: "I never for a moment seriously contemplated becoming a citizen of that 'desert country by the sea.' . . . I can most effectually surprise my friends and pain my enemies by living a most conventional existence."[27]

Cather referred to Bohemia dismissively, calling the region known for its mountains and forests a "desert." The woman who earned her living as a writer also scorned romanticized portrayals of struggling artists, claiming that "despite all sentimental notions to the contrary, Bohemia was the result of an absence of money . . . not one of its many celebrated inhabitants dwelt there a day longer than his income compelled him to."[28] Pittsburgh's most famous benefactor was Andrew Carnegie, the railroad baron and entrepreneur whose article "The Gospel of Wealth" (1889) encouraged the rich to fund philanthropic ventures for the benefit of those less fortunate. Although Cather "viewed the artistic world as the locus for alternative values" that were "unrecognized, repressed, or devalued in the larger society," she also respected the capitalist who created a space for artists and their followers.[29]

In 1911 Cather published "The Bohemian Girl." The story portrays a heroine torn between her ethnic heritage, connection to place, or land of origin, and her "bohemian" tendencies: her attraction to the arts, rejection of social conventions, and feeling of restlessness. Clara is a Bohemian immigrant married to a Swedish farmer and politician in rural Nebraska. Unlike Libuša, the legendary ruler of ancient Bohemia who wed a "ploughman" and founded a dynasty, Clara shirks her domestic duties, takes no interest in her husband's career, and eventually leaves her spouse for her brother-in-law. "Bohemia" has a complex set of meanings in this early short story. In addition to representing a geographic place, it signifies a "realm of feeling and sensation opposed to conventional values and bourgeois morality."[30] Clara is Bohemian by birth. If her father died, she would lose her "race" as well as the qualities that make her unique, including her "love of life" and "capacity for delight."[31]

Clara is bohemian in the sense that she loves music and dancing. She is a "wild tune" whom her Swedish lover Nils "can't resist" (119-20). The couple play musical instruments, dance a waltz together, and sing songs from *The Bohemian Girl* (1843). The opera—about a Polish nobleman who joins a band of gypsies and kidnaps the daughter of an Austrian count—features an aria called "Then You'll Remember Me," sung by Thadeus to the beautiful maiden Arline. "We're making a legend," says Nils, similar to the one depicted in the English opera and the folkloric account of Libuša. Nils celebrates their unconventional love by singing a phrase from the song:

When other lips and other hearts
Their tale of love shall tell,
In language whose excess imparts
The power they feel so well. (124)

Cather's heroine must decide whether to remain with her husband in Nebraska or run away with Nils. She first appears on horseback (93), a symbol of restlessness. Nils is also a wanderer. Unlike other members of his Swedish family, who establish their roots in the soil, Nils is a traveler who at the beginning of the story returns from abroad on the Trans-Continental Express, sporting a foreign haircut, a blue silk tie, and a Panama hat (89). His "roving blood" (96) makes him a more suitable romantic partner for the "gypsy" Clara (101) than her settler husband Olaf. Nils shows a disregard for private property, social boundaries, and domestic conventions. After disembarking from the train he crosses the fields toward home, cutting "through a great fenced pasture, emerging when he rolled under the barbed wire at the further corner, upon a white dusty road which ran straight up from the river valley to the high prairie" (90). Later he enters Clara's house through an open window, nonchalantly swinging his legs over the sill (104).

The ethnic characters in Cather's fiction are immigrants as well as settlers. Although they thrive on the U.S. frontier, they are nevertheless haunted by "homesickness," Cather's term for the diasporic longing experienced by the region's non-native residents. Nils feels homesick when he returns to Nebraska, blaming this sensation on "the mention of a name or two, perhaps; the rattle of a wagon along a dusty road; the rank, resinous smell of sunflowers and ironweed" (92). Similarly, Clara gets "blue" when she recalls living with her father before her marriage to Olaf. Joe Vavrika's saloon serves Bohemian immigrants (110) and is reminiscent of the boulevard cafés that feature in contemporary English and European accounts of bohemian life. Instead of being located in the nearby town, it is situated in "a cheerfuller place, a little Bohemian settlement . . . at the other end of the county" (109). Although they have adapted to their new environment, Bohemians remain separate from other immigrants, dreaming of a homeland to which they can never return. At the end of the story Clara and Nils leave Nebraska, visiting her family's hometown in Bohemia. They eventually settle in Norway, becoming permanent exiles (127).

It remains unclear whether Cather admires her characters for rejecting societal norms or whether she views them as two lonely misfits, united by their contempt for convention. A farmer tells Nils when the young man returns to Nebraska that his family owns "most of the country now. I remember the preacher's fav'rite text used to be, 'To them that hath shall be given.' They've spread something wonderful—run over this here country like bindweed. But I ain't one that begretches it to 'em. Folks is entitled to what they kin git; and they're hustlers" (91). Nils's father was a minister as well as a farmer who preached the Gospel of Wealth, quoting the Bible to justify his accumulation of property. The speaker seems unoffended by this capitalistic interpretation of Christianity, though he calls the Ericson family "hustlers" and compares them to "bindweed," a creeping perennial that crowds out other plants and crops. By running away the adulterous lovers reject religion by sinning against the institution of marriage. In addition Nils relinquishes his share of the family property and Clara leaves Olaf with the substantial dowry that she brought to her marriage, as if the couple were unconcerned with money matters or their future financial security.

The story ends without readers learning if Clara will seek a divorce, marry Nils, and start a family in Norway. Commenting on the sterility of bohemian life, one critic notes that "seldom are Bohemians the sons and daughters of Bohemians and begetters of Bohemians in their turn."[32] They are either too impoverished to provide for children or too independent to become domesticated. In this sense bohemians lead a futile existence. Those who belong to this community live in existential isolation from the rest of the world. Nils and Clara also share a lonely fate. Instead of following her characters to Norway and describing their newfound bliss, Cather allows them to disappear from the story, focusing in the end on those who remain in Nebraska; especially on Nils's younger brother Eric, who decides not to follow his brother but to stay with his mother, as "happiness filled his heart" (132).

Cather published "The Bohemian Girl" five years after moving to New York City. Like her characters, she seemed restless. Although she no longer lived in Nebraska, she returned periodically, seeking inspiration as a writer. At the same time she began building a life with her new companion Edith Lewis in Greenwich Village—a bohemian enclave where Cather felt at home to a certain extent. The author "preferred to spend what money she had on flowers, music, and entertaining." She covered the walls of their apartment with copies of paintings by European masters, placed oriental rugs on the floors, and hired a French housekeeper who created "a French household atmosphere."[33] But Cather also shared "a quiet domestic life" with Lewis, "protecting her privacy and shunning the Village's avant-garde" residents.[34] The city's bohemian residents at the turn of the century were not as unconventional in their behavior as their fictional counterparts. By the early 1900s U.S. cities were welcoming a new generation of artists who were more socially respectable than their predecessors. The first generation of bohemians—represented by such writers as Edgar Allan Poe—were believed to be drunks or drug addicts, sexual perverts, and impoverished artists. Now the Village included men as well as women who "posed" as bohemians. The publication of George du Maurier's *Trilby* (1894)—a novel about a Parisian model who falls under the hypnotic spell of the evil Svengali—had made it "respectable and highly desirable" to be a bohemian artist. As one skeptical commentator noted: "American girls wanted to be Trilbies without undressing; they wanted to be Bohemians and yet remain virgins." By the mid-1890s, the Village was filled with so many conventional middle-class artists and writers that it became facetiously known as "The Republic of Washington Square."[35] As a result the term "bohemian" became associated with the word "poser": "someone pretending to an identity to which he or she could have no preexisting claim."[36]

Cather wrote "The White Mulberry Tree" at the same time as "The Bohemian Girl." Instead of submitting the first story for publication she incorporated it into her novel *O Pioneers!* (1913). Initially Marie Shabata resembles Clara. The Bohemian immigrant is an attractive young married woman who falls in love with the son of a Swedish farmer. However, Cather reveals her ambivalence about what it means to be "bohemian" by subjecting Marie to a different fate than Clara. As O'Brien notes, "The Bohemian Girl" is one of the few instances in Cather's fiction where "romantic love has a happy ending."[37] In *O Pioneers!* Marie and her lover Emil are shot by her jealous husband Frank as they lie in an orchard under a mulberry tree, staining its white berries with their blood.

Marie is Bohemian in terms of her ethnicity as well as in keeping with other connotations the word had begun to acquire by the mid-nineteenth century. She appears as a gypsy fortune-teller at a local fair, performing her ethnicity by wearing a "kirtle" and a "yellow silk turban."[38] She is also bohemian in the sense of being "an unconventional person."[39] Ruled by her emotions, Marie runs away from a convent to marry Frank (61) and later falls in love with Emil. Unlike Clara, Marie cannot escape from Nebraska. Cather foreshadows her fate by noting her character's restlessness and her desire to transcend the confines of her body. One evening Marie wanders outside in the dark, thinking of Emil. She "stole slowly, flutteringly, along the path, like a white night-moth out of the fields. The years seemed to stretch before her like the land; spring, summer, autumn, winter, spring; always the same patient fields, the patient little trees, the patient lives; always the same yearning, the same pulling at the chain—until the instinct to live had torn itself and bled and weakened for the last time, until the chain secured a dead woman, who might cautiously be released" (128). The passage recalls an earlier scene in which another character quotes from Franz Schubert's "Der

Wanderer": "Wo bist du, wo bist du, mein geliebtest Land?" ("Where are you, where are you, my beloved land?") (60). Marie can't return to her homeland or to that mythical place

Wo meine Träume wandeln gehn,
Wo meine Todten auferstehn;
Das Land, das meine Sprache spricht,
Und alles hat, was mire gebricht?

(Where my friends wander
Where my dead ones rise from the dead
That land, so hopefully green,
That land, where my roses bloom?)

Marie is a tragic figure, a secondary character in a novel that transfers the positive aspects of being bohemian to the artistic heroine, Alexandra Bergson. The farmer metaphorically transforms the prairie into a mosaic; into a patchwork canvas "marked off in squares of wheat and corn; light and dark" (39). Alexandra's friend and future husband, the artist Carl Linstrum, notes after returning to Nebraska: "I've been away engraving other men's pictures, and you've stayed at home and made your own" (59). Later Alexandra tells Carl that Marie is "the kind that won't be downed easily. She'll work all day and go to a Bohemian wedding and dance all night, and drive the hay wagon for a cross man next morning" (61). But Cather never shows Marie farming the land. Instead, the author associates Marie and Emil with the community's graveyard and her private orchard, in which they eventually die (137).

Alexandra is unorthodox in the same sense as her bohemian counterpart, George Sand.[40] The protagonist first appears in the novel wearing "a man's long ulster (not as if it were an affliction, but as if it were very comfortable and belonged to her)" (4). Unlike Sand the *provocateur*, Alexandra dresses practically for a farmer in winter. Her androgynous appearance draws no criticism from other characters; whereas Marie's femininity makes her seem exotic. At the beginning of the novel she is described as "a stranger in the country," a "city child from Omaha" wearing a "Kate Greenaway" dress (6-7)—an eighteenth-century garment favored by female characters in Greenaway's popular children's books. Marie resembles Cather as a young girl in terms of her fondness for theatrical apparel, according to friends who remembered meeting the Virginia immigrant when she first arrived in Nebraska, "dressed in a leopard-skin fabric coat and hat."[41] As an adolescent Cather cultivated an androgynous look, before returning to the East as an adult, where the bohemian writer adopted a more conventional manner of dress. Here she also portrays Marie in paradoxical fashion, suggesting that the most "feminine" female character is also the most unnatural. As a child Marie flirts coquettishly with men in the general store, looking like a "doll" or one of Greenaway's fictional characters (7-8). Later her gypsy costume transforms her into an ethnic stereotype and makes her enhanced femininity—including her pierced ears (111), which distinguish her from other farm women—seem like a pose. Marie becomes a "bohemian, in the modern sense . . . a second-order figure, an imitator defined through the appropriation of an exotic image."[42] The less glamorous Alexandra becomes engaged to Carl at the end of the novel, while Marie has a vexed relationship with Frank. Her attractiveness to the opposite sex ultimately leads him to murder his wife.

*My Ántonia* features Cather's most memorable Bohemian character, a successful farmer, wife, and mother—a woman who symbolizes "the country, the conditions, the whole adventure" of pioneer life as well as the figure who inspires Jim Burden's childhood memoir (xxii). Ántonia combines the contradictory qualities of a Bohemian/bohemian; the attributes associated with both meanings of the word. Cather stresses the ethnicity of her heroine at the beginning of the novel, stating in a footnote that "the Bohemian name *Ántonia* is strongly accented on the first syllable" (3). Yet in spite of being a foreigner, the character adapts to Nebraska more easily than her father, who commits suicide. Her mother yearns for their homeland, while one of her siblings has "webbed" fingers like "a duck's foot," emphasizing his difference from other people (23). Ántonia is stronger than other women and more assertive than most men. She is "almost a race apart," demonstrating "a vigor" that develops into "a positive carriage and freedom of movement" (192). At the same time, the Bohemian girl's motion is uniquely American, a characteristic ascribed to the Nebraska prairie. Watching the tall grass sway in the breeze, Jim observes that "the whole country seemed, somehow, to be running. . . . I felt motion in the landscape; in the fresh, easy-blowing wind, and in the earth itself, as if the shaggy grass were a sort of loose hide, and underneath it herds of wild buffalo were galloping" (15).

Although Ántonia learns to speak English, she retains command of her native language and raises her children to be bilingual. Scholars have observed that while immigrant families often adapt to the customs of their host countries, women within those families are simultaneously tasked with preserving their native cultures.[43] Learning a second language is a challenge as well as an opportunity for Ántonia. It enables her to express herself in a freer fashion and act more independently than traditional Bohemian women, such as her mother, Mrs. Shimerda.[44] Ántonia uses English to defy her employer in the community of Black Hawk, who warns her that she must not attend an upcoming dance if she wants to avoid getting a bad reputation (200). Prior to marrying a Bohemian man and raising a family, Ántonia acts like a bohemian in terms of her unconventional behavior. She wears her father's boots on the farm (117) and "a man's long overcoat" during the winter (308). She also scandalizes the community by having a child out of wedlock, continuing to work as a single mother (309).

Ántonia is not an artist figure, unlike Alexandra in *O Pioneers!* Other foreigners and ethnic minorities assume this role—including the itinerant Italian dancing troupe (188) and the traveling African American pianist, Blind D'Arnault (178–87)—illustrating Cather's belief that the artist was an exotic figure or an outcast from conventional society. Although Ántonia is a farmer, she transforms into a work of art; into the subject of the artist's gaze. Before writing the novel Cather set a Sicilian vase filled with flowers in the middle of a table, telling a friend: "'I want my new heroine to be like this—like a rare object . . . which one may examine from all sides.'"[45] The same character becomes the subject of Jim's memoir. As the narrator recalls: "Ántonia had always been one to leave images in the mind that did not fade—that grew stronger with time. In my memory there was a succession of such pictures, fixed there like the old woodcuts of one's first primer" (342).

At the same time Ántonia has material value and social utility. The farmhand Jake says the character most closely associated with nature looks "bright as a new dollar" (4). Writing during World War I Cather portrays U.S. farmers as patriotic and self-sacrificing workers who support the troops abroad. Jim understands that the crops would eventually "enlarge and multiply until they would be, not the Shimerdas' cornfields, or Mr. Bushy's, but the world's cornfields; that their yields would be one of the great economic facts, like the wheat crop of Russia, which underlie all the activities of men, in peace or war" (132). The role her heroine plays in the global marketplace suggests Cather's respect for money, and for those who make financial contributions to society, as well as her contempt for unemployed, impoverished, and ineffectual "bohemian" artists. Although Ántonia retains aspects of her Bohemian heritage, she also becomes a successful American farmer who participates in the international war effort.

Cather's Nebraska is "a transnational, American empire in the process of formation."[46] Here, immigrants from Russia, Scandinavia, and other distant lands mingle with U.S. pioneers. In Black Hawk a Danish laundry and an Italian dancing pavilion exist side by side (188). The author compares the former Indian trails that leave traces on the prairie with Chinese "strokes" on a canvas (60). An elder tree reminds Cather of a Japanese pagoda (228). The conductor on the train that brings Jim to Nebraska has cuff-buttons "engraved with [Egyptian] hieroglyphics" (4). Men harvesting corn, "with long caps pulled down over their ears and their feet in red-lined overshoes," resemble "Arctic explorers" (63). Even the cowboy in My Ántonia looks nothing like the western hero of popular myth. Otto is an Austrian immigrant who wears a Mexican sombrero and bears a mysterious scar on his face (6).

Cather transforms the frontier into a cosmopolitan space, reminiscent of the bohemian colonies that existed in England, Europe, and major U.S. cities. In her fiction Nebraska seems like a version of the cultural melting pot the nation had become by the early twentieth century, at a time when "it was possible to imagine a multinational America in which different cultures coexisted." *My Ántonia* appeared two years after the publication of Royal Dixon's *Americanization* (1916), in which he argued that a "new world could only be created with due appreciation of [its] European heritage." Like Dixon, Cather believed "that a heterogeneous, Europeanized Midwestern society could nurture cosmopolitan culture," even though the communities depicted in her fiction were "mainly white and northern European."[47]

Cather wrote about empires in *My Ántonia*, comparing and contrasting the rise and fall of Rome with nineteenth-century U.S. westward expansion. Gaston Cleric, Jim's classical tutor at the University of Nebraska, is an ailing European who has immigrated to the New World for health reasons. The university on the prairie is a thriving institution, dedicated to transforming the children of pioneers into productive members of society. "There were many serious young men among the students who had come up to the University from the farms and the little towns scattered over the thinly settled State. Some of those boys came straight from the cornfields with only a summer's wages in their pockets, hung on through the four years, shabby and underfed, and completed the course by really heroic self-sacrifice. Our instructors were oddly assorted; wandering pioneer school-teachers, stranded ministers of the Gospel, a few enthusiastic young men just out of graduate schools. There was an atmosphere of endeavor, of expectancy and bright hopefulness about the young college that had lifted its head from the prairie only a few years before" (250). *My Ántonia* fictionalizes "the transfer of European empires to America" and charts the subsequent growth of the new nation through Ántonia's agricultural labor and Jim's education. Cather examines various empires in the novel, portraying the Spanish Empire as "an example of power in decline," illustrated by Jim's account of the Spanish explorers' failure to locate the Seven Cities of Gold. The Roman

Empire is an "ambivalent" example because it eventually succumbs to "barbarians"; whereas the U.S. Empire has triumphantly achieved its goals through Manifest Destiny.[48]

Although Ántonia's family chooses to immigrate to the U.S. West, other Bohemians feel compelled to leave their homeland when it loses its independence during World War I. Jelnick tells Jim: "By 'n' by wartimes come, when the Prussians fight us. We have very many soldiers in camp near my village, and the cholera break out in that camp, and the men die like flies" (102). Two events coincided with Cather's decision not to write about Bohemian immigrants and bohemian artists after publishing *My Ántonia*.[49] Many of these artists, who were conscripted to fight in the war, temporarily disappeared from view. After the war Bohemia was incorporated into the new nation of Czechoslovakia, losing its regional identity.

In later years Cather wrote about the war and other forms of conflict, conquest, and colonization, including the enslavement of Black people in the United States (*Sapphira and the Slave Girl*), France's settlement of northeastern Canada in the seventeenth century (*Shadows on the Rock*), and attempts by the Catholic Church to extend its worldwide influence (*Death Comes for the Archbishop*). It becomes increasingly difficult in these novels for the artist to achieve happiness or success, or to exist in a separate creative and contemplative realm, removed from impinging pressures of the outside world. In *One of Ours* (1923), Nebraska farmer Claude Wheeler becomes friends with the Erlichs, a family of artists and intellectual radicals. But that association ends when Claude is forced to assume more responsibilities at home, becomes mired in an unhappy marriage, and finally enlists to go to war, losing his life overseas. In *The Professor's House* (1925) Tom Outland, a cowboy and self-taught inventor, also enlists in the military, sacrificing his life on a battlefield in Flanders. In *My Mortal Enemy* (1926) Myra Henshawe regrets her romantic elopement with the impoverished Oswald, while learning that the theatrical world is filled with professional disappointments and petty jealousies. In *Lucy Gayheart* (1935) the Nebraska heroine is a second-rate singer/musician, a piano accompanist who fails to find love or artistic fulfillment. Although Bohemian farmers and bohemian artists no longer appear in her fiction, the characters who take their place illustrate certain continuing themes in Cather's work: the conflict between personal artistic achievement and public service or self-sacrifice; a respect for ethnic minorities and gender nonconformists as well as for immigrants who assimilate; the tension between regional autonomy or racial homogeneity and the growth of a transnational U.S. empire.

Bohemian people and bohemian artists share one thing in common: they are immigrants and vagabonds; dispossessed citizens and marginal figures existing on the fringe of society. Cather was "acutely aware of the continuum between her own sense of homelessness" and the feeling of homesickness that afflicts her immigrant characters, including Clara and Nils in "The Bohemian Girl," Carl in *O Pioneers!* (27), and Mr. Shimerda in *My Ántonia* (97). As a result she populated her fictional world with immigrants, artists, and other characters seeking secular and religious fulfillment during a period of global migration, regional development, national expansion, and international turmoil in the late nineteenth and early twentieth centuries.[50]

# A Homeless Snail

## Yone Noguchi and Japanese Self-Invention

Willa Cather once called Yone Noguchi's poetry "conspicuously Oriental."[1] She intended this phrase as a compliment. In the 1890s Noguchi became acquainted with the white male members of San Francisco's Bohemian Club. While the club excluded people of color, its associates simultaneously fetishized the Japanese poet whose mystical musings seemed to represent the wisdom of an ancient civilization. The sophistication of Noguchi's work, combined with his youthful innocence and appreciation of nature, appealed to San Franciscans at a time when the frontier Gold Rush town was transforming into the U.S. West's first cosmopolitan city.

*The American Diary of a Japanese Girl* (1902) was the first English-language novel published in the United States by a Japanese writer. The author of the fictional diary, "Miss Morning Glory," was a Japanese man who assumed multiple identities during his life. Yone Noguchi (Noguchi Yonejirō) was known in the United States as Yoné Noguchi or, more commonly, Yone. Other American nicknames, terms of endearment, and literary pseudonyms included "wee brown man," "*Le Jeune*," "an unconventional child of nature," and "a homeless snail."

Noguchi was born and raised in a small town in western Japan. He left home in 1893, going to San Francisco, where he worked as a houseboy for poet Joaquin Miller. His employer's membership in the Bohemian Club provided Noguchi with access to local authors and publishers who promoted the Japanese immigrant's career as a writer. Noguchi nurtured these connections, navigating racial prejudice and negotiating complex personal relationships in order to further his literary aspirations. At the time San Francisco was perhaps the only place in the nation where Noguchi could reinvent himself. It was the cultural capital of the U.S.

West, with a large Asian population, as well as being one of the most sexually liberated cities in the nation. Noguchi took advantage of the late nineteenth-century craze for Orientalist art and culture and exploited his attraction to both men and women, who were seduced by Noguchi's somewhat feminine, exotic appearance. Leveraging his minority status and his ambiguous sexuality to his advantage, the immigrant son of a middle-class merchant became a Japanese servant whose professed humility and admiration for Miller earned him an entrée to those in positions of power. Thereafter Noguchi capitalized on his identity as an object of white desire, conquering the West as a writer before returning to Japan, where he became a muse for the country's nationalist movement prior to World War II.

From the mid-nineteenth through the early twentieth century San Francisco was the site of rapid development, destruction, rebuilding, and reinvention. After gold was discovered in central California in 1843, the former mission town transformed "as if by magic" into a city of 35,000 residents. By 1870 it had more than quadrupled in size, becoming a major metropolis as well as the center of banking, finance, and maritime trade.[2] During this period San Francisco also suffered extensive damage, which required rebuilding major portions of the city. Five major fires occurred in 1850 and 1851, devastating the mining town where most residents lived in tents or flimsy wooden structures, lit by kerosene lamps.[3] By the early twentieth century San Francisco had become a West Coast metropolis. When an earthquake devastated the city in 1906, politicians, civic leaders, and business magnates funded massive construction projects that included a new opera house as well as the city's first subway.[4]

Nothing represented this growing cultural center and site of transformation better than the Bohemian Club, where the most famous and flamboyant member was Joaquin Miller. The self-proclaimed "Poet of the Sierras" arrived in San Francisco in 1870, sharing tall tales about his frontier adventures and wearing "a broad sombrero, blue denim pants that were too small for him, beaded moccasins and a white linen duster that fell to his heels."[5] Like Miller, most club members and their literary associates were poseurs more than writers. These "bohemians" belonged to the conventional white middle class, and although they claimed to be "liberated from the Puritan past,"[6] they were better known for their "affectations" than their "sins,"[7] unlike their neighbors in the Barbary Coast, a vice district filled with gambling dens and brothels. Some, like Miller, cultivated their eccentricities, while others hid their pasts or pretended to conform to social norms to avoid scandal. Ina Coolbrith concealed the fact that her uncle was Joseph Smith, fearing a public backlash if readers discovered her Mormon heritage.[8] Charles Warren Stoddard was homosexual, though his friends referred to him as a gentleman bachelor and as a connoisseur of "Chopin at twilight, Oriental bric-a-brac, incense, lounging [robes], and fragrant cigarettes."[9]

Stoddard's colleagues shared his fascination with the Orient. To celebrate the club's acquisition of an Egyptian mummy in 1890, Stoddard read a poem entitled "The Daughter of Pharaoh." In one stanza the animated mummy exclaims: "With gay Bohemia is my portion cast; / Born of the oldest East, I seek my rest / In the fair city of the youngest West."[10] Although San Francisco was a metropolis with an international population, the club was racially restricted. It was "gay" in the festive sense and exotic in its fetishization of foreigners and racial minorities.

Yone Noguchi came to California three years after this celebration. Although Stoddard later called him "an unconventional child of nature,"[11] the college-educated aspiring poet was a product of modern Japan. After the Meiji Restoration in 1868 the country had begun a process of modernization, welcoming foreign technology and trade with the West. (Meiji means "enlightened rule.") During this period Japan also sought to extend its realm of influence. Viewing the Western hemisphere as its own frontier, the country pursued a policy of eastern expansionism, encouraging emigration to such places as the western United States. In its colonialist discourse, the government referred to California as "an imperial beginning" and "a new Japan." Emigrants pursued their homeland's policy by "building a collective economic base" on the West Coast, purchasing farms, and starting Japanese "colonies" within racially segregated areas allowed by U.S. law.[12]

Manifest Destiny had earlier resulted in the conquest of California, the displacement and killing of its indigenous residents, and the unequal treatment of Asian immigrants who had gone there to build railroads and to work as merchants and servants in cities such as San Francisco. Eastward expansion coincided with the next phase of westward expansion, beginning at the turn of the century. Looking beyond its national borders, the U.S. government established an Open Door Policy in 1899, encouraging trade with Asia. Though Japan did not seek to dominate the West, its emigrants had similar economic incentives. The nation's adoption of capitalism after the Meiji Restoration "contributed to the blurring of the boundaries between emigration and colonization."[13]

The Naturalization Act of 1870 prevented Japanese immigrants from becoming citizens, while alien land laws discouraged them from owning homes and businesses. Racial segregation led to the creation of Japantowns throughout California, leading at least one white writer to view immigrants from an Occidental perspective. In her history of San Francisco, Gertrude Atherton referred to "Chinatown and [other] foreign 'colonies'" within the city.[14] While the Japanese considered such colonies proof of their expanding international presence, Atherton portrayed them as a blot on San Francisco's urban landscape, a fact she admitted in a chapter entitled "Yes, We Have Our Slums."[15]

Unlike other Japanese immigrants, Noguchi never intended to settle permanently in the United States. The aspiring poet also realized writing would never be as lucrative as farming or mercantile labor. But Noguchi did become involved in nationalist politics as soon as he arrived in San Francisco, joining a political club called the Patriotic League and working for a newspaper associated with the Freedom and People's Rights Movement. He also "wrote essays extolling Japan's expansionist policy"[16] and used the Sino-Japanese War (1894–95) as an opportunity to improve his English, telling "anybody [he] came across" why his homeland deserved to win the "fight" to control Korea.[17]

Noguchi hoped to advance his career—if not his nation's political ambitions—by ingratiating himself with San Francisco's literary elite. While working as a hotel dishwasher, Noguchi heard about Joaquin Miller, who lived at the Heights (Miller spelled it Hights), a rustic retreat in the Oakland Hills. Miller often hired Japanese houseboys and displayed his interest in the Orient by building paper houses in the woods surrounding his residence and creating "a meandering little stream 'Japanese style' beautifully arranged with gardens and rocks."[18] Realizing that the "fastest way to achieve recognition as a poet in Japan was to establish a reputation abroad,"[19] Noguchi visited Miller, who offered him a place to live as well as the opportunity to write in a scenic setting. Thus began Noguchi's process of reinvention, transforming himself from an educated member of the Japanese middle class into a lower-class American servant.

Immigrants were often "forced by circumstances" to adopt "roles and identities that greatly diverged from their social, economic, cultural, or religious identities in the [countries] of their birth."[20] Noguchi understood that he was playing a role during the four years he lived at the Heights. (Later he claimed his "Orientalism was born in the West." It was part of his "plan of operation," his "strike" or attack on California.[21]) Noguchi also was not fooled by Miller's histrionics, accepting the local celebrity as a lovable fraud—or, as he wrote in his autobiography, a "symbol of romance and poetry." In the book he delighted in describing Miller's mode of dress. "I must not forget to tell you that he wore top-boots and, wonder of all, a bear-skin over his shoulders even while eating." Miller sometimes sprinkled rose petals over the dinner table as a meal-time benediction.[22] When Ina Coolbrith came to visit, the poet put on a show, chanting a Native American song as rain appeared to fall from the skies. In reality the water came from a sprinkler system, secretly operated by Noguchi.[23]

At the same time the servant performed a second role, appearing as queer to members of the Bohemian Club. Noguchi exploited the Occidental perception that Japanese men were "artfully feminine."[24] By contrast, Miller was rampantly heterosexual. During his lifetime he abandoned his wife and family, lived with an Indian woman, and had an affair with actress Adah Isaacs Menken, who was best known for starring in a play in which she appeared naked, riding a horse.[25]

Yet there was also something feminine about the long-haired poet. In his fictional autobiography, *Life Amongst the Modocs* (1873), the author claims as a young man he had blond hair like a "schoolgirl."[26] In his novel *The Danites in the Sierras* (1878), his alter ego, a Mormon woman, escapes from polygamy, working in a mining camp where she cross-dresses as a man.

Miller mentioned Noguchi in an interview with the *San Francisco Chronicle* in 1896. "He's one of my class. . . . I like queer folks—the queer are always good."[27] Although it is not clear what Miller meant by the word "queer," he apparently identified with Noguchi. (The poet returned the compliment, calling Miller a "brother soul" and a "sister spirit in a rose."[28]) Others used the word "queer" to suggest differences between Noguchi and other Japanese immigrants. One of his friends wrote to an American: "Yone is most queer boy among all Nipponese. . . . He is dreamer. Yes, he are [*sic*] dreaming always of his sweet dream, mostly of his native country."[29] By the mid-1890s Noguchi had developed a multi-faceted identity. He shared a kindred spirit with San Francisco's bohemians, while maintaining a patriotic allegiance to his native country.

Through Miller Noguchi met the editor of a literary magazine called the *Lark*. Gelett Burgess published five of Noguchi's poems in 1896, marking the beginning of his career as a poet. To commemorate his new public identity Burgess nicknamed Noguchi *Le Jeune*, a term of endearment he bestowed on male contributors to his journal. Before coming to the United States Noguchi had taken English lessons, knowing his success as a writer depended on his mastery of the language. In the first chapter of his autobiography, entitled "How I Learned English," Noguchi compares the excitement he experienced when he purchased his first spelling book to the later "sensation" he felt when crossing the Atlantic Ocean. When he arrives in San Francisco, he continues his education by eavesdropping on native speakers like a Japanese spy. "Once I saw in the street a Western woman with a little girl, whom I followed, again with the same purpose, that is, to test my ears to find whether I could understand their words; I followed after them still further in despair of catching them. The girl suddenly turned back and shouted: 'Mamma, what does this fellow want?'"[30]

Ironically, Noguchi's inability to master English contributed to his early success as a poet. A year after making his literary debut, Noguchi published two small collections of poetry, *The Voice of the Valley* (1897) and *Seen and Unseen; or Monologues of a Homeless Snail* (1897). His biographer claims Noguchi's early work contains no explicit references to the Orient.[31] But his faulty English and strange metaphors appealed to fans of Japonism, a western fetish for Japanese culture in all its forms. In her review of his work Willa Cather sensed an "oriental melancholy" in Noguchi's poetry.[32] The "homeless snail" carried his home on his back, like the Japanese immigrant. Cather was sensitive to the way foreigners experienced the American West. Her early novels featured Scandinavians and Eastern Europeans farming on the Nebraska prairie. Traces of Orientalism also appear in *My Ántonia* (1918). Marks on the grass, resembling "strokes of Chinese," indicate where Indians used to ride before they were displaced by white pioneers. The plains are scattered with "pagoda-like elders," their shape reminiscent of Japanese temples.[33]

In his introduction to *Seen and Unseen* Burgess praised Noguchi's atmospheric poems: "wrapped in the warm darkness of the invisible night—shrouded in the gray mystery of mist—under the brave, upright rains, or swept by the boneless winds;—[Noguchi] has revealed himself a visitor in this sense-world, hid in a corner of the Universe, delighted in his dreams and reveries, with its shadows, its audible silence, and the poetic garments of its clouds."[34] In a later book about Japanese landscapes Noguchi contrasted the realism of Western art—the attempt "to imitate nature or to make a copy"—with the "abstraction" favored by Japanese artists, "who truly [understand] her inner soul."[35] A similar abstraction appeared in the nature photography produced by Japanese and Japanese American artists practicing in California and the Pacific Northwest at the turn of the century. These photographers created "hazy" atmospheres meant to align "with the impasto brushwork of romantic painting." An American reviewer claimed these works were not "pictorial in our sense of the word, but rather queer."[36]

Japanese pictorialism imbued western regional art with "a transnational complexity."[37] So did Noguchi's poetry. *The Voice of the Valley* was inspired by his trip to Yosemite. In one poem Noguchi is humbled by a majestic mountain. "I proffer my stainful body and leprous / soul with blackest shame unto / thee."[38] Noguchi differs from his American contemporaries John Muir and Clarence King in his relationship to Yosemite. Muir experiences the transcendental sublime, enabling him to commune as one with nature. King feels more than equal to his surroundings. He conquers mountains by climbing them and surveys them while mapping territories during the era of westward expansion. In a later essay, entitled "Japanese Art" (1935), Noguchi suggests Americans are acquisitive—they want to possess nature, unlike Japanese artists, who reside in "the extra-territorial kingdom of self-effacement."[39] The poet defines modesty as a Japanese characteristic, while simultaneously asserting a militaristic sensibility, claiming "extraterritorial" privilege, which is normally granted to foreign embassies and military bases.

In order to further his career Noguchi moved to New York City in 1900. While he completed *The American Diary of a Japanese Girl*, which featured a young woman searching for a husband abroad, Noguchi corresponded with Charles Warren Stoddard. Like his female protagonist, the version of Noguchi who appears in these letters is both romantic and calculating. Noguchi had first written to Stoddard while living at the Heights in the late 1890s. By then Stoddard had left San Francisco and accepted a teaching position at the Catholic University of America—a post he would be forced to resign in 1902, due to the Church's stand on homosexuality. Stoddard had a predilection for dark-skinned young men, as he acknowledged in his personal travelogues *Summer Cruising in the South Seas* (1874) and *Cruising Among the Caribees* (1893). In response to Noguchi's 1897 letter of introduction, which included a bouquet of pressed flowers, Stoddard had written: "Dear friend who has come to me out of the Orient! Long I have waited to hear from you." Noguchi had reciprocated by sending poems and a photograph. In later letters he emphasized "their difference in stature, gender, as well as nationality," professing that he wished to be Stoddard's "most feminine dove." Eventually Noguchi asked his friend for financial assistance. Claiming he yearned to see Stoddard in person, Noguchi wrote:

"Oh, my dearest Charlie, are you not rich enough to provide me a ticket across the continent?"[40]

By the time they met in 1900 Noguchi had already found someone else to help further his career. Through his literary connections in San Francisco the writer had become acquainted with Blanche Partington, an older woman from a socially prominent family who had offered Noguchi "editorial assistance" with his poetry. Partington had been smitten by the young man's "olive skin" and "haunting eyes," which Noguchi had exploited for romantic effect on one occasion, casting Partington a "tender frolicsome side-glance" during her visit to the Heights.[41]

After moving to New York City Noguchi met another woman, Léonie Gilmour, who helped him revise and edit *The American Diary of a Japanese Girl*. As Stoddard languished in Washington DC, Gilmour took an increasingly active role in the manuscript's production, not only correcting Noguchi's language and syntax but attempting "to capture the sense of his original words and transform them into literary form."[42] In the process she and Noguchi began a sexual relationship, which led to the birth of his son in 1904.

Noguchi's biographer has speculated that the author was most likely bisexual, that his feelings for Stoddard were genuine, and that their relationship was an "ill-fated affair," inhibited by contemporary prohibitions against same-sex desire.[43] However, there is no evidence that the relationship was consummated or that Noguchi did anything more than profess his love in a series of letters and poems.[44] Noguchi's "performance" may have been merely a form of flirtation, intended to persuade Stoddard into serving as his literary patron.

A need for money also inspired Noguchi to write *The American Diary of a Japanese Girl*. Although he hoped to establish his literary reputation as a poet, he knew such efforts paid poorly. Even Miller, San Francisco's most acclaimed poet, was forced to live modestly at the Heights, a fact Noguchi noted in his autobiography and *The American Diary of a Japanese Girl*. His own dramatic instincts enabled Noguchi to realize that the "impoverished poet" was also a stereotype, a role he and his fictional character performed at times. "In New York, where my first attempt to sell my poetical wares and my California fame as a poet of two or three years back seemed quite nicely forgotten, I decided to play a sad young poet whose fate was to die in a garret," he writes in *The Story of Yone Noguchi*.[45] Noguchi's fictional protagonist, Miss Morning Glory, also imitates people whom she meets on her American journey. "Shall I pose as poet?" she asks herself. Deciding poetry is no longer popular, she gives it up "for some more brilliant up-to-date pose."[46]

*The American Diary of a Japanese Girl* capitalized on the recent popularity of diaries, journals, and autobiographies written by young women at the turn of the century, such as *The Story of Mary MacLane* (initially entitled *I Await the Devil's Coming*), published by a proto-feminist bisexual author from Butte, Montana.[47] At the same time it exploited American stereotypes about the Japanese while subtly ridiculing Japonism. On the surface Miss Morning Glory appears submissive to her uncle, whom she accompanies overseas, and demure in her general comportment, an alternative to the new American woman who is liberated and independent. In her diary, however, the narrator displays a fiery spirit, asserting she will not be forced into an arranged marriage like her countrywomen. "The Jap 'gentleman'—who desires the old barbarity—persists still in fancying that girls are trading wares." At times Miss Morning Glory seems vain, spoiled, and insipid—a girl from a wealthy Japanese family who has been taught to value nothing but her own appearance. However, she occasionally mocks U.S. perceptions of Japanese women and Oriental culture. Taking advantage of the West's fascination with *The Mikado, Madame Butterfly*, and other works in which white actresses played Japanese characters, Noguchi simultaneously reveals that his narrator despises these portrayals of Oriental women as infantile and self-sacrificing.[48] He also satirizes the "imitation" Japanese garden Miss Morning Glory visits in California, the home of an affluent American woman decorated with Japanese lanterns, as well as another woman's presentation of a Japanese guitar and the request that her guest "tinkle a little gamboling music in the parlour before dinner."[49]

Before Noguchi disguised himself as Miss Morning Glory there had been an ancient tradition of female impersonation in Japanese theater.

Originating in the fourteenth century, Noh was a form of musical drama featuring actors who wore masks representing men and women, children, and ghosts. Kabuki theater evolved out of Noh. This new art form, combining dance and drama, was created by a woman named O Kuni during the Keicho era (1596–1614). Early troupes reportedly included "women of easy virtue," causing government officials to issue a decree in 1629, banning women from the stage. They were replaced by the Wakashu (Young Men's Kabuki), who were also outlawed twenty-three years later, when officials decided "the physical charms of the boys were an equal menace to the community." The Yarō Kabuki, made up of adult males, appeared in 1654. The men who performed in female makeup and costume were called "onnagata."[50]

Pictures of Noguchi explain why he attracted Stoddard in the same way Kabuki boy actors appealed to audiences with their "physical charms." Noguchi was not a performer in the same sense as Miller. Unlike his patron, a literary showman who relished the limelight, Noguchi was soft-spoken, unassuming, and somewhat shy. The young man did not sell his favors like the alleged prostitutes who worked in early Japanese theater, though his relationships—with Stoddard, as well as with heterosexual men and women—were situational and self-serving. Noguchi performed various roles during his career in the United States—as a same-sex admirer and heterosexual lover, and as a houseboy, poet, and pseudonymous author of *The American Diary of a Japanese Girl*. The novel was a double performance, written by a man masquerading as a woman, including revisions and editorial changes made by Gilmour, whose contributions were not acknowledged by the author.

Noguchi sought to further his career through his geographic travels. As Japan pursued its policy of eastern expansionism, the writer's politics also became more overtly nationalistic. In 1903 Noguchi journeyed to England, where he met Thomas Hardy, William Butler Yeats, and other well-known writers. Britain and Japan had recently formed the Anglo-Japanese Alliance, promising to safeguard their respective interests in China and Korea. Shortly afterward Noguchi self-published his third volume of poetry, *From the Eastern Sea*, which was well received in both Britain and Japan. In his introduction to the Japanese edition, Inazo Nitobe praised Noguchi's "virile versatility and the great vitality of our race." Alluding to Noguchi's foreign travels, Nitobe wrote: "The memories of his native land have never died within his ardent breast. All the Sierra have failed to make him oblivious of our peerless [Mount] Fuji." While acknowledging the poet's masculine style and national pride, he also noted something winsome, delicate, and strangely ambiguous about the chameleonic writer:

> His lines betray both the land of his birth and the land of his sojourn. They are the offspring of a happy union between the East and the West. [Noguchi] makes the most daring use of English, imparting to his work now a bizarre quality, then a quaint picturesqueness and again a näive Japanese tenderness. There is color in his words, there is fragrance in his phrases. Perhaps because he writes in a foreign tongue, or perhaps because his themes are often of an ethereal nature, or it may be because his mood is more often too dreamy for verbal expression, his lines give us a felicitous impression of something felt but left unsaid—something vaguely guessed but inexpressible.[51]

Noguchi's earlier writings had contained subtle political allusions and traces of nationalist sentiment. The first poem in *The Voice of the Valley* includes the lines: "Aye, mighty Yosemite!—a glorious troop / of the unsuffering souls of gods / Marches on with battle-sound against the / unknown castle of Hell!"[52] Noguchi appeals to U.S. readers by transforming his subject into Christian allegory. But his militaristic tone resonates with the later poetry he published when he returned to Japan, supporting the country's war with Russia. In *The American Diary of a Japanese Girl* the reader learns that the narrator's uncle, a Yale graduate, is the chief secretary of the Nippon Mining Company. As a young man he went to the United States to prepare for his later career, then returned to Japan, assuming a leadership position at one of the nation's largest corporate enterprises. (Nippon means "the sun's origin." It refers to the Land of the Rising Sun, a reference to imperial Japan.) The businessman has taken a leave of absence to travel with his niece and has no intention of expanding overseas.[53]

Noguchi returned to Japan in 1904, abandoning Gilmour and their son, Isamu. He married a Japanese woman, became a university professor, and continued to publish poetry and literary criticism. Noguchi supported the Russo-Japanese War (1904), collaborating with Miller on a book praising the nation's culture and military endeavors, entitled *Japan of Sword and Love* (1905). The book's nationalist agenda was undermined by the men's conflicting sensibilities. Noguchi sounded combative and fiercely patriotic in "Fight, Fight, Fight!" and "Let Us March Toward Manchuria!" The latter poem proclaimed:

Let here be the red Judgement Day!
Let us build a god's world as our fathers built!
Behold, Sun and Moon never disturb one
another's realm!
Let us drive the nation invading a neighbour's domain![54]

Miller had a history of supporting the political causes of ethnic and racial minorities. (His chosen name, Joaquin, alluded to the legendary Mexican California bandit Joaquin Murieta.) But his allegiances were merely literary gestures that revealed condescending Orientalist attitudes. In one poem Miller warns the Russians not to underestimate the Japanese soldier. "Beware this sober, wee brown man, / Who yesterday stood but a span / Beneath his blossomed cherry-trees, / Soft singing with his brother bees!" In another poem he professes his love for

this sudden, Orient star,
This lithe Venetian, lover true,
This isle-born elf, so old, so new,
Wee neighbor of the stalwart Czar—
His thousand isles, his million flowers,
His terraced steeps, his cloud-topt towers.[55]

Noguchi's poetry reflected Eastern and Western influences. While Nitobe admired this mixture of sensibilities, others did not appreciate Noguchi's work or welcome the author when he returned to Japan. His "collaboration" with Miller was a double-edged sword: a literary co-production and a kind of cooperation with the enemy.[56] The Americanized Noguchi became less popular in Japan as the country became increasingly nationalistic. During the 1930s, as tensions between Japan and the United States escalated, Noguchi published an appreciation of French composer Claude Debussy and a collection of poems inspired by his travels in India.[57] Noguchi's reputation in the United States began to decline after World War II, and his nationalist views have continued to alienate critics. An American obituary published in 1945 condemned Noguchi for discarding "his Western wife and ideas" and becoming "a great booster of Japanese imperialism," while a contemporary scholar lists among the writer's faults his "overbearing nationalism."[58]

First-generation Japanese immigrants were "faced with the need to reconcile simultaneous national belongings as citizen-subjects of one state and yet resident-members (denizens) of another."[59] Noguchi experienced a similar unease when he returned to Japan. In an essay published in 1936 the author wrote: "I often wonder whether I am an Orientalist or Occidentalist, whether I am Japanese or western. This strange question baffles me, and makes me sink into thought." At the end of his meditation, the man who had arrived with optimism in San Francisco decades earlier now concludes that "two people, the Oriental and the Occidental, on one pair of shoulders are too painful to carry about."[60]

# 7 The Past Is the Biggest Country of All

*Remembering Helena Modjeska*

"California has a more settled population than almost any State in the Union." So claimed nineteenth-century journalist Charles Nordhoff. "It does not change; our people can not 'move West,' and very few of them return to the East."[1] The fact that thousands of miners failed to strike it rich in the Gold Rush, and returned home with empty pockets, suggests the state's population may not have been as stable as Nordhoff maintained. In addition, immigrants such as Yone Noguchi came to the Western Hemisphere and returned to the "Orient" after prospering in their chosen professions. Actress Helena Modjeska charted a similar path. She left Poland at a time when her homeland was occupied by outside political forces and returned in triumph, having conquered audiences in the United States, England, and western Europe.

Helena Modjeska reigned as Poland's most acclaimed stage actress during the late nineteenth century. Her life was marked by a series of dramatic incidents, most of which she omitted from her autobiography. Modjeska was born out of wedlock to the widow of a Kraków merchant. Her first husband was a bigamist and her daughter died in infancy. Her husband kidnapped their son before their divorce, though Modjeska ransomed him back four years later.[2] Her second husband posed as a member of the Polish nobility, as did the actress, who referred to herself Countess Modjeska after their marriage. She reportedly took numerous lovers during her decades-long career.

Poland had lost its status as an independent commonwealth in the previous century. During Modjeska's lifetime the country was partitioned into territories governed by the Russian kingdom, the Prussian empire, and the Austrian Hapsburg monarchy. Fleeing from oppression at home, Modjeska and her husband emigrated to California in 1876, accompanied by a group of fellow artists. On a ranch near Anaheim they established an agricultural commune based on the socialist principles of French philosopher Charles Fourier. For the Polish exiles California was a land of possibility, the ideal site for an experimental society. It was a place of potential transformation, offering the actress an opportunity to reinvent herself anew.

When the utopian experiment failed, Modjeska resumed her acting career, touring the United States and England, starring in classic European dramas and Shakespearean plays. Although the time spent at the commune represented a brief chapter in the artist's career, it allowed Modjeska—the grand dame of Polish high society turned socialist émigré and western pioneer—to add another role to her repertoire. As the actress suggested in her memoir, and as biographers and novelists such as Willa Cather and Susan Sontag have more recently shown, Modjeska was the quintessential "actress"—a symbol for the transformative power of art.

The difficulty in identifying the "real" Helena Modjeska begins in Kraków, Poland, where a widow named Jósefa Benda gave birth to a girl in 1840. Later the daughter was given her godfather's surname and baptized as Helena Opid. In *Memories and Impressions of Helena Modjeska: An Autobiography* (1910) Modjeska claimed her childhood music teacher was her biological father. There were also rumors that Opid was the product of her mother's love affair with a Polish prince.[3]

During adolescence Opid married an actor who had previously served as her paternal guardian. Gustave Sinnmayer was also known by the stage name Gustaw Modrzejewski. He encouraged his wife to adopt the feminine version of his surname when she became an actress in 1861. Helena Modrzejewska eventually left her husband when she discovered he was legally married to another woman. In 1868 she married "Count" Karol Chaplowski, an actor who sought to garner publicity by posing as a Polish nobleman.[4]

While the identity of Helena Benda/Opid/Modrzejewska/Sinnmayer was in the process of evolving, her country was undergoing its own transformation. During the actress's childhood Kraków was "like a play from the past. Once the city had been the thriving, bustling capital of a powerful state, playing an important role in world affairs. Now it was . . . dead, a provincial town in the Austrian province of western Galicia." After getting married, the Sinnmayers moved to a small, impoverished salt-mining town, where "history ended for Helena" and the legend of Poland's greatest actress was born. Here, "Modrzejewska stepped forth upon the boards. She was never again to be Helena Benda or Helena Opid."[5]

Modrzejewska first achieved success starring in *Adrienne Lecouvreur*, a play about a famous eighteenth-century actress who revolutionized European theater by pioneering a naturalistic acting style.[6] Although Modrzejewska was a flamboyant performer, she matched the playwright's conception of the character, a creature of the theater who expresses her feelings by quoting lines from other dramas. In the play Lecouvreur denounces her lover by reciting a passage from Jean Racine's *Phèdre*, ironically claiming: "I scorn to wear a mask; I know not how to feign." Elsewhere, however, she acknowledges her artifice in a speech taken from Molière's *Psyché*.[7] The action takes place off stage, during a performance of *Bajazet*, another play by Racine. But the audience never sees Lecouvreur perform in this work. Instead she appears in a personal backstage drama, reciting the words of other writers and behaving in the guise of their theatrical heroines.

After forging her reputation in regional theater, Modrzejewska triumphantly returned to Kraków in 1865. Three years later, having separated from her husband, she moved to Warsaw, where she subsequently became established as the reigning prima donna at the city's Imperial Theatres. In 1876 Modrzejewska and her second husband decided to emigrate to California, accompanied by author Henryk Sienkiewicz and other fellow artists. Allegedly the exiles hoped to establish a socialist commune based on universalist principles, though—as in other instances concerning Modrzejewska's life—accounts differ. In her autobiography the actress maintained she came to "the land of freedom" seeking political refuge, although a recent biographer argues "her reasons for leaving were also supercharged with artistic and social ambition. Modrzejewska had conquered Warsaw . . . but she could not command universal obedience" by remaining in Poland.[8]

The author claimed Sienkiewicz was the first one to propose emigration,[9] though another biographer states that the writer "disliked [America], was cynical of our customs, manners,—or lack of manners— and was the one member of that remarkable foreign colony who never acquired even the commonplace phrases of English."[10] In fact Sienkiewicz seemed to have no particular feelings about his host country. In the introduction to his short story "A Comedy of Errors: A Sketch from American Life" (1876), the author wrote: "Whether the incident which serves as the core of the following sketch took place in the east or in the west, I could not find out. But really it does not matter."[11]

It is unclear whether the Poles intended to create an artists' retreat, an agricultural collective in which the labor was divided equally among its members, or a refuge for political exiles. In the late nineteenth century more alternative communities were founded in the West than anywhere else in the country. La Réunion, Texas, was based on Fourier's controversial theories, while Octagon City, in Kansas cattle country, became a haven for vegetarians. Nicodemus, Kansas, was incorporated as a Negro township after the Civil War, allowing former slaves to govern themselves. But this unnamed community of Polish émigrés was not based on any particular ideology.

Modrzejewska and her followers were acting in a play without a script, unsure of their roles. The ranch she and her husband purchased near Anaheim had an overgrown orchard, untended fields, a lawn that looked like a "graveyard," and a two-bedroom house (the single men slept in tents outside). The first day the workers approached their tasks with enthusiasm. "Next morning some of the party were late for breakfast; the third day some of them complained of a lame back; and a week later there were only two who insisted still on working." Modrzejewska wore a "pretty" apron in her new role as domestic goddess but became irritated when her housemates treated her like a short-order cook.[12]

Realizing she was temperamentally unsuited to her new life, and her husband and colleagues were doomed to fail in their communal experiment, the actress reinvented herself as a comic character in her autobiography. Modrzejewska recalled how she had imagined living on a farm before coming to California. "'Oh, but to cook under the sapphire-blue sky in the land of freedom! What joy!' I thought. 'To bleach linen at the brook like the maidens of Homer's 'Iliad'!'" It was more natural for Modrzejewska to compare herself to fictional characters than it was for the diva to keep house for a bunch of manual laborers. Elsewhere the author described a visit from a Polish friend, humorously recalling how her housemates were too squeamish to kill a turkey for dinner, how the overweight guest broke his bed, and how he fell in a ditch while chasing a servant girl across the ranch.[13]

Unlike communes or "intentional communities" composed of individuals who shared political or religious beliefs, the California compound was a haven for artists and intellectuals unaccustomed to fending for themselves. Although Modrzejewska was appalled by American materialism,[14] she and her husband and colleagues preferred to hire servants to perform the farm work and household chores. Another commune near Anaheim— founded by a group of German farmers, machinists, and tradesmen—had been thriving for almost twenty years. But the Polish émigrés lacked the practical skills necessary for running a ranch as well as the optimism other immigrants typically experienced when they arrived in the American promised land. The Poles were a conquered people, fleeing a homeland controlled by foreign powers, bred to accept defeat. As Modrzejewska's fictional counterpart notes in Sontag's novel *In America*: "We are natural pessimists, believing that what has happened will happen again. Perhaps that is the definition of an optimist: someone who denies the power of the past. The past is not really important here [in America]. Here the present does not reaffirm the past but supersedes and cancels it."[15]

Modrzejewska was less pessimistic than Sontag's protagonist. Whether she planned to continue acting before leaving Poland or whether she resumed her career because the ranch had failed, in either case the actress agreed to perform at the California Theatre in San Francisco the following year. She chose *Adrienne Lecouvreur* for her U.S. debut and changed her surname to Modjeska for the convenience of non-Polish-speaking theatergoers. Beginning in San Francisco, "Modjeska sought to win her public not as an ethnic artist or a visiting foreign star, but as an Americanized success." Unaware of her "scandalous youth," U.S. audiences welcomed the self-styled Polish countess. At the same time, Modjeska worried that her "quest for a world-class stage elsewhere, which implied the backwater status of her native theater, could be construed by Poles as a national betrayal." From now on, the actress realized she risked "permanent double exposure. . . . Her binational stardom demanded her proficiency in two languages and cultures so that she could shine before both publics and effectively explain one to the other, persuading Americans of her homeland's cultural prowess" at a time when Poland had become a weakened player on the international stage. At the same time Modjeska hoped to educate Poles about "the fine people and accomplished artists she managed to find in the land of big business." Her success was dependent on her ability to represent herself "as a model citizen of both countries—as an American star devoted to American audiences . . . and [as] a Polish star who reliably demonstrated the genius and loyalty her Polish public expected."[16] In a sense Modjeska served as a "cultural ambassador" of European culture, rather than as a "rebellious Polish artist in exile."[17]

The actress chose to resume her career in the American West, where audiences were more likely to welcome the self-appointed ambassador. Before settling in California, Modjeska and her compatriots had visited New York City, where the actress had "surveyed the major theaters." Realizing Polish productions were consigned to "ethnic" venues, unlike Sarah Bernhardt's "French-language spectacles [which] attracted a large, generally educated American public," Modjeska returned to the West Coast.[18] Although San Francisco had an opera house and several major theaters, its residents—one generation removed from the Gold Rush—were less formal and critically exacting than their East Coast counterparts. After completing her engagement at the California Theater, Modjeska toured the western territories. In October 1877 a reviewer for the Virginia City *Chronicle* described Modjeska's memorable death scene in *Adrienne Lecouvreur*. "First time I see her fall down by the fireplace it paralyzed me. Blast me if I'd felt so since my old mother died." Writing in the same comic vernacular style as Mark Twain, another Virginia

City journalist and western observer who had published *Roughing It* five years earlier, the reviewer recognized a fellow *poseur*, exclaiming: "Look at her actin'. Why, it just walks into a man's soul without knockin' and takes possession of the whole ground floor."[19]

In general, spectators were not overly bothered by Modjeska's heavily accented English, mispronunciation of words, and tone-deaf delivery of Shakespearean poetry. Some critics believed Modjeska may have over-emoted to compensate for her lack of fluency in a foreign language. Reviewing the same performance in San Francisco, another journalist had earlier noted how Modjeska conveyed the "madness of agony and death" by grotesquely contorting her face and body. A twentieth-century biographer notes: "She could make you laugh or cry, scowl or smile, rejoice or be plunged into deepest despair, by the magic of her voice, though you did not understand a word."[20]

Modjeska lived in "a state of constant self-translation." Most Polish immigrants who came to the United States at the turn of the century sought to avoid "the denigration and exploitation they faced in the American workplace, where they were stereotyped as ignorant peasants," by living in "large, self-sufficient communities" that resembled "foreign ghettos."[21] Modjeska's attempt to create a similar commune had failed and her successful return to acting eventually brought her sufficient "wealth, worldliness, and stardom" to distinguish her from other Polish exiles. Yet her broken English posed a problem. Modjeska was unable to persuade audiences that she was not a foreigner, yet she was determined not to be an ethnic caricature, like the Indians in Buffalo Bill's Wild West shows and the Irish working-class characters frequently seen on the public stage.[22] By the end of the nineteenth century, Modjeska had become one of the most celebrated, non-native-speaking actors or actresses in the American theater.[23]

The actress and her second husband returned to California in 1888, purchasing a ranch near their former commune, on the banks of Santiago Creek in Orange County. This investment was more lucrative than their previous "ranch," yielding annual crops of barley and alfalfa as well as olive oil, honey, and popping corn, harvested by workers whom the couple could now afford to pay.[24] But it was also a showplace for the actress, featuring extensive gardens and a mansion that bore little resemblance to their earlier rural dwelling. Modjeska named the place after the forest of Arden in Shakespeare's *As You Like It*. Having played Rosalind many times throughout her career, the actress now appeared on the domestic stage as a kind of frontier chatelaine, receiving distinguished visitors and members of the press. "Recognizing that her fans would want souvenirs of this important component of her legend . . . [Modjeska] consented to the production of photo postcards featuring her on Arden's grounds by the vine-covered old well, seated on the edge of one of its reflecting fountains, or standing with flowers in her arms."[25]

The horticulturist, botanist, and landscape designer Theodore Payne served as the head gardener at Arden until 1896. In his posthumous memoir, *Life on the Modjeska Ranch in the Gay Nineties* (1962), Payne barely mentioned his famous employer. Although he attended one of her plays in Los Angeles, he failed to comment on Modjeska's performance. Interested in California's native plants and flowers, Payne viewed Modjeska as a non-indigenous species. The actress planted English yew trees and roses in her Shakespearean forest and sometimes lay in a hammock on the lawn, according to the author, reading and chatting with visitors, or doing "fancy work," when she was not on tour.[26]

Payne was the only biographer who seemed immune to Modjeska's charm. In the introduction to a later biography, another writer enthuses: "Modjeska! Helena Modjeska. The name . . . ah yes, she was the one."[27] Others have also praised Modjeska, not for her western authenticity but for her theatrical genius. In "A Scandal in Bohemia" (1891), Arthur Conan Doyle based Irene Adler partly on the Polish actress.[28] Like the biographer who hails Modjeska as a muse ("she was the one"), Doctor Watson begins the story by confiding: "To Sherlock Holmes she is always *the* woman." Described as a former diva at the Imperial Opera of Warsaw, Adler dons a disguise that fools the sleuth and eludes capture at the end of the story.[29]

A more recognizable version of Modjeska appears in Willa Cather's novella *My Mortal Enemy* (1926). The protagonist, Myra Driscoll, is a young woman from a small midwestern town who displeases her family by eloping with a penniless suitor. She soon regrets her decision and spends the rest of her marriage wishing she were able to move in the same circles as the artists and socialites whom she meets in New York City. Modjeska is a symbol of romance; a woman who represents culture, refinement, and mystery. The actress appears without her real-life husband and son in the story, suggesting she is the embodiment of the protagonist's fantasy: a woman who chose a career over marriage and motherhood. In one scene she reigns over the assembled company "in a high-backed chair, her head resting lightly on her hand, her beautiful face half in shadow. How well I remember those long, beautifully modelled hands, with so much humanity in them. They were worldly, indeed, but fashioned for a nobler worldliness than ours; hands to hold a sceptre, or a chalice—or, by courtesy, a sword."[30] Modjeska has a genius for transforming into various characters, yet she lacks "humanity," despite the narrator's claim to the contrary. Although her "modelled" hands are her most expressive feature, they rest quietly in her lap, seemingly detached from the rest of her body.

Sontag transforms Modjeska into a fictional actress named Maryna Zalewska, making her the centerpiece of *In America* (1999) and portraying the character as a less romantic, more complex figure than her counterpart in Cather's novella. In a prefatory note Sontag claims she was "inspired by the emigration to America in 1876 of Helena Modrzejewska, Poland's most celebrated actress."[31] Accompanied by her husband and a group of fellow artists, Zalewska attempts to found a commune in California. After failing in this impractical venture, she returns to the stage, where she reestablishes her reputation as a prima donna. Like Modjeska, Zalewska remains an enigma throughout Sontag's novel. The actress is a "self-transfiguring" entity (32), a "transforming presence" who is defined by the "roles she [has] played" (199). Zalewska does not draw on her own emotions or personal experiences when performing on stage. "What would I show if I were playing myself?.... An actor doesn't need to have an essence.... An actor needs only a mask" (306). Each time she gives an interview to an American journalist, Zalewska rewrites her past, changing "her age (she lopped off six years), her antecedents (the secondary-school Latin teacher became a professor at the Jagiellonian University), . . . her reasons for coming to America (to visit the Centennial Exposition) and then to California (to restore her health)." Eventually she begins "to believe some of the stories herself" (268).

The West is also a figment of the artist's imagination. Zalewska's husband wants to immigrate to the U.S. frontier after reading novels by Thomas Mayne Reid and James Fenimore Cooper (90), both of whom wrote westerns without visiting the region. For Count Demboski, a fictional version of Modjeska's husband, the West is an imaginary space as well as a place where people (real or fictitious) can reinvent themselves. As Natty Bumppo transforms into the Deerslayer, so Ryszard Kierul (the fictional version of Henryk Sienkiewicz), changes his name in the process of becoming a writer. No one questions his transformation because in a "free country" one does not need an "identity document" (115–16). Sienkiewicz also played a crucial role in marketing Modjeska to U.S. audiences when she made her debut in San Francisco. The "Barnum-esque press agent" persuaded local residents and Polish American theatergoers that his friend's motives for returning to the stage were "altruistic and patriotic, not materialistic and self-interested." The actress represented "Poland on trial and Poland triumphant, a national incarnation whose human warmth and incomparable artistry moved [the theater's] 'naturally cold audience' into uncharacteristic ecstasies," according to Sienkiewicz.[32]

Years later, after returning to Poland, the author won the Nobel Prize for Literature, based largely on the popularity of his international bestselling biblical epic, *Quo Vadis* (1896). The Latin title ("Where are you going, Lord?") refers to a question Peter asks Christ on the road to crucifixion. In Sontag's novel a Pole asks Kierul the same question as he prepares to embark for America (21), the promised land, a place "where nothing is permanent" (210), including dreams. The members of the commune soon discover farming is a laborious, unrewarding activity. As the renamed Kierul writes to Zalewska: "We thought we were choosing freedom and leisure and self-cultivation. Instead, we have committed ourselves to day after day of repetitive agricultural duties." He contends artists "should not *settle* in this country" (204). They are itinerant folk who must constantly seek fresh sources of inspiration, or—in Zalewska's case—new venues in which to perform.

Modjeska and her biographers never refer to the California colony as a utopia. Yet Sontag uses this word to describe her characters' ill-fated enterprise (46). The narrator disagrees with Kierul, stressing the similarities between settlers and actors. "The communal impulse is strong among theatre people. And this newly rooted life hardly differed from the life of traveling players. If some of the simplest tasks of farm life still eluded them, no wonder, they had prepared hastily, conning their parts as farmers at the last minute, just off stage" (174). Zalewska notes that "every community is a failed utopia" (175) and that loyalty "to an imperiled group enterprise [is] a virtue rooted in [my] professional life. You accept the leading role in a new play, you go into rehearsal, and then realize that, for all your efforts and those of others, it's not working, the play is less good than you thought" (199).

For Maryna, acting is reality. In a similar sense, *In America* is both truth-based and fictional: a historical novel based on the life and career of Modjeska. It is also a work of metafiction in which the protagonist is a version of an actual actress celebrated for her theatricality. The unnamed narrator may be an entirely fictional character or one based on Sontag. Like the author, the speaker lived in Tucson, Arizona, as a child and later moved to southern California (16–17). The narrator does not speak Polish and cannot hear the other characters speak to each other. Yet "somehow, I didn't question how, their words reached me as sense" (3). Having never met the speakers, the narrator correctly guesses their identities.

Unlike other historical novels, *In America* has a non-chronological plot and no clear sense of time. The action begins in an unspecified location, sometime in the past, when women wore gowns and gentlemen sported frock coats (3). Yet the narrator speaks in a contemporary colloquial style, keeping the characters "in my sightline" while watching them interact (4). After this prologue, entitled "Zero," the novel shifts to Zalewska's point of view, and later to the perspective of other characters, who are sometimes only indirectly identified. The novel consists of a series of interior monologues, performed by disembodied actors who move backward and forward in time, narrating a story that parallels the life and career of Modjeska, while lacking the concrete sense of setting and character one would expect in a historical novel. At times Zalewska, her husband, and friends seem to be products of the author's imagination rather than actual people who inhabit the material world.

In an interview with a journalist from the *Irish Times*, Sontag revealed that "writing through the medium of the past [was] intensely liberating" because it allowed her to be as "operatic and expressive and romantic" as her actress protagonist. The narrator describes America as a transformative space in which people can freely reinvent themselves.[33] "Picture-taking transported everyone into the future, when their more youthful selves would be only a memory." According to Zalewska, photographs were "evidence that [the immigrants] were really here, pursuing their valiant new life" (194). Over time, however, pictures age, revealing the colonists' youthful idealism and foreshadowing their eventual failure. "The brash light of the hot March afternoon will become the sepia grace of bygone days. *Then* we were like *that*. Young and innocent-looking. And so picturesque" (187).

*In America* is a metafictional meditation on the process of self-transformation and cross-identification, exploring the relationships between actors and the roles they play on and off stage; between authors and their characters; between autobiographical narrators and fictional representations of historical figures. After the novel was published, some critics accused Sontag of plagiarizing historical sources. The most serious accusation was lodged by Ellen Lee, a member of the Helena Modjeska Foundation, an organization devoted to the preservation of Arden. Lee cited passages from the novel that were taken from "Polish verse, old newspaper articles, [Modjeska's] diaries, and autobiography," as well as from Cather's novel.

Sontag's supporters dismissed her accuser, referring to Lee as "an 81-year-old amateur historian" and "volunteer museum docent."[34] The fact that Sontag quoted other novelists, as well as journalistic sources and other primary materials, suggests the metafictional nature of her enterprise. Modjeska also took liberties with the truth in her autobiography, further blurring the line between fact and fiction. (The author's imperfect command of the English language, in contrast to the book's impeccable style, leads one to speculate whether the memoirs were ghostwritten.) Sontag complicated the matter, claiming: "All of us who deal with real characters in history . . . transcribe and adopt original sources in the [public] domain. I've used these sources and completely transformed them. . . . There's a larger argument to be made that all of literature is a series of references and allusions."[35] In a separate interview Sontag called *In America* "a work of art," contending she had invented a new genre that "doesn't require the footnotes of traditional histories. . . . Willa Cather is a writer, but the others are sources. The sources themselves are working from sources and they are using quotations of actual words. I don't consider Modjeska's memoirs the work of a writer." Refusing to explain why she considered Cather a "writer," but not Modjeska, Sontag stated she was interested in transforming the actress into someone who both was and was not Modjeska. Claiming the actress's fans should be glad Sontag resurrected the long-forgotten actress, she then contradicted herself, calling Modjeska's fictional counterpart "a completely different character." In a puzzling non sequitur, she added: "The real Modjeska was a horrible racist."[36]

In fact the "real" Modjeska never existed. She was the daughter of an unwed mother, a romantic partner to husbands and lovers, a woman who assumed a title and frequently changed her name for professional reasons, and an actress who overcame her lower-middle-class origins and lack of education by transforming on stage into well-known historical figures and fictional characters.

Modjeska was raised in a country that had been ruled by other European nations for more than a century. Despite her own fragmented identity, she was a unifying symbol for people living in Poland during partition, proof that their homeland was not "politically eclipsed and culturally undistinguished," as many Americans assumed. Yet the actress could not claim "the iconic martyrdom of political exile." She had come to the United States voluntarily, "and the Poles she met there were not rebel leaders to be worshiped, but isolated immigrants longing for the temporary repatriation she could effect with her performances."[37] Modjeska was not a resistance figure, unlike Chaplowski, who had been imprisoned in Prussia because of his subversive political activities. Nor was she a socialist whose primary purpose in immigrating was to found a Polish utopia on foreign soil. Modjeska did not leave home "to become a cook or housemaid. She came with the avowed purpose . . . to win fame abroad."[38]

For working-class men and women who comprised the majority of Polish refugees in the late nineteenth century, emigration expressed a desire for national liberation. Reuniting in a foreign country awakened their "sense of ethnic distinctiveness," leading to the creation of Poland's "fourth partition."[39] As Adam Mickiewicz explained in *Books of the Polish Nation and the Polish Pilgrims* (1830): "No Pole on his pilgrimage is called a wanderer, for a wanderer is a man straying without a goal; nor is he an exile, for an exile is a man exiled by the decree of the government." The pilgrim journeys to "the holy land, the free country," the western New World, intent on preserving a people whose homeland has come under siege.[40] Describing Zalewska's childhood, Sontag writes that the actress initially "wanted to be a soldier; and when it occurred to her that, being a girl, she would never be allowed to bear arms, she wanted to be a poet whose patriotic odes men would recite as they marched to demand their country's freedom" (42). By contrast, Cather's narrator imagines Modjeska holding "a sceptre, or a chalice—or, by courtesy, a sword." She isn't a pilgrim, a religious icon, or a queen, but an actress playing a role, equipped with the appropriate props. Cather's character seems closer to the "real" Modjeska, an actress whose favorite part was Rosalind in *As You Like It*. The Shakespearean heroine escapes to Arden after her father's European duchy has been overtaken. In the forest she assumes a different character, falling in love instead of working to restore her father's rule.

According to Polish propaganda, a woman's role as a pilgrim was to rear children and train them to be patriotic defenders of their ancestors' homeland.[41] In a speech at the Chicago Columbian Exposition in 1893, Modjeska celebrated Polish women for their "courage, industry, patriotism, and patience" during a time of political oppression. Exchanging "her customary persona as ambassador" for "the dangerous role of nationalist fire-brand," she became "a real-life heroine," using "words instead of weapons"—and her talent as an actress—to inspire the audience.[42] Modjeska's own role as a woman was more complex. She was a wife and mother as well as an actress working in a profession that seldom attracted well-bred, educated, and socially reputable women. By the time Modjeska conquered Warsaw in 1868, she had reinvented herself through her "talent, learned upper-class behavior, and marriage to Chaplowski." Her U.S. debut eight years later coincided with the transformation of San Francisco from a frontier boom town into a cosmopolitan city "connected by the transcontinental railroad with the civilized East."[43] The theater's newly sophisticated patrons welcomed the "Countess," while the audiences she later encountered on tour were less impressed by her aristocratic persona and ladylike attributes. In mining camps—where entertainment consisted of bear-wrestling matches, prize-fighting exhibitions, gambling, and drinking, and where women were scarce—men purchased tickets merely to catch a glimpse of Modjeska's ankles and to gaze at her corseted yet voluptuous figure.[44]

The actress negotiated various, sometimes contradictory, expectations throughout her career. She was a Polish exile and an American immigrant; a woman of lowly birth and a supposed European aristocrat; a person with a scandalous past and a forward-looking careerist who posed on the stage as a symbol of female propriety. The unidentified narrator in the introduction to Sontag's novel claims "the past is the biggest country of all," adding "almost everything good" seems located there (23). Zalewska may or may not share this impression. She notes that the past "is not really important [in America]," a young country filled with optimistic pioneers and enterprising citizens. Late in the novel Zalewska attends a dinner party where she meets Henry James, who describes himself not as a novelist but as a "future playwright." For the writer, Zalewska is "a contemporary *type*, . . . the most brilliant embodiment of feminine *success*" (343). Yet she appeals to U.S. audiences because she represents Poland's glorious past and because she excels at playing classic characters in history and literature.

According to a recent biographer, "Modjeska realized that winning [U.S. acclaim] would enable her *reconquest* of her native stage, provided she lay her overseas laurels at Poland's feet." The actress was not a pilgrim on a political mission to garner foreign support for her beleaguered country. She was a "careerist" who sought to broaden her audience by touring throughout the world, eventually returning to her homeland in triumph.[45] After her death in 1909, Modjeska embarked on her final U.S. tour, traveling by train from Los Angeles to New York City. Along the way there were funerals, staged for the benefit of her fans. In Los Angeles attendees received "a black-bordered funeral card" with a photograph of Modjeska dressed in one of her most popular roles as Queen Constance, accompanied by an admission ticket. At another ceremony in southern California "two hundred Knights of Columbus and representatives of two local Polish societies" escorted the casket to the church. In New York City "Modjeska's compatriots and colleagues co-produced in the same space a moving farewell to their fellow immigrant and thespian."[46]

Modjeska toured by train throughout her career in the United States. The narrator boasts about her fictional alter ego in Sontag's novel: "Hers would be the very first company to travel the theatrical circuit by a means hitherto reserved for railroad magnates and slain presidents. Maryna liked being part of the wave of the future." Yet numerous references to death and the past appear in the passage. The train is a mode of conveyance for wealthy businessmen and "slain presidents." Zalewska's luxurious compartment includes a "portrait of the great actress on horseback in Western garb," as well as funereal furnishings ("black-walnut" paneling and "velvet window hangings"). The "watery legends on the frescoed ceiling" include scenes depicting different stages of life: "Moses in the bulrushes, Narcissus at his looking-glass pond, King Arthur on his funeral barge" (330).

The tour continued in Poland, concluding with Modjeska's burial in Kraków on July 17, 1909. The funeral was attended by "delegates from Poland's three partitions." At least for a moment, Modjeska succeeded in reuniting her country. Yet her death also underscored the inability of her homeland to triumph over foreign rule. During the partitioning of their country, Poles referred to themselves as "a large nation in a stateless body,"[47] an apt description of Modjeska's corpse, deprived of its animating spirit. The funeral was her final performance, recalling a speech from her favorite play.

All the world's a stage,
And all the men and women merely players;
They have their exits and their entrances,
And one man in his time plays many parts.[48]

# 8

## Deutschland über Alles

### Germany's Literary Colonization
### of the U.S. Frontier

Much of the action in William Shakespeare's play *As You Like It* (1599) takes place in the Forest of Arden. The forest is a magical place where men and women change identities, cross-dress, and act out of character. Arden might be described as a fictional counterpart to the U.S. frontier, where Helena Modjeska founded a utopian commune and subsequently transformed into a series of theatrical figures. For western novelist Karl May, the woods represented the German frontier; the site where ancient Teutonic warriors had defeated Roman invaders in the Battle of the Teutonberg Forest (9 AD). Beginning in the late nineteenth century May reimagined that wilderness, transferring it onto the American prairie and peopling his novels with immigrant white German males who conquered their rivals, this time on foreign soil.

Although May died more than a century ago he remains one of Germany's bestselling authors. His most popular novels, set on the U.S. frontier, feature a German emigrant hero, nicknamed Old Shatterhand, and his Apache sidekick, Winnetou. Unlike earlier German authors who had traveled overseas to gather material for their fiction, May based his novels on other books he had read about the American West.[1] In addition to concealing this fact from readers, the author claimed he had personally experienced many of the adventures he later attributed to his protagonist.

May transformed the U.S. frontier into an outpost of German civilization, populated by his alter ego and fellow countrymen, all of whom drink German beer, sing German songs, and read German newspapers.[2] His westerns appealed to contemporary readers and later generations of fans because they restored to Germans something they had lost centuries earlier: a national wilderness. May projected a new frontier onto his literary version of the U.S. West, writing novels that depicted the triumph of German characters over other western pioneers and indigenous peoples, thus exemplifying the superiority of the Aryan race. By posing as the real-life inspiration for Old Shatterhand, the author also gave Germans a national folk hero with whom to identify.

May was born in rural Germany in 1842. His father was a weaver who struggled to support the family, like other craftsmen who were replaced by machines during the Industrial Revolution. May was the fifth of fourteen children, nine of whom died in infancy. Shortly after birth he lost his eyesight, most likely due to malnutrition. After regaining his sight, May was sent to a teacher training school, where he was later expelled for stealing candles, a charge he denied in his autobiography, *Mein Leben und Streben* (*My Life and My Efforts*, 1910).[3] Although he successfully appealed the case and returned to school, May was imprisoned a second time for stealing his roommate's watch and had his teacher's license revoked, making it difficult for him to find work after he completed his sentence.

During the next six years May committed a series of crimes involving theft and fraud. He impersonated an eye doctor as well as a copper engraver. He ordered expensive clothes and furs from tailors and furriers, refusing to pay for goods received. After serving a third prison sentence May continued posing as various characters, including a fictitious American consul named General Burton. On one occasion the incorrigible ex-convict confiscated money from store owners, claiming he was an undercover agent pursuing a ring of counterfeiters. After being arrested for fraud he escaped from his handcuffs and disappeared, only to be caught six months later impersonating a wealthy plantation owner from Martinique.[4]

Years later May used the proceeds from his successful writing career to purchase a house called "Villa Shatterhand." The author converted his home into a "personal diorama," filled with artifacts he had allegedly collected during his western adventures. May signed autographs and posed for photos looking like Buffalo Bill, dressed in "authentic" frontier regalia.[5] He offered tours of his villa-museum, showing visitors scars he had supposedly received in skirmishes with outlaws and Indians. When a visitor asked May why he had let his Indian sidekick die as a heathen at the end of the *Winnetou* trilogy, the author said he had performed an emergency baptism before the character died, omitting this information from the book out of respect for readers of different faiths.[6]

Writing fiction allowed May to exploit his talents as a shape-shifter and fabricator without breaking the law. It was also more profitable than his earlier criminal endeavors. In the first volume of the *Winnetou* trilogy, Old Shatterhand admits that he writes books for money, recording his adventures for "others to read."[7] The U.S. frontier also gave men such as May an opportunity to experience vicariously what Theodore Roosevelt called "the strenuous life."[8] Having suffered from blindness and malnutrition as a child, May reinvented himself as a German hero known for his strength, bravery, and superiority to Indians and white frontiersmen. In the first volume of the *Winnetou* saga the protagonist receives his nickname after an incident in which he pummels his opponents with his fists (21). The "greenhorn" also tans buffalo hides (30), lassoes mules (40), and is an excellent rider and marksman (8). Unlike May, Old Shatterhand has perfect eyesight and can see farther than other characters with the aid of his telescope (451, 624).

May transforms the American West into a wilderness resembling the forests that had once covered much of Germany. In the first volume of the *Winnetou* series, a grove of trees suddenly appears on the prairie (173). In *The Treasure of Silver Lake* (1891), the plains are populated by lumberjacks instead of homesteaders.[9] In *The Son of Bear Hunter* (1892), the reader learns Colorado is known not for its mineral deposits but for its maple syrup.[10] In the European sense there had always been frontiers—or borders—in Germany. Those borders had frequently been reconfigured over the centuries, as different European territories, kingdoms, and provinces shifted allegiances prior to the formation of the modern German nation-state in 1871. But a wilderness space no longer existed, and the memory of one barely lingered in Germany's collective consciousness. The Ur-forest—a realm inhabited in the folkloric imagination by "demons and spirits"[11]—was replaced in May's westerns by an alien, yet vaguely reminiscent landscape, inhabited by Anglo-Saxons, Native Americans, and displaced Germans.

American westerns chronicled the expansion of empire, featuring people who settled the frontier, making it safe for the establishment of white civilization. One critic claims May similarly transformed the West into a "German colony."[12] But Old Shatterhand disavows any such intent. Initially, he accepts a job working for a group of surveyors who are charting a railroad route across land that belongs to Winnetou's tribe. When the Apache persuades the protagonist the government is committing an act of illegal appropriation, the white man quits his job (170-71).

Railroads had destroyed the rural region in Saxony where May was born and raised, thus accounting for their negative portrayal in his fiction as unwelcome harbingers of civilization.[13] His westerns feature German emigrants who have lost their jobs due to the industrial, social, and political changes occurring at home. One man is a "revolutionary" who escapes from prison and flees the country at a time when monarchists in the Kingdom of Saxony are resisting national unification (56). In *The Son of Bear Hunter* a character says he left Germany because his working-class family could not afford to pay for his education (5); while in *The Ghost of the Llano Estacado* (1888), two frontiersmen discover they were both foresters who lost their jobs when the woods in their native homeland were consumed by industry.[14] Although Old Shatterhand explains that poverty was his main reason for immigrating to the United States (1), he pursues adventures on the western frontier without benefit of remuneration, rather than mining for gold (190, 421), purchasing land to farm, or engaging in other forms of capitalist enterprise.

During these exploits Old Shatterhand and his Teutonic companions— Shortleg Frank, Tubby Jemmy, Long Davy, and Helmer—demonstrate their intellectual and physical superiority over their non-German counterparts, especially Native Americans. Like many U.S. writers in the nineteenth century, May romanticized "noble savages" such as Winnetou, while portraying them as members of a vanishing race.[15] (Unlike other Indians, Winnetou converts to the white man's religion before he dies, thus ensuring his heavenly immortality.) May's depiction of Native Americans as members of a dying species was consistent with Georg Hegel's "Lectures on the Philosophy of World History," presented as a series of talks at the University of Berlin between 1822 and 1830. In his comparative analysis of different races, Hegel argued Native Americans had been unable to defeat the U.S. military and white pioneers due to their inherent inferiority.[16]

In *The Son of Bear Hunter*, a German immigrant cannot decide whether to hunt bison or rescue Oglala warriors who are being held hostage near the Yellowstone River, claiming one activity "is just as much fun as the other" (28). The character shares the same outlook as Huck, who treats Jim's rescue as nothing more than an entertaining diversion in Mark Twain's *The Adventures of Huckleberry Finn* (1885). May's protagonists are typically adolescent males. The word "old" is a term of endearment rather than a sign of maturity, conferred on Shatterhand when he exchanges his greenhorn status for admission into a western fraternity of frontier heroes. May's male characters escape the responsibilities of adulthood by fleeing to the U.S. West, where they participate in activities that test their strength and bravery, serving as rites of passage into adulthood. As D. H. Lawrence noted in *Studies in Classic American Literature* (1923), characters like May's western heroes come to the U.S. frontier to "slough the old European consciousness completely," growing "a new skin underneath, a new form."[17] May's male characters are reborn in the American West. They mature through a process that sometimes involves the reunion of sons with their fathers. Old Shatterhand restores a kidnapped son to his father in volume two of the *Winnetou* series (434). He also locates a boy's missing father in the concluding novel of the series (551). In *The Son of Bear Hunter* Shortleg Frank helps a young man of German heritage solve the mystery concerning his father's disappearance (4–5).

The unification of May's homeland in the late nineteenth century required the reconciliation of "conflicting democratic and authoritarian, Prussian and German, unitary and federal elements."[18] May's westerns appealed to readers who supported the creation of a Fatherland and who found a fictional corollary to the process of unification in plots involving the reunion of fathers and sons. His novels "provided imaginary resolutions to the violent contradictions experienced by society in turn-of-the-century imperial Germany—a society simultaneously transformed by the effects of rapid urbanization, industrialization, and cultural modernization"; a region "politically immobilized by the constraints of an authoritarian, largely preurban, preindustrial, and premodern social structure." May created "a utopian counterworld that invariably remains confined within the ideological parameters of imperial Germany." His characters reject "the complexity, anonymity, and social constraints of European civilization and bourgeois society in pursuit of personal liberty and individualist ambition in a literally limitless exotic space, only rapidly to superimpose on that 'new' space the social positions and relations, the values and hierarchies of nineteenth-century Europe."[19]

There had been no preexisting literary tradition or national epic to unite the residents of Germany's various geographic regions and social classes.[20] Now, as a result of nation formation, German culture underwent a transformation. During this period of modernization, highbrow works of literature coexisted with avant-garde art, middlebrow kitsch, and commercialized mass entertainment. Traditional culture "fragmented and new forms of mechanical reproduction"—such as the printing press—combined with rising literacy rates in modern Germany, changing "the way culture was consumed."[21] As the division between high and low culture began to disappear, *Heimat* literature, like westerns, became one of the nation's most popular genres. This distinctive German art form evolved in reaction to "rapid industrialization [and] the concomitant shift from rural to urban living," generating a national desire for an earlier pastoral era; for an idealized past that presented an "archaic image [of] German community."[22]

*Heimat* novels were the German equivalent of sentimental literature, featuring "saccharine" and romanticized stories of village life.[23] In the United States the sentimental novel and the western were believed to be incompatible. The first genre appeared in England and the U.S. in the late eighteenth century. These stories, set in the domestic sphere, attracted a predominantly female audience. The second genre evolved in the late nineteenth century. Westerns offered an alternative to male readers, allowing them to escape vicariously into the wilderness, away from the woman's realm of influence.[24] By contrast, *Heimat* literature and German westerns appealed to both sexes from an ideological perspective. Both were associated with rustic or wilderness landscapes, targeting readers who sought to escape from modernity. May's novels, in particular, shared certain characteristics with domestic fiction. The deathbed conversion of Old Shatterhand's sidekick—the most famous scene in the *Winnetou* trilogy—was also a convention of the sentimental genre.

May's westerns are more sentimental than their American counter-parts. The relationships between the hero and his Indian companion, between fathers and sons, and between other German men are described in emotional detail. Yet these novels are also consistent with westerns. May's frontier is a homosocial realm as well as a domestic space turned inside out; a place where the author's male characters unite as a meta-phorical family, transforming the landscape into an intimate meeting place. German characters conquer their environments in the tradition of western heroes. The white men—and sometimes their Indian partners— "roam the West without concern for family,"[25] constantly moving through unsettled regions and across geographically inhospitable landscapes. At the same time the western frontier, like "all really inhabited space," bears "the essence of the notion of home."[26] In the process of forming alliances these German and Native American characters create nomadic homo-social communities. Untamed by civilization, they domestic space itself, transforming the West into a German version of *heim*—into "a zone of pro-tection."[27] The cavern hideout in *The Son of Bear Hunter* (152), the Indian village in *The Treasure of Silver Lake* (62), and the Spanish mission and the pueblo built on a terraced hillside in *The Oil Prince* are domiciles as well as defensive structures where characters seek refuge from enemy forces.[28]

Although he imagines the West as a masculine version of home, May seldom furnishes his natural settings in a concrete fashion. Having never visited the region, the author was usually vague, if not factually inaccurate, when describing a particular landscape. In *The Treasure of Silver Lake* an Indian tells a group of German frontiersmen his village is located in "the West" (77). In the *Winnetou* series, characters travel thousands of miles in the narrative span of a single paragraph (328), pursuing various adventures (511, 627, 732), while reducing their distinct settings to a scenic blur. May's lack of attention to regional climates, topographies, and geographic distances suggests the landscape is neither an alien presence nor an oppositional force. Instead, the frontier—generally conceived—is an easily traversable space, quickly mastered by his protagonists and their followers.

Old Shatterhand's decision to quit his job as a surveyor has symbolic consequences. Surveyors measure space in quantifiable units, mapping it, establishing boundaries and property lines, and facilitating travel and exploration across land that is geographically difficult to navigate. May's hero shows a disregard for boundaries, regional zones, and impenetrable settings (outlaw hideaways, enemy Indian camps, and caches containing hidden treasure) that only he can locate or enter due to his shrewd thinking, independent nature, and fearlessness. The author shows a similar disregard for literary boundaries, writing a series of adventure novels filled with continuous movement but lacking narrative form. The first three novels in the *Winnetou* saga—labeled I, II, and III—are arbitrarily divided into sections. The divisions create a semblance of structure for the repetitious narrative, which one critic has described as a "collage of innumerable variations of the same tactical elements" involving white men and Indians: "reconnaissance, ambush, siege, the stalking movement, capture and release, [and] the commando strike."[29]

*Heim* provides a sheltering structure and a narrative focal point that May's fiction would otherwise lack. *Heimat* is a concept as well as a place: "a spiritualized province (a mental state turned inside out) and a provincial spirituality (a spatially perceived small world turned outside in)."[30] The western version of home is typically a wilderness dwelling—an interior space located within the exterior world; an imaginary site which the German reader may also inhabit, in a fictional universe bearing no resemblance to his or her own reality. May divides the frontier into a series of small spaces, domestic and intimate in their personal associations, yet related to the surrounding landscape with its threat of imminent danger. The reciprocal relationship between familiar and alien sensations—between comforting and fearful environments—recalls Gaston Bachelard's notion of "intimate immensity." It is a realm within oneself, an internalized dream. May's westerns represent the external expression of an inner idea, a manifestation of human desire in literary form. In his autobiography, May explained his popularity as a writer. "No matter how strong and how inventive a poet's mind might be, he would still never succeed in forcing the plot of a great, national drama upon the history of a people, if it was not already in the people's soul." Noting that "the greatest and most beautiful deeds of a nation were born out of its inner self," May suggested he had transplanted a German frontier onto U.S. soil in order to satisfy the country's yearning for its preindustrial past and its need during a time of regional and political unification for a national epic. As Bachelard states: "Immensity is within ourselves."[31]

On March 22, 1912, eight days before he died, May made his final public appearance, delivering a speech at the Academy of Literature and Music in Vienna, Austria. A young Adolf Hitler attended the talk, which was entitled *"Empor ins Reich der Edelmenschen"* ("Upward to the Realm of Noble Men"). Like millions of other Germans and Austrians, Hitler had read May's westerns as a youth. Later, during World War II, he recommended these works to his general staff and distributed copies to Nazi soldiers fighting in the trenches.[32]

May's fiction appealed to male adolescents who identified with his western protagonists. Hitler exploited the author's writing for political purposes, appealing to soldiers who yearned for a return to Germany's mythic past and racial purity. A former Nazi later claimed that when soldiers joined the war, "our Karl May days became reality; sneaking up on each other, shooting from ambush, surprise attacks and beatings. . . . The only thing we couldn't find a practical substitute for was scalping."[33] In May's westerns Germans were superior to members of other races. Yet his heroes sometimes aligned with Native Americans, an inconsistency that members of the National Socialist Party attempted to reconcile through a process of racial cross-identification.[34] U.S. indigenous peoples were native to the North American continent and thus "pure," according to Nazi ideology. *Indianer* literature romanticized Native Americans, expressing what Germans called *Indianthusiasm.* Winnetou and his historical counterparts—Pontiac, Tecumseh, and Sitting Bull—"became fascist *Führer* figures involved in a . . . battle for blood, soil, language, culture, and the independence of the 'red race' from foreign rule."[35] Historically, Anglo-Saxon pioneers and the U.S. military had been the enemies of native *volk* (a German word meaning "folk," "people," "nation," or "race").[36] During Hitler's reign German readers equated the fictional counterparts of these pioneers and military troops in May's westerns with their opponents in World War II.[37]

The National Socialist Party considered Germans to be *Volk ohne Raum* (people without space). They identified with Native Americans, who had been dispossessed by colonizers, as well as with mixed-race characters, despite the Party's belief in the importance of racial purity. May's westerns featured many such characters, including a boy in the *Winnetou* saga whose father is German and whose mother is Native American (441) as well as a biracial Indian in *The Oil Prince* who has recently returned from a visit to his father's European homeland (46, 58–59). Readers considered these characters to be pure despite their mixed heritage because they were the offspring of indigenous people and members of the Aryan race.

During World War II Germans who identified as *Volk ohne Raum* justified their invasion of other countries by subscribing to Hitler's theory that "external colonization" was necessary for the nation's transformation into a global power.[38] Hitler claimed: "Nature knows no political frontiers." Inconsistently, like the enemies of Native Americans who dispossessed or exterminated the indigenous residents of the U.S. West, Nazis sought to enact their own version of Manifest Destiny, invading other European nations to claim territory they believed was rightfully theirs. Like western cartographers, whose maps refused to acknowledge the preexisting presence of native inhabitants, Nazis engaged in similar acts of erasure. Since Jews and other non-Aryans were considered racially inferior, the space they occupied was rendered invisible. The

Nazi soldier's perception of "empty space" was produced by "an act of devivification" that was both "concrete and hallucinatory." It was easier to murder people if the military believed the space had "all along been devoid of things living."[39] In addition to motivating military action (the slaughter of Jews and other non-Aryan groups), this imaginary act produced personal "sensations of pleasure," creating the perception among troop members that nothing unwelcome "swarmed around or penetrated" the individual self.[40] This primal desire could be traced back to childhood—to an infant's need for security, symbolized by the home, which Bachelard describes as a womb, a domestic space, or an inviolable zone of self-preservation.[41]

In *Mein Kampf*, Hitler noted that the masses were often inspired by visual images, suggesting film could function as wartime propaganda.[42] Yet despite his enthusiasm for May's fiction, Hitler never ordered the German film industry to adapt May's works for a larger audience. Hollywood westerns had played in Germany prior to World War I, conquering "the hearts" of adolescent males, who later volunteered for military service once the war began.[43] However, no westerns were produced by the Nazi regime in the 1930s and 1940s. Instead the nation released comedies and melodramas during this period. Many of these comedies—such as the 1940 film *Jud Süss* (*Jew Süss*)—cast Jewish characters in villainous roles. The humor in such films derived from the Jewish male's pursuit of the Aryan heroine and her rejection of his sexual advances.[44] Melodramas were even more popular during the Nazi era. Domestic melodramas depicted the turbulent love lives of Germans and were morally resolved by the main character's choosing the appropriate partner to marry. While anti-Semitic comedies stressed the necessity of maintaining the purity of the Aryan race, domestic melodramas emphasized the necessity of "controlled mating and breeding," reinforcing "traditional family structures" and repudiating mixed marriages. Romantic melodramas served as an even more effective form of propaganda, "receiving far more screen time than war films." Instead of pitting good characters against their evil counterparts, these works internalized the erotic feelings of the heroine, rather than the male protagonist, forcing the woman to suppress her "illicit desires" by attaching herself to the "correct" suitor.[45]

Westerns attracted male readers in Germany, making the prospect of war seem like an entertaining adventure, rather than a political means of achieving world domination. Romantic melodramas appealed to a female audience, suggesting that "sacrifice and passive suffering" were expected of women living in a totalitarian system and that reproductivity with the appropriate spouse was required during wartime to swell the ranks of the Aryan race.[46] (These films found their ironic corollary in earlier Hollywood silent westerns, in which native women sacrificed themselves or betrayed their tribes to "save European Americans."[47]) Melodramas were popular with men as well as women. Hitler "thought of the masses as essentially feminine and thus easily manipulable," writing in *Mein Kampf* that "das Volk" preferred "emotional sensation" to "sober reflection." At the same time the notion of a gendered spectatorship and gendered cinematic genres did not develop in Germany until after World War II. A doctor writing in the journal *Der Film* argued men have "feelings too, and the manly man is even superior to the feminine woman when it comes to the depth and persistence of his emotional life."[48]

In literature, however, genres such as the western appealed primarily to men. In the introduction to the English translation of May's autobiography the writer speculates that May escaped from his "failing marriage" by retreating into the homosocial world of his fiction.[49] Yet May's westerns were also sentimental, playing on the male reader's emotions. The author describes Winnetou's feminine features, claiming many "ladies" would have envied his hair, which "rolled down his shoulders" (49). Blurring the distinction between the sexes, the author notes that Winnetou's sister "brushed her hair in the same way as her brother. . . . Her appearance was quite militaristic, yet girlish" (183). The homoerotic nature of Old Shatterhand's friendship with his Indian companion becomes apparent after Winnetou's death, which leaves the hero emotionally distraught (770–71). May's westerns feature the same type of relationships as those depicted in western American literature.

They tell "the story of a White Man and a Red who find solace and sustenance in each other's love."[50]

One critic has defined comedies and melodramas as "genres of integration," in contrast to war, crime, and action films (as well as westerns), which are "genres of order." The latter genres allow "for a violent removal of adversaries or threats to the social system," while the former emphasize "their reeducation and a more subtle reestablishment of harmony."[51] However, melodramas and westerns share certain characteristics, which explains why they were popular as ideological forms of entertainment. Both genres offer a morally simplistic view of the world, reducing conflicts to good versus evil, right versus wrong. Characters in Third Reich melodramas had to be "immediately legible types rather than complex individuals," like May's German protagonists and non-Aryan villains. The simplistic nature of westerns appealed to male adolescents, as well as to more sophisticated adults, who were persuaded to support the war by reading works in which "the hero had but one course to follow."[52]

In addition to indoctrinating German citizens, Hitler sought to annex "new audiences abroad," using film to seduce foreign viewers during World War II. The Nazi führer and his minister of propaganda, Joseph Goebbels, hoped to rival Hollywood, which had become the leading exporter of worldwide entertainment. (Goebbels especially admired the 1939 epic *Gone with the Wind*, noting: "The mass scenes are captivatingly well done. A huge achievement for the Americans. . . . We will follow this example.") German directors cast "erotic" actresses in leading roles and used the racy content in romantic melodramas to "liberate spectators from the constraints of nineteenth- and early twentieth-century sexual mores." These films were intended to create the impression that Germany was a nation of free-thinkers, rather than a totalitarian state. Instead of stereotypical *hausfraus*, the heroines were single, athletic, and physically attractive, the female equivalent of the German frontiersmen in May's fiction. Unlike westerns, however, these melodramas attracted male viewers, while giving women cinematic role models to emulate.[53]

May became one of Germany's all-time bestselling authors by appealing to his country's nostalgia for its rural past. An avowed pacifist, May never realized his westerns would one day be used as propaganda to justify Hitler's military invasion of other nations during World War II.[54] Yet the German definition of "nostalgia" is more complex than the English meaning of the word. Whereas "nostalgia" suggests a yearning for the past, *heimweh* means "homesickness." The antonym *fernweh* means "a longing for far-off places." It was the opposite of "nostalgia"—a fascination with the U.S. frontier—that appealed to German fans of May's fiction. His success as a writer was due to his ability to capitalize on the public's need, while simultaneously transforming the West into a German version of *heim*, thus combining the nation's contradictory desires: its wish to retreat into the past and its ambition to conquer the world.

# 9

# The Problem of Representation

*Isadora Duncan Sleeps With the Russian Navy*

Of all the men and women featured in *Geographic Personas*, Isadora Duncan was the only one who altered, disguised, or transformed her identity while paradoxically remaining herself. As the artistic director of the Isadora Duncan Dance Ensemble recently argued, the woman known as the creator of modern American dance was famous for her "reputation not her repertory." She "invented herself as an icon and gained immortality."[1] In an otherwise sympathetic biography another writer seems to diminish Duncan's achievements. Suggesting her fame was undeserved, the critic claims Duncan became a celebrity merely because the public needed "stars" to satisfy their demand for entertainment.[2] Indeed Duncan transformed into an ethereal creature on stage. But her behavior off stage played an equally significant role in shaping her public persona.

In her autobiography, published in 1927, Duncan recalled how her art had been influenced by her western heritage. Her maternal grandmother had come to California with her husband in 1849. She had given birth to Duncan's mother in the back of a covered wagon, while it was crossing the plains and simultaneously being chased by a band of Indians. After defeating the attackers, her grandfather had stuck his head inside the wagon to greet his newborn daughter, "with a smoking gun still in his hand." Years later Duncan remembered watching her Irish grandmother dance. Into these "jigs had crept some of the heroic spirit of the pioneer and the battle with the Redskins."[3] Duncan channeled that same spirit in her art. In his biography of the dancer Sewell Stokes described walking with Duncan through the streets of Paris as she performed one of her signature moves. Noting how Indians used to "sloop" through the grass as they traversed the prairie, she advised her companion to "make yourself as limp as you can, and let the weight of your body carry you forward." Then she followed suit, slinking down the promenade while passersby stared in amazement.[4]

Duncan's mother was born at the beginning of the Gold Rush era. Her father was a banker who managed the wealth accumulated by many of the miners who had struck it rich in California. Duncan was unlucky by comparison. In an essay entitled "I Was Born in America" (1924), the author declared she was born on the day in 1877 "when all the banks in San Francisco went bankrupt."[5] Her mother's birth marked the dawn of the Golden Age, while her own birth—a generation later—concluded a cycle in the region's boom-bust economy.

Although it was only her father's business that crashed, Duncan suggested his failure symbolized the end of an era and the start of a prosperous new chapter in American history, one in which the collapse of civilization was followed by a return to nature. According to Frederick Jackson Turner, the pioneers' settlement of the frontier and their subsequent search for new lands to conquer was a uniquely American process. In "The Significance of the Frontier in American History" (1893) the historian claimed: "The wilderness masters the colonist." Eventually the pioneer "transforms the wilderness." Then he embarks once again on his continuing quest to settle the continent. Turner argued that "this perennial rebirth, this fluidity of American life, this expansion westward with its new opportunities, its continuous touch with the simplicity of primitive society, furnish the forces dominating American character."[6]

Living in California, Duncan was unable to move farther westward. Instead she returned to nature by going to London, where she visited the British Museum in 1898. Turner had predicted this move in his essay, published five years earlier, suggesting the "history of society" could be read like a "page"—from left to right or from West to East.[7] Reversing the direction of her grandparents' earlier migration to California, Duncan traveled back in time to an earlier civilization that was more sophisticated, yet also more in tune with nature. The classical Greek vases and sculptures she saw in the British Museum had earlier inspired John Keats's "Ode on a Grecian Urn" (1819). Like many California natives,

Duncan considered her home to be the American Mediterranean. Comparisons between the West Coast and Greece were especially common in the late nineteenth century. Ancient Greece had been the cradle of western civilization, as well as a country "half-wild," "mysterious and semi-divine," a place "mediated through myth and communicated with through outdoor rites," emphasizing the relationship between nature and humankind.[8] Like Keats, who imagined unheard melodies sung by figures on the urn, Duncan studied pictures of dancers who cavorted in sylvan glades while appearing frozen in time: in the words of one critic, their bodies were "in arrested gesture promising further action."[9] In creating modern American dance Duncan combined her love for California with her reverence for ancient Greek artifacts. She stated in her autobiography that she had discovered the source of movement by "the Pacific Ocean, by the pine-waving forests of the Sierra Nevada. I have seen the ideal figure of youthful America dancing over the top of the Rockies."[10] But she fulfilled the promise of the "arrested gesture" by reanimating classical bodies, maintaining the early Greeks were more "natural" than the modern-day "savage," who had become alienated by society from "his spiritual being."[11]

While transforming nature into civilization, Turner's pioneer underwent a process of reverse self-transformation. The experience "takes [the pioneer] from the railroad car and puts him in the birch canoe. It strips off the garments of civilization" and replaces them with a "hunting shirt" and "moccasins."[12] Instead of dressing like an Indian, Duncan wore a loose-fitting tunic, similar to a Greek toga, without undergarments, revealing the outline of her body when she danced barefoot on stage. In 1908 a New York reviewer—comparing Duncan to a figure from Keats's poem—described her as "a pagan spirit, stepping naturally from a bit of broken marble."[13]

Duncan was a dancer rather than a storyteller, an impressionistic performer rather than an ideologue who struggled to articulate a theory about her craft, sometimes leaving audiences confused or amused by her exuberant displays. One biographer admits Duncan's importance as an innovator might now seem "baffling" to those who did not understand her purpose.[14] While the majority of spectators were entranced "by [her] vision of unknown worlds,"[15] certain critics found her performances "impossibly corny and camp."[16] Unable to explain her work and control her public image, Duncan was eventually appropriated by writers, sculptors, painters, and filmmakers, who transformed the dancer into a symbol of sexual liberation, an example of inchoate genius, or a tragic victim whose professional accomplishments were later overshadowed by her scandalous personal life.

In classical Greek art Duncan detected a spirit that was missing in contemporary U.S. culture. The dancer claimed the Puritans had tamed "the wild men, the Indians, and the wild animals in a remarkable manner. But they were always trying to tame themselves as well, with disastrous results artistically."[17] Duncan sought to combine nature and civilization, creating an art form that expressed the performer's inner spirit of freedom and creativity. She shocked her audience's puritanical sensibilities with her scantily clad exhibitions and sexual escapades. After her parents divorced Duncan vowed "to fight against marriage and for the emancipation of women, and for the right for every woman to have a child or children as it pleased her," disregarding social conventions.[18] Although this wildness of spirit was contained on the stages where Duncan performed, it overwhelmed the rest of her life. Duncan took a series of lovers and bore three children out of wedlock. Two of her children drowned in 1913 when the car in which they were riding accidentally plunged into the Seine River. The third child died shortly after birth a year later.

Fellow California native Gertrude Stein might have been referring to Duncan when she wrote: "It is something strictly American to conceive a space that is filled with moving."[19] Duncan was a force of nature, even when she was not dancing. She performed around the world, preferring to travel in open-air cars. This constant motion was another expression of her Protestant heritage, not unlike Manifest Destiny, which had earlier provided a rationale for U.S. expansion. One critic traced the arc of Duncan's career in similar terms, describing how the dancer emerged "on the very edge of western civilization, in California, vibrating to some wave of Whitmanesque affirmation, starting eastward with absolute self-confidence, conquering all of America and all of Europe for her idea, by a revelation, a presentation of her dance, in this picture of the march of the spirit of Isadora Duncan across the world."[20]

Although she claimed to be an atheist, Duncan believed dance was "the divine expression of the human spirit through the medium of the body's movement."[21] She dedicated her life to spreading "the gospel," arguing "dance is a religion and should have its worshippers."[22] Duncan was a prophet speaking "a unique world language,"[23] an artist who sought to establish dance schools as part of her "global mission" to liberate girls from the conventions of Victorian culture.[24] As Manifest Destiny was an expression of God's will, so Duncan's dancing was a representation of her inner emotions, a manifestation of the divine spirit.[25]

After the frontier "closed,"[26] the United States continued to expand overseas by initiating trade with Asia. As part of the government's Open Door Policy, the U.S. established missions in countries such as China, run by "muscular Christians" who sought to convert foreigners while profiting from these new economic partnerships. The imperialistic movement extended "American Christianity overseas in a forceful way," based on a belief that the male body was a visual symbol of U.S. supremacy as well as "a tool for good, an agent to be used on behalf of social progress and world uplift."[27] Agnes de Mille compared Duncan to an evangelical preacher, claiming she danced to arouse the audience's emotions. Yet Duncan rejected the three main components of U.S. imperialism: patriarchy, capitalism, and Christianity. (The non-doctrinaire artist shunned organized religions in general, repulsed by their rigid moral strictures.) In typically inconsistent fashion, Duncan wrote that she would have "preferred to teach boys, for they are better able to express the heroism of which we have so much need in this age."[28] But she only taught girls, stressing the importance of graceful movements rather than muscular feats of prowess. She dismissed gymnastics, which had become popular with the rise of the Young Men's Christian Association (YMCA), pronouncing in her autobiography: "For the gymnast, the movement and culture of the body are an end in themselves, but for the dancer they are only the means."[29]

In creating the graceful movements of modern dance Duncan was inspired by the wind-blown grass of the American prairie and the ebb and flow of the Pacific Ocean.[30] These gestures—no longer "arrested" but given full expression by the dancer's choreography—mimicked the process of westward expansion. Like the critic who described one of Duncan's performances as a "wave of Whitmanesque affirmation," Turner called the frontier "the outer edge of the wave—the meeting point between savagery and civilization." He imagined a "tide of immigrants" rushing into a region where gold had been discovered, or where land was available, then receding when those resources disappeared, flooding into other regions that offered better opportunities for pioneers.[31] Duncan's technique was equally fluid. One critic used a classical Greek metaphor, combined with nautical imagery, to conjure the memory of one of her performances. "Her figure moved forward with the weight placed as in the Nike statue or the figurehead of a ship—the upper torso leaning forward and the limbs following."[32]

In 1928, a year after Duncan's death, German dance theorist Rudolf Laban developed a system for analyzing human motion called Labanotation. The system charted the movement of a body through space, noting its direction and degree of extension in a series of horizontal and vertical graphs. Laban distinguished between personal space, contained within the boundaries of a dancer's body (the "kinesphere"), and general space, the area surrounding the subject. Labanotation tracked the movement of the kinesphere through general space. As its author stated: "Extension in space is a fundamental function of matter. Living matter is organised in bodily units, and has, apart from the natural extension of growth, the gift of extending and contracting these bodily units. Such a bodily unit is the body of a moving person; it follows the inner impulse of a mysterious autonomic will."[33]

Laban defined the dual phenomenon implied by Stein's phrase, a space "filled with moving." The kinesphere was one such space, and the surrounding area into which the body extended was another. Turner described a similar duality, referring to the frontier as a site of activity (exploration, settlement, industry) and migration as a process of movement that led to the creation of new frontiers where similar activities recurred. Yet Laban's scientific approach to the study of human movement could not account for the "mysterious" will that inspired such behavior. It recalled the "divine" spirit that coursed through Duncan's body in her quasi-pagan dances or the holy agency that motivated Manifest Destiny.

Like Duncan, the German theorist failed to articulate fully a phenomenon that was partly instinctive or resistant to analysis. For performing artists, or those who attempted to re-create an artist's work in another medium, this inexpressibility created a crisis in representation. In ancient Greece artists captured the ephemeral nature of dance by sculpting performers and depicting them on vases and urns.[34] Yet the act of *ekphrasis* (the representation of one art form by another) was difficult to achieve, as painters struggled to depict three-dimensional dances on two-dimensional surfaces.[35] Because he also feared something would be lost in translation when he wrote about the dancers on the Grecian urn, Keats modified the traditional Pindaric ode to accommodate his subject matter.[36] Duncan took similar liberties when she translated classical Greek poses into modern American dance. Lacking a formal pedagogical method to explain her process, Duncan instructed students merely to imitate her movements. They often did so without understanding why.[37]

Martha Graham influenced dancers more than Duncan because she pioneered "the Graham technique," which combined breath control, specific torso movements, the use of pelvic and abdominal muscles, spinal flexibility, and distinctive hand gestures—a technique that continues to be taught in music, dance, and drama schools around the world. In addition Graham's performances were often thematically driven, enabling audiences to appreciate her craft within a narrative context. Duncan sought to reconcile her frontier heritage with her childhood in metropolitan San Francisco, seeking a balance between nature and civilization—a compromise Graham was able to achieve more successfully. Her first major solo dance, "Frontier" (1932), was inspired by her family's move from Pennsylvania to California in 1908. "The train was taking us from our past," wrote Graham in her autobiography, "through the vehicle of the present, to our future. Tracks in front of me, how they gleamed whether we went straight ahead or through a newly carved-out mountain. It was these tracks that hugged the land, and became a living part of my memory. Parallel lines whose meaning was inexhaustible, whose purpose was infinite."[38] The set design featured a log fence with two pieces of rope stretched from opposite ends of the stage, meeting at a distant point beyond the fence, symbolizing the transition from the fenced-in range to the modern West, the ropes representing the train's parallel lines.

Unlike Graham, Duncan was unable to preserve her legacy by translating her theories about dance into a codified set of instructions or to explain her performances by using concrete symbols to create supplementary visual narratives. As a result she and her work were appropriated by other artists, writers, and filmmakers for their own personal or ideological reasons. Duncan was a proto-feminist; a "new" woman who preceded the Jazz Age, when such emancipated figures became commonplace. Most of her appropriators were men who transformed the dancer into an object of the male gaze, sexualizing, misrepresenting, or ridiculing the eccentric artist. Because most of the dancers depicted on Greek vases and sculptures were male, Duncan's modern interpretation of classical art was an act of female self-assertion.[39] Her later appropriation by male artists was a retaliatory attempt by the opposite sex to reclaim the power of representation.

Men began manipulating Duncan while she was still performing at the peak of her powers. Auguste Rodin tried to seduce her in his Paris studio, kneading "my whole body as if it were clay," the dancer complained in her autobiography.[40] When she rejected his advances, Rodin drew her instead. Although his pictures failed to convey a sense of movement, they revealed his attraction to Duncan, who appears naked with her nipples visible in a series of sketches (circa 1906). Rodin may have realized that painting was a more accurate means of representation than sculpture. Such depictions of Duncan—shown in stationary poses, cast in bronze—produced a feeling of heaviness, transforming the dancer into an earth-bound monument.[41]

By contrast, modernist American painter Abraham Walkowitz used watercolors to reproduce a feeling of physical motion. He painted impressionistically in broad strokes that allowed the colors to bleed on canvas, creating a wavy effect that made Duncan's tunic—and the curtains in the background—appear to move. His paintings produced between 1908 and 1917 show Duncan wearing a series of red, blue, and yellow garments (in contrast to the white tunics she usually wore), the primary colors symbolizing the elemental nature of Duncan's art. The individual disappears in the paintings and the Dancer takes her place: an outlined body with a featureless face abstractly representing the spirit of genius.

In sketches Walkowitz and French artist Antoine Bourdelle employed a technique called "gesture drawing" to achieve similar effects. They watched Duncan perform in five-to-ten-second intervals, rendering the subject in rapidly executed, spontaneous lines to capture a feeling of fluidity. They portrayed the dancer's vibrating body by using multiple lines—instead of a single outline—to depict waving limbs and a rhythmic torso. (Duncan claimed the solar plexus was the source of her body's energy.[42]) Shaded areas in these minimalist sketches indicate where the dancer places her weight when she moves: on the ball of one foot, in a leg muscle or the arch of her back. These drawings come closest to releasing the arrested "gesture" Duncan observed in classical Greek art.

The dancer's flamboyant personality interested male writers more than her craft. When Stokes published *Isadora Duncan: An Intimate Portrait* (1928), critics and fans accused him of trashing the artist's reputation. Stokes met Duncan toward the end of her life, when she was overweight, broke, and drinking heavily. Initially he describes her as "a stupid woman" who "waddl[ed] slightly as she walked." Although he later corrects his first impression, admitting Duncan had an "amazing" personality, elsewhere Stokes recalls a decrepit figure with "an uncovered head of [dyed] flaming red hair, whose pale features had been badly touched up with rouge." All that remains of Duncan is a pathetic opportunist who claims "I love potatoes—and young men."[43]

Other writers cared about Duncan's artistry only to the extent that it paralleled their own experiments in literary modernism. Gesture drawing was based on the same premise as stream-of-consciousness writing—on the theory that a subject could be most authentically rendered in the moment, instinctively, without resorting to editing or self-revision. Duncan appeared in *The Big Money* (1936), the final installment in John Dos Passos's *U.S.A.* trilogy. Here the author transforms the dancer into a vessel for his ideological message; into a tragic example of the effect on society caused by "capitalism, industrialism, and mechanized civilization."[44] Initially he describes Duncan as a westerner, "for whom the world was a goldrush." Her success, however, ultimately compromises her artistic integrity. Feeding on "lobster and champagne," Duncan eventually becomes accustomed to "the millionaire life," a *gauche* American traveling through Europe, speaking "with the strong California accent her French never lost."[45]

The dancer also featured in a series of novels by Upton Sinclair, where she initially appeared in a more favorable light. In *World's End* (1940), protagonist Lanny Budd visits Duncan at her dance studio in Paris. "She would make a few simple movements against the background of her blue curtains, and something magical would happen, a spirit would be revealed, an intimation of glory."[46] However, when he meets her again in *Between Two Worlds* (1941), Budd encounters an older woman ravaged by grief, having lost her children and experienced the devastation of World War I. "The hotel at Bellevue which she had planned to make the temple of a new art had served as a hospital for broken bodies and was now being made into a factory for poison gases."[47] No longer the object of Budd's desire, Duncan once again becomes the author's ideological muse, representing the modernist crisis provoked by the war and the plight of the artist living in an existential world.

Decades later Duncan became the subject of an absurdist play by Jeff Wanshel, entitled *Isadora Duncan Sleeps With the Russian Navy* (1977). The slapstick comedy emphasized the random nature of human existence by dramatizing the highs and lows of Duncan's life as well as the dancer's multiple personas. "I remember me," she admits, looking back on her career. "But which me? [*As Isadora Duncan deliberates, the Chorus moves and freezes, exemplifying each quality.*] Anguish? Delight? Filth? Luminous purity? Hellfire? Heroism?" Actors portraying Wanshel and the play's producer acknowledge their desire to exploit Duncan for financial gain. The author tells himself: "With the drowning of her kids ... how can you go wrong?" Later, the producer reminds the playwright, "Look—nobody cares about ancient Greece. What our audience wants to know is, who made love to Isadora?" He threatens the playwright: "If she doesn't fuck anybody in Greece, the Greek sequence goes."[48]

Film would seem to be the most effective medium for capturing Duncan in motion, allowing the artist to control her own representation. But the celebrity, once referred to as "the most portrayed woman in the world,"[49] never consented to be filmed. De Mille regarded this lack of documentation as a misfortune. The choreographer noted in other representations of Duncan that "she stands, she gazes, she yearns, but she does not balance, or hover, or take to the air in any way, and any fleeting or passing expression is lost." In photographs this "overpowering personality [looks] like a normal woman." Her "broad, placid forehead, the mild eyes, the chin drawn in without aggression ... the sweet yielding mouth, bespeak impatience, understanding, and, yes, conformity."[50] However, one critic believes Duncan wanted to be remembered by future generations of dance enthusiasts. "That is why she refused to be filmed, because she wanted to become a legend: an absence rendered perpetually present. The sense of longing that was so much a part of Duncan's dancing reproduces itself in our always thwarted but never-ceasing desire to see her dance, if not in the flesh or on celluloid, then at least in the mind's eye."[51]

Filmmakers filled this void after Duncan's death, once again transforming her into an object of the male gaze, creating celluloid tributes to the legendary dancer that were stylistically at odds with her philosophy about her craft. The artist avoided "abrupt transitions between kneeling and sitting" in her performances, making the legs appear connected to the torso, "not cut off at the hips as is sometimes done in ballet."[52]

However, Ken Russell's *avant-garde* biopic, *Isadora Duncan: The Biggest Dancer in the World* (1966), builds "upon abrupt transitions." In addition to choppy editing, the film shifts in tone "from the sublime to the ridiculous, from placid beauty to surreal absurdity." It "swings wildly between moments of near transcendental splendor and sudden outbreaks of vulgar showmanship as Russell meditates upon the gap between Duncan's artistic drives and the effect of time that gnaws at the dancer's physical and personal stamina."[53] Russell's cinematic pastiche resembles Dos Passos's collage technique. The director intersperses his fictional documentary with fake newsreel footage of actual historical events, reminiscent of the author in his kaleidoscopic trilogy, which incorporates literary newsreels, fiction, and biographies of famous people to illustrate "the fragmented nature of the individual social and historical experience of modern America."[54]

Russell and fellow British filmmaker Karel Reisz competed for the opportunity to tell Duncan's story. Reisz bought the rights to *My Life* and other copyrighted source material, forcing his rival to rely on Stokes's critically disparaged biography. In *Isadora* (1968), Duncan is controlled by a succession of lovers. After seeing her perform, theater designer Gordon Craig calls her the dancer "I've always imagined." Dressed like Svengali, in a black cape and hat, Craig treats Duncan as his muse, creating sets filled with "light and air," though they also resemble prisons in which the artist is held captive. In a later scene wealthy patron and lover Paris Singer sits in his opera box, stroking his imperial mustache while viewing Duncan through a lorgnette. After being subjected to the male gaze and passing inspection, the dancer is installed in one of Singer's mansions, where she performs like a bird in a gilded cage.[55] Duncan also becomes objectified by the director's gaze. An early scene shows her staring into a mirror. The viewer sees the back of her head but not her face. In a later scene she stares into another mirror and the viewer sees her face instead of the mirror. The camera becomes a reflecting lens as Duncan, her image, and the viewer scrutinize one another. When Craig and Duncan make love, he declares while disrobing her: "You belong to me." The camera assumes Craig's point of view as Duncan succumbs to the camera, rolling around on the floor as if she were simultaneously dancing, experiencing ecstasy, and wrestling to escape.

The title of Wanshel's play alludes to a period in the early 1920s when Duncan moved to the Soviet Union. Continuing her eastward migration, which had taken her from California to England and Europe in search of new lands to conquer with her pioneering form of dance, Duncan believed her radical art and support for women's emancipation would be welcome in the post-revolution Communist state. She concluded her autobiography by announcing she was leaving the "Old World" of her native homeland and immigrating to the "New World," the "World of Comrades," the "dream that Lenin had by a great magic turned to reality."[56] Initially she was embraced by the government, which had denounced ballet as an imperial art form associated with the recently overthrown Emperor Nikolai II.[57] An individualist whose performances seemed spontaneous and self-inspired, Duncan also rejected ballet. In her autobiography she complained that the classical art form required rigid poses and unnatural contortions of the body, transforming performers into "articulated puppet[s]" who produced "artificial mechanical movement not worthy of the soul."[58] An expressive dancer rather than a political ideologue, Duncan failed to comprehend that her personal mission was incompatible with the goals of the Soviet Union. Although her host country viewed Duncan as "a cultural messenger whose [art] could be adapted for political purposes," it eventually realized modern dance, "whose form demanded individual expression as the core of its language," conflicted with "the collectivist tenets of the state."[59]

When Duncan returned to the United States in 1924 she was regarded by socialist artists as "passé." A new generation of artists had begun to replace expressive dance with "a canon borrowed from the abstract modernist painters and sculptors."[60] Seeking to depict the history of class struggle, which *The Communist Manifesto* (1848) defined as the story of all nations throughout time, dancers rejected individual expression in favor of choreographed routines featuring collective bodies that celebrated the labor of social protest and class resistance. Dance became part of "movement culture," a "world of working-class education, recreation, and entertainment built by the [U.S.] Communist Party, the new industrial unions, and the fraternal benefit lodges, particularly those of the International Workers Order (IWO)."[61] Duncan had liberated dance from the conformity of classical ballet with her radical moves. Now she was replaced by a cultural movement that used socialist dance to convey the struggle of political groups and economic underclasses.[62] The term "movement" referred to the motion of dance as well as to the dialectics of Marxism, which maintained that "change, development, and progress take place by way of contradiction and conflict," representing the perpetual flux of human existence.[63]

After her exile from the "New World" and a brief return to her postlapsarian homeland, Duncan wandered the earth, becoming indigent, neglectful of her craft, and undisciplined in her personal life, relying on alcohol to sustain her spirits. This decline in her later years made it easier for her contemporaries to dismiss her without compassion after she died. One evening in 1927 Duncan went for a ride with a French mechanic in her favorite means of conveyance, an open-air automobile. Her long flowing scarf became entangled in the spokes of one of its rear wheels, snapping her neck and instantly killing her. Referring to the diva's penchant for wearing dramatic garments, Gertrude Stein reportedly commented afterward: "Affectations can be dangerous." Jean Cocteau claimed with a lack of feeling that "Isadora's death [was] *perfect*" because it provoked "a kind of horror that [left] one calm." In fact the accident nearly decapitated the dancer, who was yanked from the car as the scarf wrapped around its wheel, and she was "dragged some twenty or thirty meters before [it] came to a stop," reducing her face to a bloody pulp.[64]

Duncan's death has been represented by various writers and filmmakers. Perhaps the most fitting ending to the story of America's modern dance pioneer is not the accident but a fictional scene that concludes Ken Russell's pseudo-documentary film. Having failed to accomplish her mission in the "New World," Duncan retreats to the Soviet countryside, where she considers selling her love letters to support her students.

Parking her car in a field, she places a gramophone on the ground. As she lies in the grass, a breeze scatters the letters while a record plays "Bury Me Not on the Lone Prairie."

It matters not, I've oft been told,
Where the body lies when the heart grows cold;
Yet grant, oh, grant this wish to me:
Oh, Bury me not on the lone prairie.[65]

# Afterword

*Burials and Exhumations*

In the song "Bury Me Not on the Lone Prairie" the dying singer pleads with his fellow cowboys not to leave him on the barren frontier, where "the wild coyotes will howl o'er me."[1] However, at the time the song was composed in the late nineteenth century, the prairie was no longer a sparsely populated region.[2] The song re-created a frontier that no longer existed, and its subject was a performer who sang for an audience made up of other fictional cowboys. "Bury Me Not on the Lone Prairie" has several metadramatic dimensions. Addressing his last words to the men who "gathered to see him die," the singer performs his own demise. In addition he asks to have his body sent back East, so his family and friends can "weep o'er me" (49).

Early cowboy songs were orally and collectively composed by ranch hands. Subsequently these works circulated among other members of their profession. They were sung in bunkhouses, around campfires, and during trail drives. In order to make it easier to remember lyrics, cowboys borrowed melodies from other popular songs, such as "My Bonnie Lies over the Ocean." The song that plays on Isadora Duncan's gramophone at the end of director Ken Russell's film was based on "The Ocean Burial" (1839), with music by George N. Allen and different lyrics by Edward Hubbell Chapin. Many western songs explored elegiac themes, such as the decline of the cattle industry, the imminent extinction of the cowboy, his solitary life or his inability to marry, and his yearning for an afterlife, where his earthly sacrifices would be rewarded. At the same time these songs romanticized cowboys as members of a vanishing breed; symbols of a disappearing frontier that was rapidly becoming mythologized in popular culture.

The "real" cowboy was an unromantic figure: a manual laborer who worked for a menial wage. The people in *Geographic Personas* also had dual identities. They were seemingly exotic, glamorous, or celebrated public figures with relatively mundane or secret personal lives. Some of them died tragically, after sinking into obscurity, going to prison, or becoming socially ostracized. Others became victims of alcoholism, depression, or suicide. Each individual represents the two conflicting theories that have dominated western scholarship for more than a hundred years. On one hand, these subjects created self-narratives in which they appeared as frontier heroes, noble savages, intrepid scientific explorers, and writers who depicted the American West as a sublime or pastoral landscape. On the other hand, their personas testified to the fact that these people and places no longer—or had never—existed; that the history of the region was more complex and problematic than what they represented. Almost a century before the New Western historians began revising Turner's thesis, these individuals revised their personal stories, concealing certain truths that modern scholars eventually exposed.[3]

"Bury Me Not on the Lone Prairie" is constructed around a series of inherent contradictions. The singer fears his carcass will be eaten by buzzards, yet asks the other cowboys to leave roses on his grave (50–51). The song is composed in rhyming verse, which facilitates the reconciliation of opposing ideas and provides narrative closure. But it also ends with the cowboys ignoring their friend's request, leaving his body in a shallow pit, where it can be dug up and eaten by predators (51). The singer asks not to be buried in "a narrow grave six by three,"[4] contrasting the existential terrors of the wide open spaces with the gothic confinement of his burial site (49). The song depicts male camaraderie on the western frontier and the absence of men in civilization. The cowboy wants to be buried at home next to his father. Only his mother and sister survive, as does a young woman whom the singer left behind (50).

"Bury Me Not on the Lone Prairie" looks forward and backward in time. Perhaps for this reason Carl Sandburg included it in his folklore anthology, *The American Songbag* (1927).[5] The poet published the book at approximately the same time the West and Midwest were developing into urban and industrial regions; when modernism was establishing its unique relationship with the nation's past and its people's earlier "primitive" cultures. Sandburg was a poet who commemorated life on the nineteenth-century prairie in *Cornhuskers* (1918). He was also a modernist who wrote "Chicago" (1916), a poem about a twentieth-century city known for its slaughterhouses and that Sandburg calls "Hog Butcher for the World."[6] The Harlem Renaissance explored the roots of African American culture, reconsidering the Negro vernacular, slave songs and spiritual hymns, and African wood carvings as great works of art. In a similar fashion Sandburg returned to the origins of western American settlement for his own poetic inspiration.

Unlike Sandburg, the earliest inhabitants in the American West were not primarily interested in creating art. Native American creation stories explained the material and spiritual worlds for religious and cultural purposes, though they could also be appreciated for aesthetic reasons. White western explorers focused on collecting scientific, geological, and anthropological data. Scholars later criticized some of these works for their factual inaccuracies and cultural biases. But they have seldom considered them in the same ways that one examines art, which is meant to be interpreted, copied, revised, reproduced, and performed. Hence the problem with the term "cultural appropriation," which is used in a pejorative sense to suggest that someone has stolen, used, or exploited the art belonging to another cultural group. In fact art has been appropriated for centuries, by various cultures and individuals, not always with nefarious motives.

The people in *Geographic Personas* sought to appropriate other cultures, false identities, and—in the case of James Addison Reavis—almost the entire U.S. Southwest territory. In turn, they were appropriated as subjects by biographers, artists, and scholars, who questioned the personas these subjects had constructed, revealing their true histories or exposing them as frauds. Some of them did so with honorable intentions, examining the intricacies of their subjects' lives and careers, while others exploited them for artistic reasons or personal gain. Helena Modjeska has been transformed by other women writers, such as Willa Cather and Susan Sontag, into a sympathetic and complex artist figure, unlike Isadora Duncan, who has been sexualized, sometimes ridiculed, and (mis)represented by male biographers, artists, and filmmakers. Like the cowboy in the song played at the end of the film, Duncan's fate was left to others. "We took no heed of his dying prayer; / In a narrow grave just six by three / We buried him there on the lone prairie" (50).

Passing is a euphemism for death. The term suggests that a person transitions from one place to another, often imagined as a spiritual realm where the corporeal self no longer exists. The word also refers to literal movement as well as the passage of time. Clarence King wrote about the passage of prehistoric glaciers through the Yosemite region, noting that the "marvelously changed condition" of the U.S. West was a feature of "recent geological times."[7] By the mid-nineteenth century the frontier had begun to develop so rapidly that individuals became transformed in the process. During this period, westward migration was the most dramatic form of literal movement. The subjects in *Geographic Personas* took advantage of modern technologies, the transformation of the region into a public space, and the creation of new modes of representation to "pass" as members of different races and to perform in a variety of roles, forever changing the way we view the American West.

# Notes

## Introduction

1. Turner, "Significance of the Frontier," 33. Roosevelt also imagined western people as archetypal characters. In *Ranch Life and the Hunting-Trail*, the author refers to the "fringed tunic or hunting-shirt, made of buckskin," worn by "hunters and trappers," calling it "the most picturesque and distinctively national dress ever worn in America." The hunter represents "the arch-type of freedom," while cowboys are "typical men of the plains" (81, 83, 88).
2. Turner, "Significance of the Frontier," 39.
3. Lewis and Clark, *Journals*, 478.
4. Bernard DeVoto, "Preface," in Lewis and Clark, *Journals*, xxv. President Jefferson explained to the Spanish government that the expedition was "a literary pursuit"; that is, "an effort to add to geographical and scientific knowledge" of the newly acquired territories.
5. Pike, "Preface to the Original Edition," in *Expeditions of Zebulon Montgomery Pike*, ii.
6. Coues, "Preface to the New Edition," in Pike, *Expeditions*, xii.
7. Coues, "Preface," in Pike, *Expeditions*, v.
8. Clappe, *Shirley Letters*, 68, 107.
9. Beckwourth and Bonner, *Life and Adventures*, 46, 120, 198. For an analysis of Beckwourth's autobiography, see Allmendinger, *Imagining the African American West*, 1–12.
10. Parkman, *Oregon Trail*, 178.
11. DeVoto quotes Parkman in the introduction to a later edition of Beckwourth's autobiography. See *Life and Adventures*, xix.
12. Twain, *Roughing It*, 96.
13. Twain, "On the Decay of the Art of Lying," in *The Stolen White Elephant*, 224.
14. Fisher, "Appearing and Disappearing," 165.
15. Certeau, *Practice of Everyday Life*, 112.
16. Cather, *My Ántonia*, ix–xiii. The first chapter of Jim's memoir also begins on a train, as his younger self arrives in Nebraska. Cather had written a similar scene six years earlier in "The Bohemian Girl" (1912), in which one of the

story's main characters returns to Nebraska aboard the Transcontinental Express (*Stories, Poems, and Other Writings*, 89).

17. For an analysis of the "transnational influences that shaped" the formula western, including the "European colonial adventure tale[s]" of Karl May, see Kollin, *Captivating Westerns*, 3.

18. Slotkin, *Gunfighter Nation*, 39–44. Roosevelt also used the term "waste spaces" to refer to the unsettled regions west of the Mississippi River in *The Winning of the West*, 1. Miller contends that Roosevelt's book was inspired by Darwinian theory, which enabled the author to see "westward migration as a distinct series of evolutionary episodes" (Miller, *Theodore Roosevelt*, 199).

19. Lowry, *"Littery Man,"* 12, 65.

20. Woodruff, "Historical Essay," in Cather, *My Ántonia*, 382.

21. Orvell, *The Real Thing*, 142.

22. Slotkin, *Gunfighter Nation*, 235.

23. Slotkin, *Gunfighter Nation*, 163.

24. Miller, *Theodore Roosevelt*, 48, 164, 277.

25. Harte, "The Luck of Roaring Camp," in *Selected Stories and Sketches*, 8.

26. Miller, *Theodore Roosevelt*, 163, 277. Roosevelt was familiar with Harte's writings, noting in *Ranch Life and the Hunting-Trail* that "a curious shooting scrape" he had witnessed out West was "worthy of being chronicled" by the author (95).

27. Crane, "The Bride Comes to Yellow Sky," 151. Subsequent references to this edition appear parenthetically in the text.

28. Certeau describes this combination of spectatorship and alienation, noting in reference to train travel that the window "is what allows us to *see*, and the rail, what allows us to *move through*. These are two complementary modes of separation. The first creates the spectator's distance . . . a dispossession of the hand in favor of a greater trajectory for the eye. The second inscribes, indefinitely, the injunction to pass on; it is its order written in a single but endless line: go, leave, this is not your country" (*Practice of Everyday Life*, 112). In "The Bride Comes to Yellow Sky," this "trajectory for the eye" enables the narrator to see further than the characters on the train. "Vast flats of green grass, dull-hued spaces of mesquit and cactus, little groups of frame houses, woods of light and tender trees, all were sweeping into the east, sweeping over the horizon, a precipice" (151).

29. For a literary example of this inverted relationship between the West and the East, see Denning, who notes that while western pulp fiction satisfied the public's craving for stories about the early frontier, eastern dime novels explored the "mysteries of the city" during the industrial era (*Mechanic Accents*, 85–117).

30. Urgo notes this paradox in reference to Cather, who also traveled back and forth between Nebraska and New York City during her writing career. See Urgo, "The Cather Thesis," in *Cambridge Companion*, 38–39.

31. White (*Eastern Establishment*, 6–27) studies gentlemen's clubs and other exclusive sites where male members of the upper classes mingled, including people from "families of established wealth and long-standing social prominence who traced their ascendancy to a period before the dawn of industrialism" as well as the *nouveau riche*. Slotkin (*Gunfighter Nation*, 37) writes about one organization to which King belonged: the Boone and Crocket Club, established by Roosevelt and Henry Cabot Lodge in 1888. The fraternity for "gentlemen hunters" brought together men who were both members of eastern society and western enthusiasts.

32. Sandweiss notes that during King's lifetime, New York City "was a collection of neighborhoods, many defined by the residents' class or race or national origin. Horse-drawn trolleys and elevated trains let New Yorkers move about from place to place, but in this presubway era, many city residents lived largely within the bounds of their immediate neighborhoods, rarely venturing into worlds where their social class or physical appearance might make them conspicuous. King lived his secret life for thirteen years [in one such neighborhood in Brooklyn], and no one, it seems, ever found him out" (Sandweiss, *Passing Strange*, 9). Scheiner adds: "By 1860 the city's Negro population could be said to be living in segregated areas, even though Negroes were not limited to a single area, nor did they constitute more than eight per cent of any ward's population." This situation persisted until the early 1920s (*Negro Mecca*, 23). Bold describes the measures taken by these organizations to exclude people of color in *The Frontier Club*, 67–68.

33. King, *Mountaineering in the Sierra Nevada*, 142.

34. Sandweiss, *Print the Legend*, 3.

35. Trzcinski, *Peralta Land Grant Mystery*, 24.

36. Twain, *Roughing It*, 225.

37. Other Native American autobiographies might also be considered unreliable because their narratives were mediated by white male translators and editors. Black Hawk, a member of the Sauk tribe, dictated his story to government interpreter Antoine Le Claire. It was subsequently edited for publication by Illinois newspaperman J. B. Patterson. Black Elk, an Oglala Lakota medicine man, told his story to his son, Ben Black Hawk, who translated his father's words into English for Great Plains ethnographer John G. Neihardt. It is impossible to determine to what extent the speakers were forthcoming in sharing their stories and information about their tribes and to what degree the narratives are inaccurate works. (See Black Hawk, *Black Hawk*, and Black

Elk, *Black Elk Speaks*.) For a detailed analysis of these works, and their status as authoritative texts, see Krupat, *For Those Who Come After*. Other autobiographies, written by Native Americans in English during this period, include La Flesche, *The Middle Five*; Zitkala-Sa, *American Indian Stories, Legends, and Other Writings*; Charles Eastman, *Indian Boyhood*; and Luther Standing Bear, *My Indian Boyhood*.

38. James, *Lone Cowboy*, 357–59.

39. Floyd, *Claims and Speculations*, 1. For further consideration of the ways in which new networks of "communication and transportation—telegraphs, railroads, and steamships—laid the foundation for this revolution," see Edwards, *New Spirits*, 38.

40. Lewis, *From Traveling Show to Vaudeville*, 316.

41. Slotkin, *Gunfighter Nation*, 231–34.

42. Darwin, *Emotions in Man and Animals*, 13, 15.

43. For an analysis of these same-sex communities, see, for example, Allmendinger, *The Cowboy*, 5–7, 48–82; and Johnson, *Roaring Camp*, 127–30, 169–74, 335–37.

44. Sueyoshi, *Discriminating Sex*, 2.

45. Sueyoshi, *Queer Compulsions*, 3.

46. Knoper, *Acting Naturally*, 24, 105.

47. Orvell notes the tendency during this period "to enclose reality in manageable forms, to contain it within a theatrical space, an enclosed exposition or recreational space, or within the space of the picture frame. If the world outside the frame was beyond control, the world inside of it could at least offer the illusion of mastery and comprehension" (*The Real Thing*, 35).

48. Yagoda writes that "Rogers' persona *wasn't* an act—or, to the extent that it was, it had been almost totally internalized by the time he reached the height of his success." The performer was "a Cherokee Indian, and also the son of a Confederate veteran who fancied himself a southern gentleman; the heir to a sizable fortune, and also an itinerant cowboy." Rogers reconciled these different aspects of his identity due to his "capacity for self-creation." At the same time, his inability to act strengthened—rather than weakened—his claim to credibility. Although "he tended to rely on a limited set of moves—the ocular double-take, the grin, the bowed head, the head scratch—his ingrained restraint and naturalism presented a refreshing contrast to the hypercharged emotionalism and/or acrobatism silent-film audiences were used to" (Yagoda, *Will Rogers*, xiv, 3, 166).

49. Chandler, "The Simple Art of Murder," 14.

50. Orvell, *The Real Thing*, xvi.

51. Chandler, "The Simple Art of Murder," 18.

52. Lewis, *Unsettling the Literary West*, 4, 67.

53. White, *Eastern Establishment*, 5.

54. See, for example, La Farge's *Laughing Boy* (1929), Clark's *The Ox-Bow Incident* (1940), Guthrie's *The Big Sky* (1947), and Schaefer's *Shane* (1949). Orvell notes that Frank Norris moved away from realism during this period, adding that what he meant by "reality" was "blood, sex, money, grime, garbage, immigrants, and killing snowstorms—a recognition of areas of experience previously excluded from polite literature," rather than innovations in the novel as an art form (Orvell, *The Real Thing*, 240). The same might be said for several of Norris's contemporaries, who were more interested in writing about controversial social and political matters than they were in experimenting with style, including the muck-racking journalist/novelist Upton Sinclair in *Oil* (1927) and the political leftist and naturalist Jack London in *Martin Eden* (1909).

55. Wister's *The Virginian* (1902) established the template for the genre, paving the way for such formula fiction writers as Zane Grey and Clarence Mulford, creator of the Hopalong Cassidy series.

56. Lewis, *Unsettling the Literary West*, 67.

57. Orvell, *The Real Thing*, 154.

58. West, *A Cool Million*, 163.

59. West, *Miss Lonelyhearts*, 108.

60. Baudrillard, *Simulacra and Simulation*, 1, 3.

61. For example, see Cohen, *Mapping the West*, and Hayes, *Historical Atlas of the American West*. Trachtenberg also disputes Baudrillard's claim, noting that "mapmaking preceded settlement and had perhaps an even greater effect on conceptualization of the land than landscape paintings" and other forms of representation (*The Incorporation of America*, 19).

62. Lewis, *Unsettling the Literary West*, 15.

63. Baudrillard, *Simulacra and Simulation*, 1.

64. Austin, *The Land of Little Rain*, 1–2.

## 1. Geographic Personas

1. Baudrillard, *Simulacra and Simulation*, 3.

2. Francis Peloubet Farquhar, "Preface," in King, *Mountaineering in the Sierra Nevada*, 11.

3. Spickard suggests that the term "shape shifting" is more useful than the word "passing," which raises issues concerning "pretending and racial authenticity." By contrast, shape shifting reveals how lives unfold "in fluid social circumstances." See "Shape Shifting: Reflections on Racial Plasticity," in Tamai et al., eds., *Shape Shifters*, 10. However, the notion of "pretending" is central to understanding King's life and career.

4. Sandweiss chronicles King's common law marriage to Ada Copeland in *Passing Strange*. No correspondence between the couple survives, and there is scant historical evidence pertaining to their marriage.

5. For a study of such clubs, see White, *Eastern Establishment*.

6. See Wilson, *The Explorer King*.

7. Nash claims that Henry Adams was the first American writer to give the term "wilderness" this new meaning, citing the author's reference to New York City in *Democracy* (1890) as a "wilderness of men and women" (Nash, *Wilderness and the American Mind*, 3). See also *The Jungle* (1905), Upton Sinclair's exposé of the meat-packing industry, and *How the Other Half Lives* (1890), Jacob Riis's journalistic and photographic account of New York City's tenement slums.

8. Van Kirk writes about sexual relations between fur trappers and Native American women in *Many Tender Ties*. Butler examines frontier prostitution in *Daughters of Joy, Sisters of Misery*.

9. Sandweiss, *Passing Strange*, 10.

10. Sandweiss, *Passing Strange*, 9.

11. King, *Mountaineering in the Sierra Nevada*, 48. Subsequent references to this edition appear parenthetically in the text.

12. Smith, *Pacific Visions*, 80.

13. Farquhar, "Preface," in King, *Mountaineering in the Sierra Nevada*, 16.

14. Wilkins, *Clarence King*, 2, 49.

15. Wyatt, *The Fall into Eden*, 47.

16. O'Sullivan, *Timothy H. O'Sullivan: The King Survey Photographs*, 29. The photograph has also been entitled "Taking a Breath." See Jurovics et al., *Framing the West*, 180.

17. Sachs, *The Humbolt Current*, 246.

18. Sachs, *The Humbolt Current*, 49–51.

19. Sandweiss, *Passing Strange*, 100.

20. King, "Catastrophism and Evolution," 450, 454.

21. O'Grady, *Pilgrims to the Wild*, 105.

22. Van Noy, *Surveying the Interior*, 3, 33.

23. Henry Adams, "King," in *Clarence King Memoirs*, 167.

24. Moore, *King of the Fortieth Parallel*, 4.

25. Wilkins, *Clarence King*, 320.

26. Sandweiss, *Passing Strange*, 17, 23–24, 51–52. Wilkins also claims that King hoped "popular sovereignty would prevail throughout the Western Territories" and that King's maternal grandmother befriended runaway slaves (*Clarence King*, 11, 36, 319).

27. As noted earlier, Sandweiss (*Passing Strange*, 9) and Scheiner (*Negro Mecca*, 23) address how until the 1920s, city residents rarely ventured beyond their

immediate neighborhoods into areas where they would be conspicuous; see note 32 to the introduction, this volume.

28. As noted earlier, (*Eastern Establishment*, 6–27) and Slotkin (*Gunfighter Nation*, 37) review organizations that brought together upper class members of eastern society and western enthusiasts; see note 31 to the introduction, this volume.

29. Muir, "Wild Parks and Forest Reservations," 10.

30. Timothy O'Sullivan is best known for his photographs of the Civil War. He was the official photographer for the U.S. Geological Exploration of the Fortieth Parallel from 1867 to 1869.

31. O'Sullivan, *King Survey Photographs*, 172, 146.

32. Jurovics, "Framing the West," 19.

33. O'Sullivan, *King Survey Photographs*, 138.

34. Jurovics, "Framing the West," 75, 142–43.

35. Jurovics, "Framing the West," 37.

36. O'Sullivan, *King Survey Photographs*, 84.

37. Craib, "Cartography and Decolonization," 23.

38. King, "Map of the Nevada Basin."

39. Rabasa, *Inventing America*, 358.

40. Farber, *Mixing Races*, 27, 29.

41. King, *Systematic Geology*, 4.

42. Santino, *Miles of Smiles*.

43. Wilson, *The Explorer King*, 12–13.

44. Wilkins, *Clarence King*, 194.

45. O'Grady, *Pilgrims to the Wild*, 87.

46. Wilkins, *Clarence King*, 39.

47. Morrison, *Playing in the Dark*, 9, 52.

48. Sandweiss, *Passing Strange*, 283.

49. Morrison, *Playing in the Dark*, 3.

## 2. Lord of the Limber Tongue

1. O'Grady, *Pilgrims to the Wild*, 87.

2. Baudrillard, *Simulacra and Simulation*, 4.

3. Briefel, *The Deceivers*, 2.

4. Grafton, *Forgers and Critics*, 12.

5. Ruthven, *Faking Literature*, 40.

6. For information about the tensions between whites and Apaches, and the competition between individuals and private enterprises, see Powell, *The Peralta Grant*, 4, 76–79, 81; and Trzcinski, *Peralta Land Grant Mystery*, 88.

7. Powell, *The Peralta Grant*, 62–68.

8. Powell, *The Peralta Grant*, 13–15. See also Cookridge, *Baron of Arizona*, 26–35.

9. Powell, *The Peralta Grant*, 17–19; Trzcinski, *Peralta Land Grant Mystery*, 317.

10. Powell, *The Peralta Grant*, 20–21. Although Trzcinski contends that Willing was poisoned by someone whom the con man had previously victimized, he offers no evidence to prove his theory (*Peralta Land Grant Mystery*, 343).

11. Powell, *The Peralta Grant*, 25–33; Cookridge, *Baron of Arizona*, 74–84.

12. Johnson, *Adverse Report of the Surveyor General*, 7. Subsequent references to this edition appear parenthetically in the text.

13. Powell, *The Peralta Grant*, 62–70; Cookridge, *Baron of Arizona*, 123–32.

14. Powell, *The Peralta Grant*, 102–34; Trzcinski, *Peralta Land Grant Mystery*, 428–55; Cookridge, *Baron of Arizona*, 242–84.

15. Powell, *The Peralta Grant*, 108; Cookridge, *Baron of Arizona*, centerpiece caption.

16. Cookridge, *Baron of Arizona*, 289.

17. See, for example, Posner, *Law and Literature*; and Dworkin, *A Matter of Principle*, 146–66.

18. Bruner, *Making Stories*, 43.

19. Griswold del Castillo, *Treaty of Guadalupe Hidalgo*, 97.

20. Ebright, Introduction to *Land Grants and Law Suits in Northern New Mexico*, 3–4.

21. Montoya, *Translating Property*, 11.

22. Correia, *Properties of Violence*, 2.

23. Trzcinski, *Peralta Land Grant Mystery*, 18.

24. *The Baron of Arizona*. DVD. Directed by Sam Fuller. Los Angeles: Lippert Pictures, 1950.

25. Peralta Land Grant Case Exhibits (1886), John Addison Reavis Collection, Arizona Historical Society Archives, Flagstaff. Exhibit AAA is a copy of the Royal Patent granted by King Ferdinand VI, King of Spain, to Don Miguel de Peralta de la Córdoba. Exhibits BBB are the will and codicil of Don Miguel de Peralta.

    For copies of original Spanish-language, handwritten documents, featuring an ornate, cursive script and "flourishes," see The Peralta Land Grant; James Addison Reavis and the Barony of Arizona Collection, University of Arizona Archives, Tucson. These include notarial records found in Guadalajara, Mexico; forged documents relating to the Peralta Grant; leaves of paper stolen from a book in the Guadalajara city council archives; and various *cedulas* or official records.

26. Grafton, *Forgers and Critics*, 50.

27. For information about the relationship between human identity and performance theory, in life and literature, see Rosenthal and Schäfer, Introduction to *Fake Identity?* 12; and Gilman, *Dark Twins*, 6.

28. Powell, *The Peralta Grant*, 62–65.

29. Cookridge, *Baron of Arizona*, 22–26.

30. Powell, *The Peralta Grant*, 53.

31. University of Arizona Archives, MS AZ 110.

32. Trzcinski, *Peralta Land Grant Mystery*, 12.

33. Horsman, *Race and Manifest Destiny*, 208–10.

34. Messent, Foreword to Twain, *The American Claimant*, 8–11.

35. Mowry, *Memoir of the Proposed Territory*, 4, 6.

36. Grafton, *Forgers and Critics*, 32.

37. Ruthven, *Faking Literature*, 58.

38. Ruthven, *Faking Literature*, 71.

39. Correia, *Properties of Violence*, 7–9.

40. Rosenthal and Schäfer, *Fake Identity?*, 16.

41. Taylor, *The Archive and the Repertoire*, 19–20.

42. As quoted in Powell, *The Peralta Grant*, 34.

43. Johnson, *Adverse Report of the Surveyor General*, 46.

44. Montoya, *Translating Property*, 8.

45. Rosenthal and Schäfer, *Fake Identity?*, 16.

46. James Addison Reavis, "Confessions of Peralta-Reavis, the King of Forgers," *San Francisco Call* 85, no. 116 (March 26, 1899), 1–2, cdnc.ucr.edu /cgi-bin/cdnc?a=d&d=SFC18990326.2.167.2.

## 3. A French Canadian Cowboy

1. During James's childhood, Bothwell estimates that approximately 80 percent of Quebec's residents maintained their linguistic and religious traditions, a "proportion that remained relatively constant" until the late twentieth century (*Canada and Quebec*, 43). The province continued to preserve this majority despite an enormous influx of British immigrants in the late nineteenth century (Dickinson and Young, *A Short History of Quebec*, 110).

2. Handler, *Nationalism and the Politics of Culture*, 37.

3. Moogk, *La Nouvelle France*, xii.

4. Linteau et al., *Quebec*, 28.

5. Amaral, *Will James*, 101–2.

6. Palmer, Preface to *The Settlement of the West*, vi.

7. Palmer, Preface, 110.

8. Allmendinger, *The Cowboy*, 16.

9. James, *Lone Cowboy*, 71–72, 119, 144, 183–87. Subsequent references to this edition appear parenthetically within the text of the essay.

10. Gunesh, "Multilingualism and Cosmopolitanism," 220.

11. Romaine, *Bilingualism*, 121.

12. Amaral, *Will James*, 152.

13. James, *The Drifting Cowboy*, viii.

14. For an analysis of this phenomenon, see Deloria, *Playing Indian*; and Huhndorf, *Going Native*.

15. For more information about James's incarceration and the prison's influence on his future career as an artist, see Allmendinger, *The Cowboy*, 99–104.

16. James, "Filling the Cracks," in *The Drifting Cowboy*, 43.

17. For a history of *Sunset* magazine, from its origin in 1898 through the early twentieth century, see Starr, *Inventing the Dream*, 168.

18. Adams, *The Cowboy Dictionary*, 32.

19. James, "Borrowed Horses," in *Horses I've Known*, 58.

20. James, "For the Sake of Freedom," in *Horses I've Known*, 61.

21. James, "Regular Folks," in *The American Cowboy*, 134.

22. Adams, *The Cowboy Dictionary*, 104, 343.

23. Allmendinger, *The Cowboy*, 17–18.

24. Allmendinger, *The Cowboy*, 261, 99, 242–43.

25. Allmendinger, *The Cowboy*, 174, 30, 191, 286.

26. James, "On the Middle," in *The American Cowboy*, 64.

27. Bouchard, *Obsessed with Language*, 20.

28. Amaral, *Will James*, 91.

29. Amaral, *Will James*, 13.

30. Branding consultancy executive Brian Collins, interviewed in Millman, *Brand Thinking and Other Noble Pursuits*, 81.

31. Mark and Pearson, *The Hero and the Outlaw*, 72, 106, 124.

32. Artist James B. Wyeth, as quoted in Amaral, *Will James*, xiv.

33. Amaral, *Will James*, 70, 96, 118.

34. Amaral, *Will James*, 80, 88–89.

35. Amaral, *Will James*, 95, 140, 158.

36. Klein, *History of Forgetting*, 1–18.

37. Godbout, Jacques, director. *Alias Will James*. National Film Board of Canada, 1988.

## 4. Making an Indian

1. Cobb, Foreword to Chief Buffalo Child Long Lance (Sylvester Long), *Long Lance*, xxxvi.

2. Whether Wild West shows demeaned Native Americans by requiring them to reenact their status as conquered subjects, or whether the indigenous peoples who participated in these extravaganzas were able to find satisfaction in their roles, or means of subverting the intentions of the shows' creators, continues to be debated. Recent scholarship tends to focus on the

surprisingly positive aspects of working in these racial performance settings. Warren notes that Indians refused to play "humiliating roles" for Buffalo Bill Cody. "The dramatic presentation of white supremacy only became possible through the cast's enthusiasm for beguiling the Wild West's racial frontiers" (*Buffalo Bill's America*, 397). Officials at the Carlisle Indian School, where Long was later a student, worried that participating in these shows "would undermine government policies of assimilation, which sought to extinguish, not reinforce, traditional ways" (McNenly, *Native Performers in Wild West Shows*, 47).

3. For an account of Long's family lineage, his work with Wild West shows, and his admission to the Carlisle Indian Industrial School, see Smith, *Chief Buffalo Child Long Lance*, 22–42.

4. Turner, "Significance of the Frontier."

5. Deloria, "Foreword: American Fantasy," in Bataille and Silet, eds., *The Pretend Indians*, ix.

6. Kilpatrick, *Celluloid Indians*, 9.

7. Warren, *Buffalo Bill's America*, 400, 407.

8. Kilpatrick, *Celluloid Indians*, 16–17.

9. Fear-Segal and Rose, Introduction to *Carlisle Indian Industrial School*, 9.

10. Dickson College, Carlisle Indian School Digital Resource Center, http://carlisleindian.dickinson.edu.

11. Smith, *Chief Buffalo Child Long Lance*, 58, 51.

12. Sylvester Long, "Valedictory Address," in Chief Buffalo Child Long Lance and Forsberg, ed., *Redman Echoes*, 73–74.

13. Trafzer et al., Introduction to *Boarding School Blues*, 19.

14. Trafzer et al., Introduction, 1.

15. Sylvester Long, "The Story of Carlisle Indian Military School," in Long and Forsberg, *Redman Echoes*, 14.

16. Adams, *Education for Extinction*, 186.

17. Anderson, *Carlisle vs. Army*, 277.

18. Deloria, *Indians in Unexpected Places*, 116. Susan Kollin notes: "The sport of football is not just comparable to war but at times may even exceed some aspects of war in the violence and savagery it unleashes on the field" (*Captivating Westerns*, 11).

19. Smith, *Chief Buffalo Child Long Lance*, 55.

20. Smith, *Chief Buffalo Child Long Lance*, 71–80.

21. Smith, *Chief Buffalo Child Long Lance*, 131.

22. Smith, *Chief Buffalo Child Long Lance*, 141–42.

23. Smith, *Chief Buffalo Child Long Lance*, 147, 156.

24. Smith, *Chief Buffalo Child Long Lance*, 184, 188–89.

25. Chief Buffalo Child Long Lance (Sylvester Long), *Long Lance*, 2. Subsequent references to this edition appear parenthetically in the text.

26. Wong, *Sending My Heart Back*, 13–14. Brumble also writes that "autobiography was not a genre indigenous to Indian cultures" (*American Indian Autobiography*, 131).

27. Smith, *Chief Buffalo Child Long Lance*, 232.

28. Smith, *Chief Buffalo Child Long Lance*, 22.

29. Aleiss, *Making the White Man's Indian*, 41.

30. Carver, *The Silent Enemy*, DVD.

31. Aleiss, *Making the White Man's Indian*, 41.

32. See Davis, *Hand Talk*, and Sebeok and Sebeok, eds., *Aboriginal Sign Languages*. Volume 1 includes "Introduction to the Study of Sign Languages among the North American Indians as Illustrating the Gesture Speech of Mankind" and "A Collection of Gesture-Signs and Signals of the North American Indians with Some Comparisons," both originally published in 1880 by Garrick Mallery, an early American ethnologist.

33. For an analysis of this popular pastime, as it manifested itself in the early twentieth century, see Deloria, *Playing Indian*, 96–101.

34. Chief Buffalo Child Long Lance (Sylvester Long), *How to Talk in the Indian Sign Language*, 26.

35. Smith, *Chief Buffalo Child Long Lance*, 147.

36. Browder, "'One Hundred Percent American,'" 119; Micco, "Tribal Re-Creations," 74.

37. Smith, *Chief Buffalo Child Long Lance*, 147.

38. Carlisle founder General Richard Henry Pratt recalls this incident in his autobiography, *Battlefield and Classroom*, 136–37.

39. Deloria, *Indians in Unexpected Places*, 124.

40. Williams, "Editor's Introduction," in Chief Buffalo Child Long Lance, *How to Talk*, 1–2.

41. Kilpatrick, *Celluloid Indians*, 5.

42. Vestal, "The Hollywooden Indian," 64.

43. Dench, "Making the Movies" (1915), cited in Raheja, *Reservation Reelism*, 37.

44. Kilpatrick, *Celluloid Indians*, 34.

45. Raheja, *Reservation Reelism*, 8, 13.

### 5. L'Ouest Bohème

1. Sayer, *The Coasts of Bohemia*, 6.

2. For a history of the term "Bohemian," see Levin, *Bohemia in America*, 4; Cottom, *International Bohemia*, 4; Parry, *Garrets and Pretenders*, xxi; and Durrans, *Influence of French Culture*, 125.

3. Parry, *Garrets and Pretenders*, xxi; Harris, *George Sand*, 128–29; and Graña, Preface to Graña and Graña, eds. *On Bohemia*, xv.

4. Levin, *Bohemia in America*, 243, 286; Cottom, *International Bohemia*, 4, 23.

5. Butler, *Bodies That Matter*, 149; Roberts, *The New Immigration*, 4. In "The Immigrant Experience in the Gilded Age," Daniels explains the difference between "old" and "new" trends in nineteenth-century U.S. immigration. In the early and mid-nineteenth century, the majority of immigrants came from western Europe. However, by the early 1880s more immigrants began arriving from eastern and southern Europe. See Calhoun, ed., *The Gilded Age*, 87.

6. Evelyn I. Funda suggests that Cather may also have known Bohemian immigrants later when she lived in Pittsburgh and New York City. See Funda, "Picturing Their Ántonia(s)," 355.

7. Porter, *On the Divide*, 4, 8.

8. The legend of Libuša, as well as other stories in early Czech folklore and history, are discussed in *The Chronicle of the Czechs*, written by Cosmas of Prague between 1119 and 1125 (trans. Wolverton, 40–52) and by Agnew in *The Czechs*, 12, 83. According to legend, Libuša eventually married a "ploughman" named Premysl, who assumed leadership of the family dynasty. This term recalls the plough in Cather's *My Ántonia*, which symbolizes the settlement of the Nebraska prairie by farmers such as the Bohemian immigrant Mr. Shimerda (237). Subsequent references to this edition appear parenthetically in the text.

9. See, for example, Lindemann, who writes about Cather's sexual "coming of age" in *Willa Cather*, 2–4, and in her introduction to *The Cambridge Companion to Willa Cather*, 3–4. Faderman examines Cather's transition from women's to men's clothing in *Odd Girls and Twilight Lovers*, 53; while Lee notes that at least one Nebraska local called Cather "that morpheedite" (*Willa Cather*, 3).

10. Brown and Edel, *Willa Cather*, 49; Bennett, *The World of Willa Cather*, 30–31.

11. Shaw, *Willa Cather and the Art of Conflict*, 67.

12. O'Brien, *Willa Cather: The Emerging Voice*, 99.

13. Shively, ed., *Writings from Willa Cather's Campus Years*, 122.

14. For a discussion of Cather's interest in French culture and its impact on her writing, see Durrans, *Influence of French Culture*.

15. Slote, ed., *Kingdom of Art*, 410.

16. Lee, *Willa Cather*, 11.

17. Porter, *On the Divide*, xx.

18. Lindeman, Introduction to *The Cambridge Companion to Willa Cather*, 6.

19. Rosowski, *The Voyage Perilous*, 5.

20. Reynolds, *Willa Cather in Context*, 46, 73.

21. Sergeant, *Willa Cather: A Memoir*, 25.

22. Byrne and Snyder, *Chrysalis*, 3.

23. Rosowski, *The Voyage Perilous*, 224.

24. Rosowski, *The Voyage Perilous*, 225.

25. Byrne and Snyder, *Chrysalis*, 43, 55.

26. Rosowski, *The Voyage Perilous*, 230.

27. Cather, *Selected Letters*, 39.

28. Slote, ed., *Kingdom of Art*, 410. César Graña claims that Bohemia is usually represented by "people of excitable imaginations and modest talent, a combination which disables them for an ordinary existence and forces them, as consolation, to a life of dedicated unconventionality." See "The Ideological Significance of Bohemian Life," in Graña and Graña, *On Bohemia*, 3.

29. Rosowski, *The Voyage Perilous*, 224. James Woodress also writes about the relationship between business-created wealth and the arts in Pittsburgh (*Willa Cather*, 79).

30. Rosowski, *The Voyage Perilous*, 225.

31. Cather, "The Bohemian Girl," in *Stories, Poems, and Other Writings*, 126. Subsequent references to this edition appear parenthetically in the text.

32. Parry, *Garrets and Pretenders*, xxiii.

33. Bonham, *Willa Cather*, 64-66.

34. Rosowski, *The Voyage Perilous*, 226.

35. Parry, *Garrets and Pretenders*, 102, 106, 267.

36. Cottom, *International Bohemia*, 11.

37. Rosowski, *The Voyage Perilous*, 395.

38. Cather, *O Pioneers!*, 111.

39. Nelson, *Willa Cather*, 80.

40. For an analysis of Sand's literary influence on Cather, see Durrans, *Influence of French Culture*, 85-99. O'Brien also notes similarities between these transatlantic writers, describing Sand as an "androgynous figure who adopted a male pseudonym, at times wore male attire, and scandalized the bourgeoisie" (186).

41. Bennett, *The World of Willa Cather*, 3.

42. Cottom, *International Bohemia*, 5.

43. Espín, *Women Crossing Boundaries*, 7.

44. Espín notes that a second language may enable speakers to address topics that would be considered taboo in their native cultures (*Women Crossing Boundaries*, 138-39).

45. Sergeant, *Willa Cather: A Memoir*, 139.

46. Urgo, "The Cather Thesis," in *Cambridge Companion*, 42.

47. Reynolds, *Willa Cather in Context*, 73, 77.

48. Reynolds, *Willa Cather in Context*, 46–48.

49. The only other reference to Bohemians and bohemian artists appears in *The Song of the Lark* (1915), in which Cather compares the aspiring singer Thea Kronberg to a gypsy. For an analysis of this passage, see Durrans, *Influence of French Culture*, 95.

50. Urgo adds that "American culture, as examined through Cather's texts, is rooted in the vigilant maintenance of unsettled lives, impermanent connections, and continuous movements in space and time" (*Willa Cather and the Myth of American Migration*, 15–17).

## 6. A Homeless Snail

1. Cather, "Two Poets," 579.

2. Winchester, *A Crack in the Edge*, 182. For statistics relating to San Francisco's rapid population growth, see Boyd, *Wide-Open Town*, 3.

3. Winchester, *A Crack in the Edge*, 185.

4. For information about the reconstruction of San Francisco after the 1906 earthquake, see Winchester, *A Crack in the Edge*, 271; Kennedy, *The Great Earthquake and Fire*, 4–5; and Wyatt, *Five Fires*, 109–12.

5. Marberry, *Splendid Poseur*, 64.

6. Starr, *Americans and the California Dream*, 242.

7. Austen, *Genteel Pagan*, 24.

8. Rhodehamel and Wood, *Ina Coolbrith*, 58–80; George, *Ina Coolbrith*, 4–19.

9. Starr, *Americans and the California Dream*, 242.

10. Sueyoshi, *Queer Compulsions*, 49.

11. Sueyoshi, *Queer Compulsions*, 41–42.

12. Azuma, *Between Two Empires*, 10, 22–23.

13. Azuma, *Between Two Empires*, 19.

14. Atherton, *My San Francisco*, i.

15. Atherton, *My San Francisco*, 231–37.

16. Duus, *Life of Isamu Noguchi*, 14.

17. Yone Noguchi, *The Story of Yone Noguchi*, 16.

18. Sueyoshi, *Queer Compulsions*, 21.

19. Duus, *Life of Isamu Noguchi*, 18.

20. Franey, Introduction to Noguchi, *American Diary of a Japanese Girl*, xv.

21. Noguchi, "The Region Beyond the Torii: An Apology," in *Later Essays*, 125.

22. Noguchi, *The Story of Yone Noguchi*, 57–58.

23. George, *Ina Coolbrith*, 158–60.

24. Sueyoshi, *Discriminating Sex*, 2. For an analysis of the feminization and queering of Asian and Asian American men in American literature, see Eng, *Racial Castration*.

25. Austen, *Genteel Pagan*, 18.

26. Miller, *Life Amongst the Modocs*, 11.

27. Sueyoshi, *Queer Compulsions*, 24.

28. Noguchi and Hakutani, Introduction to *Selected Writings of Yone Noguchi*, 21.

29. Duus, *Life of Isamu Noguchi*, 14.

30. Noguchi, *The Story of Yone Noguchi*, 1, 6.

31. Sueyoshi, *Queer Compulsions*, 29.

32. Cather, "Two Poets," 580.

33. Cather, *My Ántonia*, 60, 228.

34. Noguchi and Burgess, Introduction to *Seen and Unseen*, vi–vii.

35. Noguchi, *Hiroshige and Japanese Landscapes*, 24–25.

36. Sailor, "'You Must Become Dreamy,'" 7, 19.

37. Sailor, "'You Must Become Dreamy,'" 1.

38. Noguchi, *The Voice of the Valley*, 18.

39. Noguchi, *Later Essays*, 63.

40. Sueyoshi, *Queer Compulsions*, 37–43.

41. Sueyoshi, *Queer Compulsions*, 47–48.

42. Duus, *Life of Isamu Noguchi*, 24–25.

43. Sueyoshi, *Queer Compulsions*, 33.

44. See, for example, "To Charles W. Stoddard," a poem in which Noguchi refers to them as "two shy stars, west and east." In Noguchi, *From the Eastern Sea*, 17.

45. Noguchi, *The Story of Yone Noguchi*, 23.

46. Noguchi, *American Diary of a Japanese Girl*, 15–16.

47. Edward Marx notes that American reviewers referred to "Miss Morning Glory" as a "Japanese Mary MacLane." See "Afterword," in Noguchi, *American Diary of a Japanese Girl*, 138.

48. Franey, Introduction to Noguchi, *American Diary of a Japanese Girl*, xi–xiii.

49. Noguchi, *American Diary of a Japanese Girl*, 35, 61, 67.

50. For a history of Kabuki theater, its relation to Noh, and its evolution over time, see Scott, *The Kabuki Theatre of Japan*, 35–36; and Kawatake, *Kabuki*, 125. For a discussion of the onnagata, see Isaka, *Onnagata*, 5, 10, 45; and Leiter, Introduction to Leiter, ed., *A Kabuki Reader*, xxviii.

51. Noguchi and Nitobe, Introduction to Noguchi, *From the Eastern Sea*, 2–3.

52. Noguchi, *Voice of the Valley*, 15.

53. Noguchi, *American Diary of a Japanese Girl*, 9.

54. Miller and Noguchi, *Japan of Sword and Love*, 4.

55. Miller and Noguchi, *Japan of Sword and Love*, 3, 8.

56. Marx writes that Japanese critics continue "to regard Noguchi as an essentially foreign writer," paying little attention to his works ("Afterword," 142).

57. See "Debussy in Japan," in Noguchi, *Later Essays*, and Noguchi, *The Ganges Calls Me*.

58. Marx, Introduction to Noguchi, *Later Essays*, 3–4.

59. Azuma, *Between Two Empires*, 6.

60. Noguchi, "The Region Beyond the Torii: An Apology," in *Later Essays*, 124–25.

## 7. The Past Is the Biggest Country

1. Nordhoff, *California*, 19.

2. Holmgren, *Starring Madame Modjeska*, 385.

3. See Modjeska, *Memories and Impressions*, 17; Coleman, *Fair Rosalind*, 1.

4. Modjeska, *Memories and Impressions*, 114, 154, 346.

5. Coleman and Coleman, *Wanderers Twain*, 11, 17.

6. For a discussion of the 1849 French drama, authored by Ernest Legouvé and Eugène Scribe, see Richtman, *Adrienne Lecouvreur*, 14.

7. Legouvé and Scribe, in Richtmann, *Adrienne Lecouvreur*, 50, 55.

8. Holmgren, *Starring Madame Modjeska*, 247. The author also cites a letter written by Modrzejewska to the wife of the editor of the *Polish Gazette* in March 1877, in which she acknowledges that "performing on the American stage 'had been my secret plan from the beginning of our venture'" (308).

9. Modjeska, *Memories and Impressions*, 248–49.

10. Coleman and Coleman, *Wanderers Twain*, 75.

11. Sienkiewicz, "A Comedy of Errors: A Sketch from American Life," in Sienkiewicz and Obst, *Henryk Sienkiewicz: Three Stories*, 3.

12. Modjeska, *Memories and Impressions*, 288–89.

13. Modjeska, *Memories and Impressions*, 296–302. Taking a cue from Modjeska, her biographer also portrayed the actress as a pampered dilettante and comic snob. "Was it for this she had come all these thousands of miles, to stand over a cookstove, and wash the linen of her inferiors?" (Coleman and Coleman, *Wanderers Twain*, 48)

14. As quoted in Coleman and Coleman, *Wanderers Twain*, 39.

15. Sontag, *In America*, 222. Subsequent references to this edition appear parenthetically in the text.

16. Holmgren, *Starring Madame Modjeska*, 355, 385, 400, 414.

17. Holmgren, *Starring Madame Modjeska*, 471.

18. Holmgren, *Starring Madame Modjeska*, 323.

19. Coleman and Coleman, *Wanderers Twain*, 117.

20. Coleman and Coleman, *Wanderers Twain*, 92, i.

21. Holmgren, *Starring Madame Modjeska*, 573, 592.

22. Holmgren, *Starring Madame Modjeska*, 593, 355–69.

23. Americans embraced Modjeska despite her "foreignness," as it did her nephew, Władysław Teodor (W.T.) Benda. The Polish immigrant came to the United States in 1899 and soon established a successful career as an artist.

At a time when magazines and other illustrated periodicals were publishing portraits of the typical "American Girl," Benda developed a reputation for drawing women who looked more ethnic or exotic. For this reason, Willa Cather chose him to illustrate the first edition of *My Ántonia* (1918), in which the titular heroine is a female Bohemian immigrant.

24. Holmgren, *Starring Madame Modjeska*, 349.

25. Holmgren, *Starring Madame Modjeska*, 335.

26. Payne, "Thomas Payne in His Own Words," 52, 20.

27. Coleman and Coleman, *Wanderers Twain*, i.

28. Polatynska and Polatynska, "Diogenes Club: A Few Words about Theatres in Warsaw, or Where Sang Irene Adler," November 21, 2000, http://www.diogenes-club.com.

29. Doyle, "A Scandal in Bohemia," in *Sherlock Holmes*, 209, 227.

30. Cather, *My Mortal Enemy*, 38.

31. Sontag, *In America*, i.

32. Holmgren, *Starring Madame Modjeska*, 414, 431.

33. Susan Sontag, "I Believe in Transformation. It's the Most American Thing to Me," *Irish Times*, June 10, 2000.

34. See Doreen Carvajal, "So Whose Words Are They? Susan Sontag Creates A Stir," *New York Times on the Web*, May 27, 2000, https://movies2.nytimes.com/library/books/052700sontag-america.html; and Ed Vulliamy, "Sontag Pleads Poetic License in Using Uncredited 'Scraps of History,'" *Guardian*, May 27, 2000, https://www.theguardian.com/world/2000/may/28/books.booksnews.

35. Vuillamy, "Sontag Pleads Poetic License."

36. Carvajal, "So Whose Words Are They?"

37. Holmgren, *Starring Madame Modjeska*, 246, 446–64.

38. Coleman and Coleman, *Wanderers Twain*, 65.

39. Jacobson, *Special Sorrows*, 18, 33.

40. As cited in Jacobson, *Special Sorrows*, 14.

41. Jacobson, *Special Sorrows*, 35.

42. Holmgren, *Starring Madame Modjeska*, 581, 587.

43. Holmgren, *Starring Madame Modjeska*, 385, 355.

44. Enss, *Entertaining Women*, vii–viii, 106–17; Holmgren, *Starring Madame Modjeska*, 339. For more information on the lives and careers of actresses in Gold Rush California, see Rourke, *Troupers of the Gold Coast*.

45. Holmgren, *Starring Madame Modjeska*, 574.

46. Holmgren, *Starring Madame Modjeska*, 675–76.

47. Holmgren, *Starring Madame Modjeska*, 68, 563.

48. William Shakespeare, *As You Like It* 2. 7. 138–41.

## 8. Deutschland über Alles

1. Earlier authors, who based their work on first-hand research, include Charles Sealsfield, Friedrich Gerstäker, Armand Strubberg, and Balduin Möllhauser.
2. Cracroft, "American West of Karl May," 255, 257.
3. May, *My Life and My Efforts*, 100. Subsequent references to this edition appear parenthetically in the text.
4. For information about May's career as a criminal, see Walther, *Karl May*, 40–50, 71–72; and Schmidt, *Karl May*, 33.
5. Wernitznig, *Europe's Indians, Indians in Europe*, 57.
6. Schmidt, *Karl May*, 43.
7. May, *Winnetou, the Chief of the Apache*, 555. The first three novels in the *Winnetou* series were originally published separately in 1893 under the following titles: *Winnetou I* or *Winnetou der Rote Gentleman I* (*Winnetou the Red Gentleman I*), *Winnetou II* or *Winnetou der Rote Gentleman II* (*Winnetou the Red Gentleman II*), and *Winnetou III* or *Winnetou der Rote Gentleman III* (*Winnetou the Red Gentleman III*). Subsequent references to this three-volume edition appear parenthetically in the text.
8. The phrase comes from a speech that Theodore Roosevelt delivered in 1899.
9. May, *The Treasure of Silver Lake*, 45.
10. May, *The Son of Bear Hunter*, 102. Subsequent references to this edition appear parenthetically in the text.
11. Nash, *Wilderness and the American Mind*, 8.
12. Cracroft, "American West of Karl May," 255.
13. Green, *Fatherlands*, 223.
14. May and Thomas, *The Ghost of the Llano Estacado*, 5.
15. Fiorentino, "'Those Red-Brick Faces,'" in Feest, ed., *Indians and Europe*, 408.
16. Wernitznig, *Europe's Indians, Indians in Europe*, 35.
17. Lawrence, *Studies in Classic American Literature*, 58.
18. Green, *Fatherlands*, 299.
19. Schneider, "Finding a New Heimat in the Wild West," 53–54.
20. Lutz, "German Indianthusiasm," in Calloway et al., *Germans and Indians*, 171.
21. Blackbourn, *The Long Nineteenth Century*, 391.
22. Kaes, *From Hitler to Heimat*, 165.
23. Blackbourn, *The Long Nineteenth Century*, 390–91.
24. Tompkins, *West of Everything*, 132.
25. Perry, "Reconsidering Winnetou," in Varner, ed., *New Wests and Post-Wests*, 216n.7.
26. Bachelard, *Poetics of Space*, 5.
27. Bachelard, *Poetics of Space*, 31.

28. May, *The Oil Prince*, 1, 135. Subsequent references to this edition appear parenthetically in the text.

29. Sammons, *Ideology, Mimesis, Fantasy*, 231.

30. Blickle, *Heimat*, 7.

31. Bachelard, *Poetics of Space*, 184.

32. Cracroft, "The American West of Karl May," 257; Wernitznig, *Europe's Indians, Indians in Europe*, 61.

33. Wernitznig, *Europe's Indians, Indians in Europe*, 65.

34. For an analysis of the ideological inconsistencies of National Socialism, see Theweleit, *Male Fantasies*, vol. 2: Male *Bodies*, 351.

35. Christian Feest, "Germany's Indians in a European Perspective," in Calloway et al., eds., *Germans and Indians*, 178.

36. For discussions of the term *volk* and its significance for the National Socialist Party, see Lutz, "German Indianthusiasm," in Calloway et al., eds., *Germans and Indians*, 170-71; and Blackbourn, *The Long Nineteenth Century*, 394. In *Mein Kamp*, trans. Murphy, Hitler wrote that "the *volkish* concept of the world recognizes that the primordial racial elements are of the greatest significance for mankind" (167).

37. Sammons, *Ideology, Mimesis, Fantasy*, 235.

38. "If a nation confines itself to 'internal colonization' while other races are perpetually increasing their territorial annexations all over the globe, that nation will be forced to restrict the numerical growth of its population at a time when the other nations are increasing theirs." In Hitler, *Mein Kampf*, 67. The book originally appeared in two volumes, published in 1925 and 1927.

39. Theweleit, *Male Bodies*, 2:272.

40. Theweleit, *Male Bodies*, 2:272.

41. Bachelard, *Poetics of Space*, 31.

42. For an account of Hitler's attitudes toward film and other forms of pictorial representation, see Niven, *Hitler and Film*, 2.

43. Kracauer, *From Caligari to Hitler*, 20. After World War I a cult of masculinity continued to prevail in Germany, as Theweleit demonstrates in his companion study, *Male Fantasies*, vol. 1. Here he explains the connection between German men's "dread of women" and their "hatred of communism and the rebellious working class." See also Barbara Ehrenreich's foreword in Theweleit, *Male Fantasies*, 1:ix-xv. This attitude shifted during the 1930s, as the National Socialist Party began to realize that it was necessary to convince women as well as men to support the war.

44. Tegel, *Nazis and the Cinema*, 150.

45. For a comparative study of domestic and romantic melodramas, see Heins, *Nazi Film Melodrama*, 46-48, 96-97.

46. Heins, *Nazi Film Melodrama*, 21, 46. Anker examines more recent uses of melodramatic political discourse, which "identifies the nation-state as a virtuous and innocent victim of villainous action" in a post-9/11 world. See Anker, *Orgies of Feeling*, 2.

47. German, "The European Imperial Gaze and Native American Representation in American Film," in Varner, ed., *New Wests and Post-Wests*, 187–88.

48. Heins, *Nazi Film Melodrama*, 14, 21.

49. Author unknown, "Translator's Introduction," in May, *My Life and My Efforts*, 6.

50. Fiedler, *Return of the Vanishing American*, 51. Wernitznig also comments on Winnetou's feminine appearance (*Europe's Indians, Indians in Europe*, 61), as does Feest, who suggests that Winnetou's "hermaphrodite beauty . . . renders this figure open to multiple desires and identifications, not only in terms of erotic attraction, but also as incorporating everything an imperialist may hope for in a colonial subject" (see "Germany's Indians in a European Perspective," in Calloway et al., eds., *Germans and Indians*, 176). Writing about May's fiction, Perry notes: "A love interest, if introduced into the plot, is either a past event, or the prospective lover is killed during the development of the narrative. . . . Interracial love interests are generally avoided" ("Reconsidering Winnetou," in Varner, ed., *New Wests and Post-Wests*, 216n.7). Cracroft also points to the absence of women and the death of Old Shatterhand's same-sex partner in arguing for a homoerotic reading of May's works ("The American West of Karl May," 253).

51. Heins, *Nazi Film Melodrama*, 14.

52. Kracauer, *From Caligari to Hitler*, 20.

53. Heins, *Nazi Film Melodrama*, 25, 47, 50.

54. May did not endorse Hitler, though his second wife, Klara, "affiliated herself with the Nazi Regime" after his death (Wernitznig, *Europe's Indians, Indians in Europe*, 61).

## 9. The Problem of Representation

1. Mantell-Seidel, *Isadora Duncan in the Twenty-First Century*, 15.

2. Blair, *Isadora*, xii.

3. Duncan, *My Life*, 305.

4. Stokes, *Isadora Duncan*, 119.

5. Duncan, "I Was Born in America," in *Isadora Speaks*, 23.

6. Turner, "Significance of the Frontier," 33, 32.

7. Turner, "Significance of the Frontier," 38.

8. Starr, *Americans and the California Dream*, 379.

9. Terry, *Isadora Duncan*, 115.

10. Duncan, *My Life*, 22.
11. Duncan, "I Was Born in America," 36; Duncan, "The Dance of the Future," in Cheney, ed., *The Art of the Dance*, 55. Anderson notes that Art Nouveau was also an influence on later practitioners of modern American dance who sought to naturalize the movement of the human body. "The product of an urban culture," Art Nouveau "claimed the importance of nature by favoring sinuous, flowing lines and shapes inspired by vines, flowers, tendrils, wind-blown grass, and swirling waves." See Anderson, *Art without Boundaries*, 10.
12. Turner, "Significance of the Frontier," 33.
13. Duncan, *My Life*, 194.
14. Blair, *Isadora*, 356.
15. Margherita Duncan, "Isadora," in Cheney, ed., *Isadora Duncan*, 23.
16. Thorpe, *Creating a Ballet*, 63.
17. Duncan, *My Life*, 11.
18. Duncan, *My Life*, 8–9.
19. Gertrude Stein, "The Gradual Making of the Making of Americans," as quoted in Daly, *Done into Dance*, 11.
20. Cheney, Introduction to Cheney, ed., *Isadora Duncan*, 6.
21. Duncan, *My Life*, 3, 60.
22. Duncan, *My Life*, 95; Terry, *Isadora Duncan*, 27.
23. Duncan, "Isadora's Last Dance," in Cheney, ed., *The Art of the Dance*, 13.
24. Duncan, in Rosemont, ed., *Isadora Speaks*, 31.
25. Cheney, Introduction, 5.
26. In "Significance of the Frontier," Turner referred to the settlement of the U.S. West as "the closing of a great historic movement" (31).
27. Putney, *Muscular Christianity*, 4, 6. See also, Vance, *The Sinews of the Spirit*, 1.
28. Rosemont, ed., *Isadora Speaks*, 58.
29. Duncan, *My Life*, 152.
30. Duncan, *My Life*, 2.
31. Turner, "Significance of the Frontier," 32, 36, 31.
32. Blair, *Isadora*, 37.
33. Laban, with Ullmann, ed., *Choreutics*, 18. Campbell discusses the theory of Labanotation in *The Ecstasy of Being*. According to Campbell, the system clarifies and maps "all the possibilities of exteriorization and extension-into-space," including "twelve primary directions" in which a dancer's body might move (129).
34. Naerebout, "In Search of a Dead Rat," in MacIntosh, ed., *Ancient Dancer*, 42–44.
35. Smith, "Reception or Deception?," in MacIntosh, ed., *Ancient Dancer*, 78.
36. Gittings, *John Keats*, 310–11.

37. Terry, *Isadora Duncan*, 58.

38. Graham, *Blood Memory*, 43-44.

39. Smith, in MacIntosh, ed., *Ancient Dancer*, 77.

40. Duncan, *My Life*, 75.

41. See, for example, sculptures by Demetre H. Chiaparus, Antoine Bourdelle, and Edmund Gomanski.

42. Magriel, Preface to Magriel, ed., *Isadora Duncan*, 5.

43. Stokes, *Isadora Duncan*, 16, 25, 30.

44. Nanney, *John Dos Passos*, 1.

45. Dos Passos, *The Big Money*, 154-61.

46. Sinclair, *World's End*, 193.

47. Sinclair, *Between Two Worlds*, 164.

48. Wanshel, *Isadora Duncan Sleeps with the Russian Navy*, 10, 13, 24.

49. MacDougall, "Isadora Duncan and the Artists," in Magriel, ed., *Isadora Duncan*, 37.

50. De Mille, Foreword to Duncan, Pratl, and Splatt, eds., *Life into Art*, 7, 9.

51. Daly, *Done into Dance*, ix-x.

52. Blair, *Isadora Duncan*, 46.

53. Lanza, *Phallic Frenzy*, 48.

54. Hook, Introduction to Hook, ed., *Dos Passos*, 1, 11.

55. *Isadora*, directed by Karel Reisz, Universal Pictures, 1968.

56. Duncan, *My Life*, 322.

57. Geduld, "Performing Communism in the American Dance," 44, 55.

58. Duncan, *My Life*, 61.

59. Geduld, "Performing Communism in the American Dance," 44, 55.

60. Geduld, "Performing Communism in the American Dance," 44.

61. Marx and Engels, *The Communist Manifesto*, 62. Franko writes about the ideological shift from modern American dance to socialist expressions of group solidarity in *The Work of Dance*, 2-3, 39-47. Denning elaborates on the role that movement culture played in promoting socialist dance in *The Cultural Front*, 67-77.

62. Franko, *The Work of Dance*, 2.

63. Daniels, *The Rise and Fall of Communism in Russia*, 25.

64. Kurth, *Isadora*, 555-56.

65. "Bury Me Not on the Lone Prairie" was orally composed and originally sung by cowboys in the late nineteenth century. In Lomax and Lomax's edited folklore collection *Cowboy Songs and Other Frontier Ballads*, the song was retitled "The Dying Cowboy" (49). It is also sometimes referred to as "The Cowboy's Lament."

## Afterword

1. Editors John A. Lomax and Alan Lomax retitled the song "The Dying Cowboy" in their landmark western folklore anthology, *Cowboy Songs and Other Frontier Ballads*, 49. Subsequent references to this edition appear parenthetically in the text.

2. Because these songs were orally and collectively composed by cowboys and then circulated among other members of their profession, it is impossible to determine when the song originated or who authored the original version. However, since cowboys worked in large numbers only during the last few decades of the nineteenth century, it is reasonable to assume "Bury Me Not on the Lone Prairie" dates from this period.

3. This process began in the late 1980s. See, for example, Limerick, *The Legacy of Conquest*; White, *"It's Your Misfortune"*; and Cronon, *Nature's Metropolis*.

4. McMurtry chose this phrase as the title for a collection of essays that examines the West from both nostalgic and revisionist perspectives. See *In a Narrow Grave*.

5. In addition to this song, the anthology includes an entire section on western music, entitled "Pioneer Memories." See Sandburg, ed., *The American Songbag*, 89–124.

6. Sandburg, "Chicago," reprinted in *The Complete Poems of Carl Sandburg*, 3.

7. King, *Mountaineering in the Sierra Nevada*, 168.

# Bibliography

Adams, David Wallace. *Education for Extinction: American Indians and the Boarding School Experience, 1875-1928*. Lawrence: University of Kansas Press, 1995.

Adams, Henry. "King." In *Clarence King Memoirs: The Helmet of Mambrino*, 167–71. New York: Putnam, 1904.

Adams, Ramon F. *The Cowboy Dictionary: The Chin Jaw Words and Whing-Ding Ways of the American West*. 1963; reprint ed. New York: Perigee Books, 1993.

Agnew, Hugh LeCaine. *The Czechs and the Lands of the Bohemian Crown*. Stanford CA: Hoover Institution Press, 2007.

Aleiss, Angela. *Making the White Man's Indian: Native Americans and Hollywood Movies*. Westport CT: Praeger, 2005.

Allmendinger, Blake. *The Cowboy: Representations of Labor in an American Work Culture*. New York: Oxford University Press, 1992.

———. *Imagining the African American West*. Lincoln: University of Nebraska Press, 2005.

Amaral, Anthony. *Will James, the Last Cowboy Legend*. 1967; reprint ed. Reno: University of Nevada Press, 1980.

Anderson, Jack. *Art without Boundaries: The World of Modern Dance*. Iowa City: University of Iowa Press, 1997.

Anderson, Lars. *Carlisle vs. Army: Jim Thorpe, Dwight Eisenhower, Pop Warner, and the Forgotten Story of Football's Greatest Battle*. New York: Random House, 2007.

Anker, Elisabeth R. *Orgies of Feeling: Melodrama and the Politics of Freedom*. Durham NC: Duke University Press, 2014.

Atherton, Gertrude. *My San Francisco: A Wayward Biography*. New York: Bobbs-Merrill, 1946.

Austen, Roger. *Genteel Pagan: The Double Life of Charles Warren Stoddard*. Edited by John William Crowley. Amherst: University of Massachusetts Press, 1991.

Austin, Mary. *The Land of Little Rain*. 1903; reprint ed. Penguin Nature Library. New York: Penguin Books, 1988.

Azuma, Eiichiro. *Between Two Empires: Race, History, and Transnationalism in Japanese America*. New York: Oxford University Press, 2005.

Bachelard, Gaston. *The Poetics of Space*. 1958; reprint ed. New York: Beacon, 1992.

Baudrillard, Jean. *Simulacra and Simulation*. Translated by Sheila Faria Glaser. 1981; reprint ed. Ann Arbor: University of Michigan Press, 1994.

Beckwourth, James P., and Thomas D. Bonner. *The Life and Adventures of James P. Beckwourth, Mountaineer, Scout, and Pioneer, and Chief of the Crow Nation of Indians, Written from His Own Dictation by T. D. Bonner*. 1856; reprint ed. Lincoln: University of Nebraska Press, 1981.

Bennett, Mildred R. *The World of Willa Cather*. New York: Dodd, Mead, 1951.

Black Elk. *Black Elk Speaks: The Complete Edition*. Edited by John G. Neihardt. 1930; reprint ed. Lincoln: University of Nebraska Press, 2014.

Black Hawk. *Black Hawk: An Autobiography*. Edited by Donald Dean Jackson. 1833; reprint ed. Urbana: Prairie State Books, University of Illinois Press, 1990.

Blackbourn, David. *The Long Nineteenth Century: A History of Germany, 1780–1918*. New York: Oxford University Press, 1998.

Blair, Fredrika. *Isadora: Portrait of the Artist as a Woman*. New York: McGraw Hill, 1986.

Blickle, Peter. *Heimat: A Critical Theory of the German Idea of Homeland*. Rochester NY: Camden House, 2002.

Bold, Christine. *The Frontier Club: Popular Westerns and Cultural Power, 1880–1924*. New York: Oxford University Press, 2013.

Bonham, Barbara. *Willa Cather*. Philadelphia: Chilton, 1970.

Bothwell, Robert. *Canada and Quebec: One Country, Two Histories*. Vancouver: University of British Columbia Press, 1995.

Boyd, Nan Alamilla. *Wide Open Town: A History of Queer San Francisco to 1965*. Berkeley: University of California Press, 2003.

Briefel, Aviva. *The Deceivers: Art Forgery and Identity in the Nineteenth Century*. Ithaca NY: Cornell University Press, 2006.

Bouchard, Chantal. *Obsessed with Language: A Sociolinguistic History of Quebec*. Trans. Luise von Flotow. Toronto: Guernika, 1998.

Browder, Laura. "'One Hundred Percent American': How a Slave, a Janitor, and a Former Klansman Escaped Racial Categories by Becoming Indian." In *Beyond the Binary: Reconstructing Cultural Identity in a Multicultural Context*, edited by Timothy B Powell, 116–32. New Brunswick NJ: Rutgers University Press, 1999.

Brown, Edward K, and Leon Edel. *Willa Cather: A Critical Biography*. New York: A. A. Knopf, 1953.

Brumble, H. David, III. *American Indian Autobiography*. Berkeley: University of California Press, 1988.

Bruner, Jerome S. *Making Stories: Law, Literature, Life*. New York: Farrar, Straus and Giroux, 2002.

Butler, Anne M. *Daughters of Joy, Sisters of Misery: Prostitutes in the American West, 1865–90*. Urbana: University of Illinois Press, 1985.

Butler, Judith. *Bodies That Matter: On the Discursive Limits of "Sex."* New York: Routledge, 1993.

Byrne, Kathleen D, and Richard Clement Snyder. *Chrysalis: Willa Cather in Pittsburgh, 1896–1906.* Pittsburgh: Historical Society of Western Pennsylvania, 1980.

Calhoun, Charles W., ed. *The Gilded Age: Perspectives on the Origins of Modern America.* Lanham MD: Rowman and Littlefield, 2007.

Campbell, Joseph. *The Ecstasy of Being: Mythology and Dance.* Novato CA: New World Library, 2017.

Carver, H. P., director. *The Silent Enemy.* DVD. Beacon Films, 1930.

Cather, Willa. *My Ántonia.* Edited by Charles W. Mignon and Kari Ronning. 1918; reprint ed. Lincoln: University of Nebraska Press, 1997.

———. *My Mortal Enemy.* 1926; reprint ed. New York: Vintage, 1990.

———. *O Pioneers!* 1913; reprint ed. New York: Vintage, 1992.

———. *The Selected Letters of Willa Cather.* Edited by Andrew Jewell and Janis Stout. New York: Alfred A. Knopf, 2013.

———. *Stories, Poems, and Other Writings.* New York: Library of America, 1992.

———. "Two Poets: Yone Noguchi and Bliss Carman." In *The World and the Parish: Willa Cather's Articles and Reviews, 1893–1902,* edited by William Martin Curtin, vol. 2, 579–80. Lincoln: University of Nebraska Press, 1970.

Certeau, Michel de. *The Practice of Everyday Life.* Translated by Steven Rendall. Berkeley: University of California Press, 1984.

Chandler, Raymond. "The Simple Art of Murder." In *The Simple Art of Murder,* 1–18. 1944; reprint ed. New York: Vintage, 1988.

Chief Buffalo Child Long Lance (Sylvester Long). *How to Talk in the Indian Sign Language.* Edited by Kenneth Williams. Akron OH: B. F. Goodrich Rubber Company, 1930.

———. *Long Lance.* Foreword by Irvin S. Cobb. New York: Cosmopolitan, 1928; reprint ed. Jackson: University of Mississippi Press, 1995.

[Chief] Buffalo Child Long Lance and Roberta Forsberg, ed. *Redman Echoes: Comprising the Writings of Chief Buffalo Child Long Lance and Biographical Sketches by His Friends.* Literary Licensing-openlibrary.org, 2011.

Clappe, Louise Amelia Knapp Smith [Shirley]. *The Shirley Letters from the California Mines, 1851–1852.* Edited by Marlene Smith-Baranzini. 1851–52; reprint ed. Berkeley CA: Heyday Books, 1998.

Cobb, Irvin S. Foreword to Long Lance, *Chief Buffalo Child Long Lance,* i–xxxviii. 1928; reprint ed. Jackson: University of Mississippi Press, 1995.

Cohen, Paul E. *Mapping the West: America's Westward Movement 1524–1890.* New York: Rizzoli, 2002.

Coleman, Arthur Prudden, and Marion Moore Coleman. *Wanderers Twain, Modjeska and Sienkiewicz: A View from California.* Cheshire CT: Cherry Hill Books, 1964.

Coleman, Marion Moore. *Fair Rosalind: The American Career of Helena Modjeska*. Cheshire CT: Cherry Hill Books, 1969.

Cookridge, E. H. *The Baron of Arizona*. New York: John Day Company, 1967.

Correia, David. *Properties of Violence: Law and Land Grant Struggle in Northern New Mexico*. Athens: University of Georgia Press, 2013.

Cosmas Pragensis and Lisa Wolverton. *The Chronicle of the Czechs*. Washington DC: Catholic University of America Press, 2009.

Cottom, Daniel. *International Bohemia: Scenes of Nineteenth-Century Life*. Philadelphia: University of Pennsylvania Press, 2013.

Cracroft, Richard H. "The American West of Karl May." *American Quarterly* 19, no. 2 (1967): 249–58.

Craib, Raymond B. "Cartography and Decolonization." In *Decolonizing the Map: Cartography from Colony to Nation*, edited by James R. Akerman, 16–47. Chicago: University of Chicago Press, 2017.

Crane, Stephen. "The Bride Comes to Yellow Sky." In *The Red Badge of Courage*, edited by Gary Scharnhorst, 149–66. 1898; reprint ed. New York: Penguin Books, 2005.

Daly, Ann. *Done into Dance: Isadora Duncan in America*. Bloomington: Indiana University Press, 1995.

Daniels, Robert V. *The Rise and Fall of Communism in Russia*. New Haven CT: Yale University Press, 2007.

Darwin, Charles. *The Expression of the Emotions in Man and Animals*. London: John Murray, 1872.

Davis, Jeffrey Edward. *Hand Talk: Sign Language among American Indian Nations*. New York: Cambridge University Press, 2010.

Deloria, Philip Joseph. *Indians in Unexpected Places*. Lawrence: University of Kansas Press, 2004.

———. *Playing Indian*. New Haven CT: Yale University Press, 1998.

Deloria, Vine. "Foreword: American Fantasy." In *The Pretend Indians: Images of Native Americans in the Movies*, edited by Gretchen M. Bataille and Charles L. P. Silet, i–xii. Ames: Iowa State University Press, 1980.

Dench, Ernest A. "'Making the Movies' (1915)." In Michelle H. Raheja, *Reservation Reelism*. Lincoln: University of Nebraska Press, 2010.

Denning, Michael. *The Cultural Front: The Laboring of American Culture in the Twentieth Century*. London: Verso, 1997.

———. *Mechanic Accents: Dime Novels and Working-Class Culture in America*. Haymarket Series. London: Verso, 1987.

Dickinson College. Carlisle Indian School Digital Resource Center. Accessed May 13, 2020. http://carlisleindian.dickinson.edu/.

Dickinson, John Alexander, and Brian J. Young. *A Short History of Quebec*. 2nd ed. Toronto: Copp Clark Pitman, 1993.

Dos Passos, John. *The Big Money*. New York: Harcourt Brace, 1936.

Doyle, Arthur Conan. "A Scandal in Bohemia." In *Sherlock Holmes: The Complete Novels and Stories*. 1891; reprint ed. New York: Bantam Books, 1986: 209–29.

Duncan, Dorée, Carol Pratl, and Cynthia Splatt, eds. *Life into Art: Isadora Duncan and Her World*. New York: Norton, 1993.

Duncan, Isadora. *The Art of the Dance*. Edited by Sheldon Cheney. 1902; reprint ed. New York: Theatre Arts Books, 1928.

———. "The Dance of the Future." In *The Art of the Dance*, edited by Sheldon Cheney, 54–55. 1902; reprint ed. New York: Theatre Arts Books, 1928.

———. *Isadora Speaks: Writings and Speeches of Isadora Duncan*. Edited by Franklin Rosemont. 1924; reprint ed. Chicago: Charles H. Kerr Company, 1994.

———. *My Life*. 1927; reprint ed. New York: Norton, 2013.

Duncan, Margherita. "Isadora." In *The Art of the Dance*, edited by Sheldon Cheney, 23–32. 1902; reprint ed. New York: Theatre Arts Books, 1928.

Duncan, Raymond. "Isadora's Last Dance." In *The Art of the Dance*, edited by Sheldon Cheney, 13–25. 1902; reprint ed. New York: Theatre Arts Books, 1928.

Durrans, Stéphanie. *The Influence of French Culture on Willa Cather: Intertextual References and Resonances*. Lewiston NY: Edwin Mellen Press, 2007.

Duus, Masayo. *The Life of Isamu Noguchi: Journey without Borders*. Translated by Peter Duus. Princeton: Princeton University Press, 2000.

Dworkin, Ronald. *A Matter of Principle*. Cambridge MA: Harvard University Press, 1986.

Eastman, Charles A. *Indian Boyhood*. 1902; reprint ed. New York: Dover, 1971.

Ebright, Malcolm. *Land Grants and Law Suits in Northern New Mexico*. Albuquerque: University of New Mexico Press, 1994.

Edwards, Rebecca. *New Spirits: Americans in the Gilded Age, 1865–1905*. New York: Oxford University Press, 2006.

Ehrenreich, Barbara. In *Male Fantasies, Volume 1: Women, Floods, Bodies, History*, translated by Stephen Conway. Minneapolis: University of Minnesota Press, 1987.

Eng, David L. *Racial Castration: Managing Masculinity in Asian America*. Durham NC: Duke University Press, 2007.

Enss, Chris. *Entertaining Women: Actresses, Dancers, and Singers in the Old West*. Guilford CT: TwoDot, 2016.

Espín, Oliva M. *Women Crossing Boundaries: A Psychology of Immigration and Transformations of Sexuality*. New York: Routledge, 1999.

Faderman, Lillian. *Odd Girls and Twilight Lovers: A History of Lesbian Life in Twentieth-Century America*. New York: Columbia University Press, 1991.

Farber, Paul Lawrence. *Mixing Races: From Scientific Racism to Modern Evolutionary Ideas*. Baltimore MD: Johns Hopkins University Press, 2011.

Fear-Segal, Jacqueline, and Susan D. Rose, eds. Introduction to *Carlisle Indian Industrial School: Indigenous Histories, Memories, and Reclamations*, 1–34. Lincoln: University of Nebraska Press, 2016.

Fiedler, Leslie A. *The Return of the Vanishing American*. New York: Stein and Day, 1968.

Fiorentino, Daniele. "'Those Red-Brick Faces': European Press Reactions to the Indians of Buffalo Bill's Wild West Show." In *Indians and Europe: An Interdisciplinary Collection of Essays*, edited by Christian F. Feest, 403–14. Lincoln: University of Nebraska Press, 1999.

Fisher, Philip. "Appearing and Disappearing in Public: Social Space in Late Nineteenth-Century Literature and Culture." In *Reconstructing American Literary History*, edited by Sacvan Bercovitch, 163–82. Harvard English Studies 13. Cambridge MA: Harvard University Press, 1986.

Floyd, Janet. *Claims and Speculations: Mining and Writing in the Gilded Age*. Albuquerque: University of New Mexico Press, 2012.

Franey, Laura E. Introduction to *The American Diary of a Japanese Girl*, edited by Edward Marx and Laura E. Franey. 1902; reprint ed. Philadelphia: Temple University Press, 2007.

Franko, Mark. *The Work of Dance: Labor, Movement, and Identity in the 1930s*. Middletown CT: Wesleyan University Press, 2002.

Funda, Evelyn I. "Picturing Their Ántonia(s): Mikoláš Aleš and the Partnership of W. T. Benda and Willa Cather." In *Willa Cather: A Writer's Worlds*, edited by John J. Murphy, Françoise Palleau-Papin, and Robert Thacker, 353–78. Cather Studies 8. Lincoln: University of Nebraska Press, 2010.

Geduld, Victoria. "Performing Communism in the American Dance: Culture, Politics and the New Dance Group." *American Communist History* 7, no. 1 (June 1, 2008): 39–65.

George, Aleta. *Ina Coolbrith: The Bittersweet Song of California's First Poet Laureate*. Suisin City CA: Shifting Plates Press, 2015.

German, Kathleen M. "The European Imperial Gaze and Native American Representation in American Film." In *New Wests and Post-Wests: Literature and Film of the American West*, edited by Paul Varner, 186–206. Newcastle, UK: Cambridge Scholars, 2013.

Gilman, Susan. *Dark Twins: Imposture and Identity in Mark Twain's America*. Chicago: University of Chicago Press, 1989.

Gittings, Robert. *John Keats*. Boston: Little Brown, 1968.

Godbout, Jacques. *Alias Will James*. National Film Board of Canada, 1988.

Grafton, Anthony. *Forgers and Critics: Creativity and Duplicity in Western Scholarship*. Princeton NJ: Princeton University Press, 1990.

Graham, Martha. *Blood Memory*. New York: Doubleday, 1991.

Graña, Marigay. "Preface." In *On Bohemia: The Code of the Self-Exiled*, edited by César Graña and Mari Graña, i–xxiii. New Brunswick: Transaction Publishers, 1990.

Green, Abigail. *Fatherlands: State-Building and Nationhood in Nineteenth-Century Germany*. New York: Cambridge University Press, 2001.

Griswold del Castillo, Richard. *The Treaty of Guadalupe Hidalgo: A Legacy of Conflict*. Norman: University of Oklahoma Press, 1990.

Gunesh, Konrad. "Multilingualism and Cosmopolitanism." In *The Multilingual Mind: Issues Discussed by, for, and about People Living with Many Languages*, edited by Tracey Tokuhama-Espinosa, 219–37. Westport CT: Praeger, 2003.

Handler, Richard. *Nationalism and the Politics of Culture in Quebec*. Madison: University of Wisconsin Press, 1988.

Harris, Elizabeth. *George Sand*. New Haven CT: Yale University Press, 2004.

Harte, Bret. "The Luck of Roaring Camp." In *Selected Stories and Sketches*, edited by David Wyatt, 7–17. 1868; Reprint ed. New York: Oxford University Press, 1995.

Hayes, Derek. *Historical Atlas of the American West*. Berkeley: University of California Press, 2009.

Heins, Laura. *Nazi Film Melodrama*. Urbana: University of Illinois Press, 2013.

Hitler, Adolf. *Mein Kampf*. Translated by James Murphy. 1939; Reprint ed. San Bernardino CA: White Wolf, 2014.

Holmgren, Beth. *Starring Madame Modjeska: On Tour in Poland and America*. Bloomington: Indiana University Press, 2012.

Hook, Andrew, ed. *Dos Passos: A Collection of Critical Essays*. Englewood Cliffs NJ: Prentice-Hall, 1974.

——. Introduction to *Dos Passos: A Collection of Critical Essays*, edited by Andrew Hook, i–xix. Englewood Cliffs NJ: Prentice-Hall, 1974.

Horsman, Reginald. *Race and Manifest Destiny: The Origins of American Racial Anglo-Saxonism*. Cambridge MA: Harvard University Press, 1981.

Huhndorf, Shari M. *Going Native: Indians in the American Cultural Imagination*. Ithaca NY: Cornell University Press, 2001.

Isaka, Maki. *Onnagata: A Labyrinth of Gendering in Kabuki Theater*. Seattle: University of Washington Press, 2015.

Jacobson, Matthew Frye. *Special Sorrows: The Diasporic Imagination of Irish, Polish, and Jewish Immigrants in the United States*. Cambridge: Harvard University Press, 1995.

James, Will. *The American Cowboy*. New York: Scribner, 1942; reprint ed., Missoula MT: Mountain Press, 2005.

——. *The Drifting Cowboy*. 1925; reprint ed. Billings MT: Will James Art Company, 1995.

————. *Horses I've Known*. 1940; reprint ed. Missoula MT: Mountain Press, 2009.

————. *Lone Cowboy: My Life Story*. 1930; reprint ed. Lincoln: University of Nebraska Press, 1985.

Johnson, Royal A. *Adverse Report of the Surveyor General of Arizona, Royal A. Johnson, upon the Alleged Peralta Grant: A Complete Expose of Its Fraudulent Character*. 1890; reprint ed. Norderstedt, Germany: Hansebooks, 2017.

Johnson, Susan Lee. *Roaring Camp: The Social World of the California Gold Rush*. 2000; reprint ed. New York: W. W. Norton, 2001.

Jurovics, Toby. "Framing the West: The Survey Photographs of Timothy H. O'Sullivan." In *Framing the West: The Survey Photographs of Timothy H. O'Sullivan*, 1–23. New Haven CT: Yale University Press, 2010.

Jurovics, Toby, Carol M. Johnson, Glenn Williamson, and William F. Stapp, eds. *Framing the West: The Survey Photographs of Timothy H. O'Sullivan*. New Haven CT: Yale University Press, 2010.

Kaes, Anton. *From Hitler to Heimat: The Return of History as Film*. Cambridge MA: Harvard University Press, 1992.

Kawatake, Toshio. *Kabuki: Baroque Fusion of the Arts*. Translated by Frank Hoff and Jean Connell Hoff. Tokyo: LTCB International Library Trust–International House of Japan, 2003.

Kennedy, John Castillo. *The Great Earthquake and Fire*. New York: William Morrow, 1963.

Kilpatrick, Jacquelyn. *Celluloid Indians: Native Americans and Film*. Lincoln: University of Nebraska Press, 1999.

King, Clarence. "Catastrophism and Evolution." *American Naturalist* 11, no. 8 (1877): 449–70.

————. "Map of the Nevada Basin." Washington DC: National Archives, Records of the War Department, 1876.

————. *Mountaineering in the Sierra Nevada*. Edited by Francis Peloubet Farquhar. 1872; reprint ed. Bison Books, Lincoln: University of Nebraska Press, 1997.

————. *Systematic Geology: Report of the Geological Exploration of the Fortieth Parallel*. Vol. 1. Washington DC: Government Printing Office, 1878.

Klein, Norman M. *The History of Forgetting: Los Angeles and the Erasure of Memory*. 1997; reprint ed. London: Verso, 2008.

Knoper, Randall K. *Acting Naturally: Mark Twain in the Culture of Performance*. Berkeley CA: University of California Press, 1995.

Kollin, Susan. *Captivating Westerns: The Middle East in the American West*. Postwestern Horizons. Lincoln: University of Nebraska Press, 2015.

Kracauer, Siegfried. *From Caligari to Hitler: A Psychological History of the German film*. New York: Noonday Press, 1959.

Krupat, Arnold. *For Those Who Come After: A Study of Native American Autobiography*. Berkeley CA: University of California Press, 1989.

Kurth, Peter. *Isadora: A Sensational Life*. Boston: Little, Brown, 2001.

La Flesche, Francis. *The Middle Five: Indian Schoolboys of the Omaha Tribe*. 1900; reprint ed. Lincoln: University of Nebraska Press, 1978.

Laban, Rudolf von. *Choreutics*. Edited by Lisa Ullmann. London: Macdonald and Evans, 1966.

Lanza, Joseph. *Phallic Frenzy: Ken Russell and His Films*. Chicago: Chicago Review, 2007.

Lawrence, D. H. *Studies in Classic American Literature*. 1923; reprint ed. New York: Penguin, 1977.

Lee, Hermione. *Willa Cather: A Life Saved Up*. London: Virago, 1989.

Leiter, Samuel L. Introduction to *A Kabuki Reader: History and Performance*, edited by Samuel L. Leiter, xix–xxxii. Armonk NY: M. E. Sharpe, 2002.

Levin, Joanna. *Bohemia in America, 1858–1920*. Stanford CA: Stanford University Press, 2010.

Lewis, Meriwether, and William Clark. *The Journals of Lewis and Clark 1804–1806*. Edited by Bernard DeVoto. 1804; reprint ed. Boston: Houghton Mifflin, 2001.

Lewis, Nathaniel. *Unsettling the Literary West: Authenticity and Authorship*. Lincoln: University of Nebraska Press, 2003.

Lewis, Robert M. *From Traveling Show to Vaudeville: Theatrical Spectacle in America, 1830–1910*. Baltimore MD: Johns Hopkins University Press, 2003.

Lindemann, Marilee. *The Cambridge Companion to Willa Cather*. New York: Cambridge University Press, 2005.

Lindemann, Marilee, ed. *Willa Cather: Queering America*. New York: Columbia University Press, 1999.

Linteau, Paul-André, René Durocher, and Jean-Claude Robert. *Quebec: A History 1867–1929*. Translated by Robert Chodos. Toronto: James Lorimer and Company, 1983.

Lomax, John A., and Alan Lomax, eds. *Cowboys Songs and Other Frontier Ballads*. 1910; reprint ed. New York: Collier, 1986.

Long, Long Lance (see Chief Buffalo Child Long Lance under C).

Lowry, Richard S. *"Littery Man": Mark Twain and Modern Authorship*. New York: Oxford University Press, 1996.

Lutz, Hartmut. "German Indianthusiasm: A Socially Constructed German National(ist) Myth." In *Germans and Indians: Fantasies, Encounters, Projections*, edited by Colin G. Calloway, Gerd Gemünden, and Susanne Santop, 169–70. Lincoln: University of Nebraska Press, 2002.

MacDougall, Allan Ross. "Isadora Duncan and the Artists." In *Isadora Duncan*, edited by Paul David Magriel, 37–53. New York: Holt, 1947.

Magriel, Paul David. Preface to *Isadora Duncan*, edited by Paul David Magriel, i–viii. New York: Holt, 1947.

Mantell-Seidel, Andrea. *Isadora Duncan in the Twenty-First Century: Capturing the Art and Spirit of the Dancer's Legacy*. Jefferson NC: MacFarland and Company, 2016.

Marberry, M. M. *Splendid Poseur: Joaquin Miller—American Poet*. New York: Crowell, 1953.

Mark, Margaret, and Carol S. Pearson. *The Hero and the Outlaw: Building Extraordinary Brands through the Power of Archetypes*. New York: McGraw-Hill, 2001.

Marx, Edward. Introduction to *The American Diary of a Japanese Girl*, edited by Edward Marx and Laura E. Franey, i–xxiii, 1902; reprint ed. Philadelphia: Temple University Press, 2007.

Marx, Edward, and Laura E. Franey, eds. *The American Diary of a Japanese Girl*. 1902; reprint ed. Philadelphia: Temple University Press, 2007.

Marx, Karl, and Friedrich Engels. *The Communist Manifesto*. 1848; reprint ed. New York: Signet, 2011.

May, Karl Friedrich. *My Life and My Efforts*. 1910; reprint ed. Hamburg: Tredition, 2012.

——. *The Oil Prince*. Translated by Herbert Windolf. 1897; reprint ed. Pullman: Washington State University Press, 2003.

——. *The Son of Bear Hunter*. 1892; reprint ed. Liverpool: CTPDC Publishing, 2014.

——. *The Treasure of Silver Lake*. Translated by M. A. Thomas. 1891; reprint ed. Liverpool: CTPDC Publishing, 2014.

——. *Winnetou, the Chief of the Apache*. Translated by M. A. Thomas. Liverpool: CTPDC Publishing, 2014.

May, Karl, and M. A. Thomas. *The Ghost of the Llano Estacado*. 1888; reprint ed. Liverpool: CTPDC Publishing, 2014.

McNenly, Linda Scarangella. *Native Performers in Wild West Shows: From Buffalo Bill to Euro Disney*. Norman: University of Oklahoma Press, 2012.

Messent, Peter. Foreword to Mark Twain, *The American Claimant*, 1–15. 1892; reprint ed. New York: Oxford University Press, 1992.

Micco, Melinda. "Tribal Re-Creations: Buffalo Child Long Lance and Black Seminole Narratives." In *Re-Placing America: Conversations and Contestations: Selected Essays*, edited by Ruth Hsu, Cynthia G. Franklin, and Suzanne Kosanke, 74–81. Honolulu: University of Hawai'i Press, 2000.

Miller, Joaquin. *Life Amongst the Modocs: An Unwritten History*. 1873; reprint ed. San Jose CA: Orion Press, 1987.

Miller, Joaquin, and Yone Noguchi. *Japan of Sword and Love*. Tokyo: Kanao Bunyendo, 1905.

Miller, Nathan. *Theodore Roosevelt: A Life*. New York: William Morrow and Company, 1992.

Millman, Debbie. *Brand Thinking and Other Noble Pursuits*. New York: Allworth Press, 2011.

Montoya, María E. *Translating Property: The Maxwell Land Grant and the Conflict over Land in the American West, 1840–1900*. Berkeley: University of California Press, 2002.

Modjeska, Helena. *Memories and Impressions of Helena Modjeska: An Autobiography*. 1910; reprint ed. New York: Benjamin Blom, 1969.

Moogk, Peter N. *La Nouvelle France: The Making of French Canada: A Cultural History*. East Lansing: Michigan State University Press, 2000.

Moore, James Gregory. *King of the Fortieth Parallel: Discovery in the American West*. Stanford: Stanford University Press, 1006.

Morrison, Toni. *Playing in the Dark: Whiteness and the Literary Imagination*. New York: Vintage Books, 1992.

Mowry, Sylvester. *Memoir of the Proposed Territory of Arizona*. Joseph Meredith Toner Collection. Washington DC: Henry Polkinhorn, 1857.

Muir, John. "The Wild Parks and Forest Reservations of the West." In *Our National Parks*, 1–18. 1901; reprint ed. San Francisco: John Muir Library, Sierra Club Books, 1991.

Naerebout, Frederick. "In Search of a Dead Rat: The Reception of Ancient Greek Dance in Late Nineteenth-Century Europe and America." In *The Ancient Dancer in the Modern World: Responses to Greek and Roman Dance*, edited by Fiona Macintosh, 39–56. Oxford: Oxford University Press, 2012.

Nanney, Lisa. *John Dos Passos*. Chapel Hill: University of North Carolina Press, 1998.

Nash, Roderick. *Wilderness and the American Mind*. 1967; reprint ed. New Haven CT: Yale University Press, 1982.

Nelson, Robert James. *Willa Cather and France: In Search of the Lost Language*. Urbana: University of Illinois Press, 1988.

Niven, William John. *Hitler and Film: The Führer's Hidden Passion*. New Haven CT: Yale University Press, 2018.

Noguchi, Yone. *From the Eastern Sea*. Tokyo: Fuzanbō, Urajinbō-chō, Kanda, 1905.

———. *The Ganges Calls Me*. Tokyo: Kyobunkwan, 1938.

———. *Hiroshige and Japanese Landscapes*. Tokyo: Board of Tourist Industry, 1934.

———. *Later Essays*. Edited by Edward Marx. 1936; reprint ed. San Bernardino: Botchan Books, 2013.

——. "The Region Beyond the Torii: An Apology." In *Later Essays*, edited by
Edward Marx, 46–59. 1936; reprint ed. San Bernardino: Botchan Books, 2013.

——. *The Story of Yone Noguchi*. Philadelphia: George W. Jacobs and Company,
1915.

——. *The Voice of the Valley*. San Francisco: William Doxey, 1897.

Noguchi, Yone, and Gelett Burgess. Introduction to *Seen and Unseen; or Monologues of a Homeless Snail*, i–vii. 1897; reprint ed. New York: Orientalia, 1920.

Noguchi, Yone, and Inazo Nitob. Introduction to *From the Eastern Sea*, 1–3. Tokyo:
Fuzanbō, Urajinbō-chō, Kanda, 1905.

Noguchi, Yone, and Yoshinobu Hakutani. Introduction to *Selected Writings of Yone
Noguchi: An East-West Literary Assimilation*, edited by Yoshinobu Hakutani,
vol. 1, 1–25. Rutherford NJ: Fairleigh Dickinson University Press, 1990.

Nordhoff, Charles. *California: For Health, Pleasure, and Residence*. New York:
Harper and Brothers, 1875.

O'Brien, Sharon. *Willa Cather: The Emerging Voice*. New York: Oxford University
Press, 1987.

O'Grady, John P. *Pilgrims to the Wild: Everett Ruess, Henry David Thoreau, John Muir,
Clarence King, Mary Austin*. Salt Lake City: University of Utah Press, 1993.

Orvell, Miles. *The Real Thing: Imitation and Authenticity in American Culture,
1880–1940*. Cultural Studies of the United States. Chapel Hill: University of
North Carolina Press, 1989.

O'Sullivan, Timothy H. *Timothy H. O'Sullivan: The King Survey Photographs*.
Edited by Keith F. Davis, Jane Lee Aspinwall, and François Brunet. New
Haven CT: Yale University Press, 2011.

Palmer, Howard. Preface to *The Settlement of the West*, i–ix. Calgary AB: University of Calgary Press–Comprint Publishing, 1977.

Parkman, Francis Jr. *The Oregon Trail*. Edited by David Levin. 1849; reprint ed.
New York: Penguin, 1983.

Parry, Albert. *Garrets and Pretenders: A History of Bohemianism in America*. 1933;
reprint ed. New York: Dover, 1960.

Payne, Theodore. "Thomas Payne in His Own Words: A Voice for California
Native Plants: A Collection of Memoirs in Three Sections." In *Life on the
Modjeska Ranch in the Gay Nineties*, 13–75. 1962; reprint ed. Pasadena CA:
Many Moons Press, 2004.

Perry, Nicole. "Reconsidering Winnetou: Karl May Film Adaptations and Contemporary Indigenous Responses." In *New Wests and Post-Wests: Literature
and Film of the American West*, edited by Paul Varner, 215–37. Newcastle, UK:
Cambridge Scholars, 2013.

Pike, Zebulon Montgomery. *The Expeditions of Zebulon Montgomery Pike*. Vol. 1.
Edited by Elliott Coues. 1810; reprint ed. New York: Dover, 1987.

Polatynska, Catharina, and Joanna Polatynska. "The Diogenes Club: A Few Words about Theatres in Warsaw or Where Sang Irene Adler," November 21, 2000. http://www.diogenes-club.com.

Porter, David H. *On the Divide: The Many Lives of Willa Cather*. Lincoln: University of Nebraska Press, 2008.

Posner, Richard A. *Law and Literature*. 3rd ed. Cambridge MA: Harvard University Press, 2009.

Powell, Donald Moore. *The Peralta Grant: James Addison Reavis and the Barony of Arizona*. Norman: University of Oklahoma Press, 1960.

Pratt, Richard Henry. *Battlefield and Classroom: Four Decades with the American Indian, 1867–1904*. 1923; reprint ed. New Haven CT: Yale University Press, 1964.

Putney, Clifford. *Muscular Christianity: Manhood and Sports in Protestant America, 1880–1920*. Cambridge MA: Harvard University Press, 2001.

Rabasa, José. *Inventing America: Spanish Historiography and the Formation of Eurocentrism*. Norman: University of Oklahoma Press, 1994.

Raheja, Michelle H., ed. *Reservation Reelism: Redfacing, Visual Sovereignty, and Representations of Native Americans in Film*. Lincoln: University of Nebraska Press, 2010.

Reisz, Karel. *Isadora*. Universal Pictures, 1968.

Reynolds, Guy. *Willa Cather in Context: Progress, Race, Empire*. New York: St. Martin's Press, 1996.

Rhodehamel, Josephine DeWitt, and Raymund F. Wood. *Ina Coolbrith: Librarian and Laureate of California*. Salt Lake City: Brigham Young University Press, 1973.

Richtman, Jack. *Adrienne Lecouvreur: The Actress and the Age*. Englewood Cliffs NJ: Prentice-Hall, 1971.

Roberts, Peter. *The New Immigration: A Study of the Industrial and Social Life of Southeastern Europeans in America*. New York: Arno Press, 1970.

Romaine, Suzanne. *Bilingualism*. 2nd ed. Oxford: Blackwell, 1995.

Roosevelt, Theodore. *Ranch Life and the Hunting-Trail*. 1888; reprint ed. Lincoln: University of Nebraska Press, 1983.

———. *The Winning of the West: From the Alleghanies to the Mississippi, 1769–1776*. Vol. 1. 1889; reprint ed. Lincoln: University of Nebraska Press, 1995.

Rosenthal, Caroline, and Stefanie Schäfer, *Fake Identity? The Impostor Narrative in Native American Culture*. Chicago: University of Chicago Press, 2014.

Rosowski, Susan J. *The Voyage Perilous: Willa Cather's Romanticism*. Lincoln: University of Nebraska Press, 1986.

Rourke, Constance. *Troupers of the Gold Coast, or the Rise of Lotta Crabtree*. New York: Harcourt, Brace and Company, 1928.

Ruthven, Kenneth Knowles. *Faking Literature*. Cambridge: Cambridge University Press, 2001.

Sachs, Aaron. *The Humboldt Current: Nineteenth-Century Exploration and the Roots of American Environmentalism*. New York: Vintage, 2006.

Sailor, Rachel. "'You Must Become Dreamy': Complicating Japanese-American Pictorialism and the Early Twentieth-Century Regional West." *European Journal of American Studies* 9, no. 3 (2014): 1–16.

Sam Fuller. *The Baron of Arizona*. DVD. Los Angeles: Lippert Pictures, 1950.

Sammons, Jeffrey L. *Ideology, Mimesis, Fantasy*. Chapel Hill: University of North Carolina Press, 1998.

Sandburg, Carl. *The Complete Poems of Carl Sandburg*. New York: Houghton Mifflin Harcourt, 1970.

———. *Cornhuskers*. New York: Henry Holt, 1918.

Sandburg, Carl, ed. *The American Songbag*. New York: Harcourt, Brace 1927.

Sandweiss, Martha A. *Passing Strange: A Gilded Age Tale of Love and Deception across the Color Line*. 2009; reprint ed. New York: Penguin, 2010.

———. *Print the Legend: Photography and the American West*. Yale Western Americana Series. New Haven CT: Yale University Press, 2004.

Santino, Jack. *Miles of Smiles, Years of Struggle: Stories of Black Pullman Porters*. Urbana: University of Illinois Press, 1989.

Sayer, Derek. *The Coasts of Bohemia: A Czech History*. Translated by Alena Sayer. Princeton NJ: Princeton University Press, 1998.

Scheiner, Seth M. *Negro Mecca: A History of the Negro in New York City, 1865–1920*. New York: New York University Press, 1965.

Schmidt, Helmut. *Karl May*. Meisenheim: Verlag Anton Hain, 1979.

Schneider, Tassilo. "Finding a New Heimat in the Wild West: Karl May and the German Westerns of the 1960s." *Journal of Film and Video* 47, no. 3 (1995): 50–66.

Scott, A. C. *The Kabuki Theatre of Japan*. London: Allen and Unwin, 1955.

Scribe, Eugène, and Ernest Legouvé. *Adrienne Lecouvreur: A Play in Five Acts*. Edited by H. Herman. London: Samuel French, 1880.

Sergeant, Elizabeth Shepley. *Willa Cather: A Memoir*. Philadelphia: J. P. Lippincott, 1953.

Shaw, Patrick W. *Willa Cather and the Art of Conflict: Re-Visioning Her Creative Imagination*. Troy NY: Whitston, 1992.

Shively, James R., ed. *Writings from Willa Cather's Campus Years*. Lincoln: University of Nebraska Press, 1950.

Sienkiewicz, Henryk, and Peter J. Obst. *Henryk Sienkiewicz: Three Stories*. 1876; reprint ed. Rockville MD: Wildside Press, 2013.

Sinclair, Upton. *Between Two Worlds*. New York: Viking, 1941.

———. *World's End*. 1940; reprint ed. New York: Viking, 1943.

Slote, Bernice, ed. *The Kingdom of Art: Willa Cather's First Principles and Critical Statements, 1893-1896*. Lincoln: University of Nebraska Press, 1966.

Slotkin, Richard. *Gunfighter Nation: The Myth of the Frontier in Twentieth-Century America*. New York: Harper Collins, 1992.

Smith, Donald B. *Chief Buffalo Child Long Lance: The Glorious Impostor*. Red Deer, Alberta: Red Deer Press, 1999.

Smith, Michael L. *Pacific Visions: California Scientists and the Environment, 1850-1915*. New Haven CT: Yale University Press, 1987.

Smith, Tyler Jo. "Reception or Deception? Approaching Greek Dance through Vase-Painting." In *The Ancient Dancer in the Modern World: Responses to Greek and Roman Dance*, edited by Fiona Macintosh, 77-98. Oxford: Oxford University Press, 2012.

Sontag, Susan. *In America*. 1999; reprint ed. New York: Picador, 2000.

Standing Bear, Luther. *My Indian Boyhood*. 1931; reprint ed. Lincoln: University of Nebraska Press, 2006.

Starr, Kevin. *Americans and the California Dream, 1850-1915*. New York: Oxford University Press, 1973.

———. *Inventing the Dream: California through the Progressive Era*. New York: Oxford University Press, 1985.

Stokes, Sewell. *Isadora Duncan: An Intimate Portrait*. London: Brentan's, 1928.

Sueyoshi, Amy Haruko. *Discriminating Sex: White Leisure and the Making of the American "Oriental."* Urbana: University of Illinois Press, 2018.

—. *Queer Compulsions: Race, Nation, and Sexuality in the Affairs of Yone Noguchi*. Honolulu: University of Hawai'i Press, 2012.

Tamai, Lily Anne Y. Welty, Ingrid Dineen-Wimberly, and Paul R Spickard, eds. *Shape Shifters: Journeys across Terrains of Race and Identity*. Lincoln: University of Nebraska Press, 2020.

Taylor, Diana. *The Archive and the Repertoire: Performing Cultural Memory in the Americas*. Durham NC: Duke University Press, 2003.

Tegel, Susan. *Nazis and the Cinema*. London: Hambledon Continuum, 2007.

Terry, Walter. *Isadora Duncan: Her Life, Her Art, Her Legacy*. New York: Dodd, Mead, 1963.

Theweleit, Klaus. *Male Fantasies*, Vol. 1: *Women, Floods, Bodies, History*. Translated by Stephen Conway. Minneapolis: University of Minnesota Press, 1987.

———. *Male Fantasies*, Vol. 2: *Male Bodies: Psychoanalyzing the White Terror*. Translated by Erica Carter and Chris Turner. Minneapolis: University of Minnesota Press, 1989.

Thorpe, Edward. *Creating a Ballet: MacMillan's Isadora*. London: Evans Brothers, 1981.

Tompkins, Jane P. *West of Everything: The Inner Life of Westerns*. New York: Oxford University Press, 1992.

Trachtenberg, Alan. *The Incorporation of America: Culture and Society in the Gilded Age*. New York: Hill and Wang, 1982.

Trafzer, Clifford E., Jean A. Keller, and Lorene Sisquoc, eds. *Boarding School Blues: Revisiting American Indian Educational Experiences*. Lincoln: University of Nebraska Press, 2006.

Trzcinski, Zigmunt. *Peralta Land Grant Mystery: Saga of Fraud*. New York: iUniverse, 2004.

Turner, Frederick Jackson. "The Significance of the Frontier in American History." In *Rereading Frederick Jackson Turner: "The Significance of the Frontier in American History" and Other Essays*, edited by John Mack Faragher, 11–30. 1893; reprint ed. New York: Henry Holt, 1994.

Twain, Mark. *Roughing It*. Edited by Franklin R. Rogers and Paul Baender. 1872; reprint, Iowa-California ed., Berkeley: University of California Press, 1973.

———. *The Stolen White Elephant, Etc*. Boston: James R. Osgood and Company, 1882.

Umiker-Sebeok, Donna Jean, and Thomas A. Sebeok, eds. *Aboriginal Sign Languages of the Americas and Australia*. Vols. 1–2. New York: Plenum Press, 1978.

Urgo, Joseph, R. "The Cather Thesis: The American Empire of Migration." In *The Cambridge Companion to Willa Cather*, edited by Marilee Lindemann, 35–50. New York: Cambridge University Press, 2005.

———. *Willa Cather and the Myth of American Migration*. Champaign: University of Illinois Press, 1995.

Van Kirk, Sylvia. *Many Tender Ties: Women in Fur-Trade Society, 1670–1870*. Norman: University of Oklahoma Press, 1983.

Van Noy, Rick. *Surveying the Interior: Literary Cartographers and the Sense of Place*. Reno: University of Nevada Press, 2003.

Vance, Norman. *The Sinews of the Spirit: The Ideal of Christian Manliness in Victorian Literature and Religious Thought*. Cambridge: Cambridge University Press, 1985.

Vestal, Stanley. "The Hollywooden Indian." In *The Pretend Indians: Images of Native Americans in the Movies*, edited by Gretchen M. Bataille and Charles L. P. Silet. Ames: Iowa State University Press, 1980.

Walther, Klaus. *Karl May*. München: Deutscher Taschenbuch Verlag, 2002.

Wanshel, Jeff. *Isadora Duncan Sleeps With the Russian Navy*. New York: Dramatists Play Service, 1977.

Warren, Louis S. *Buffalo Bill's America: William Cody and the Wild West Show*. New York: Alfred A. Knopf, 2005.

Wernitznig, Dagmar. *Europe's Indians, Indians in Europe: European Perceptions and Appropriations of Native American Cultures from Pocahontas to the Present*. Lanham MD: University Press of America, 2007.

West, Nathanael. *A Cool Million and The Dream Life of Balso Snell*. 1931, 1934; reprint ed. New York: Farrar, Straus and Giroux, 2006.

———. *Miss Lonelyhearts and The Day of the Locust*. 1933, 1939; reprint ed. New York: New Directions, 1969.

White, G. Edward. *The Eastern Establishment and the Western Experience: The West of Frederic Remington, Theodore Roosevelt, and Owen Wister*. 1968; reprint ed. Austin: University of Texas Press, 1989.

White, Richard. *"It's Your Misfortune and None of My Own": A New History of the American West*. Norman: University of Oklahoma Press, 1993.

Wilkins, Thurman. *Clarence King: A Biography*. New York: Macmillan, 1958.

Wilson, Robert. *The Explorer King: Adventure, Science, and the Great Diamond Hoax—Clarence King in the Old West*. New York: Scribner, 2006.

Winchester, Simon. *A Crack in the Edge of the World: America and the Great California Earthquake of 1906*. New York: Viking, 2005.

Wong, Hertha Dawn. *Sending My Heart Back across the Years: Tradition and Innovation in Native American Autobiography*. New York: Oxford University Press, 1992.

Woodress, James Leslie. *Willa Cather: Her Life and Art*. New York: Pegasus, 1970.

Woodruff, James. "Historical Essay." In *My Ántonia*, Willa Cather, 361–91. Edited by Charles W. Mignon and Kari Ronning. 1918; reprint ed., Willa Cather Scholarly Edition, Lincoln: University of Nebraska Press, 1997.

Wyatt, David. *The Fall into Eden: Landscape and Imagination in California*. Cambridge Studies in American Literature and Culture. Cambridge, UK: Cambridge University Press, 1986.

———. *Five Fires: Race, Catastrophe, and the Shaping of California*. Reading MA: Addison-Wesley, 1997.

Yagoda, Ben. *Will Rogers: A Biography*. Norman: University of Oklahoma Press, 1993.

Zitkala-Sa. *American Indian Stories, Legends, and Other Writings*. 1921; reprint ed. New York: Penguin, 2003.

# Index

abstraction: in Japanese art, 99
Adams, Andy, 56
Adams, Henry, 26, 164n7
*Adrienne Lecouvreur* (play), 109, 111–13
*The Adventures of Huckleberry Finn*
    (Twain), 129
*Adverse Report of the Surveyor General*
    (Johnson), 36–37
Africanist presence in American liter-
    ature, 32
agricultural communes, 108, 109–11,
    113–14, 116–17
Alberta, Canada, 66
*Alias Will James* (film), 60–61
alienation, 19, 79, 160n28
Alta California, 34
alternative communities. *See*
    communes
*The American Claimant* (Twain), 44
*The American Cowboy* (James), 53, 60
*The American Diary of a Japanese Girl*
    (Noguchi), 93, 100–104
American industry, 19
*Americanization* (Dixon), 90
American West: alternative communi-
    ties in, 110; and Bohemian immi-
    grants, 91; and Clarence King,
    22–23, 158; and cultural appropri-
    ation, 157; and erasure, 32, 134–35;
    and geological exploration, 28–29;
    and Helena Modjeska, 112, 116;
    and Hollywood westerns, 54, 60;

and Japan, 95–96; and Karl May,
    126–29, 131–32; and modernist
    writers, 18–20; and Nazi ideology,
    134–35; as "real," 7; realistic repre-
    sentations of, 49; San Francisco as
    cultural capital of, 93–94; in serial
    fiction, 64; as site of contestation,
    45–47; and Theodore Roosevelt,
    6–8, 159n1; and Willa Cather, 79–
    80, 99; and Will James, 51–52. *See
    also* U.S. frontier
Anaheim CA, 108, 110–11
"Ancient Ruins in the Cañon de
    Chelle, New Mexico Territory,
    1873" (O'Sullivan), 28
Anglo-Japanese Alliance, 103
Anglo-Saxons, 1, 43–44, 134
anti-Semitic comedies, 135
Apaches, 39, 44–45
appropriation, 142, 146, 157–58
archives, 34–36, 39, 44, 46
Arden, 113–14, 125
Arizona, 34–44, 46
arrested gesture, 141, 147
Art Nouveau, 180n11
Asia, trade with, 96, 143
Asian immigrants, 96
*As You Like It* (Shakespeare), 114,
    120, 125
Atherton, Gertrude, 96
Austin, Mary, 20
authenticity, 19, 58, 61

201

and Polish exiles, 107–9; and San Francisco, 93–98, 101, 111–13, 116, 121, 145; and Yone Noguchi, 95

California Theatre, 111–12

Campbell, Joseph, 180n33

Canada, 49–51, 54, 57, 66–67, 70, 72, 77, 167n1

Canadian Expeditionary Force, 66

capitalism, 47, 96, 143

*Carlisle Arrow* (newspaper), 64

Carlisle Indian Industrial School, 63–66, 69–70, 169n2

Carnegie, Andrew, 81

Carson City NE, 53

catastrophism, 25, 28

"Catastrophism and Evolution" (King), 25

Cather, Willa, 77–92; on Bohemia, 81; "The Bohemian Girl," 81–85, 159–60n16; and bohemian sensibility of, 78; early fiction of, 78; early life of, 78; and ethnic characters in fiction, 82–83; Evelyn I. Funda on, 171n6; and fictional account of Helena Modjeska, 114–15, 120; and gender norms, 78, 80; and Joseph Urgo, 161n30, 173n50; *Lucy Gayheart*, 91–92; as modernist, 19; *My Ántonia*, 5, 7, 87–91, 99, 159n16, 171n8, 176n23; *My Mortal Enemy*, 91, 114–15; in New York City, 84–85; not writing about Bohemian immigrants and artists, 91–92; *One of Ours*, 91; *O Pioneers!*, 85–87; in Pittsburgh, 80–81; *The Professor's House*, 91; *The Song of the Lark*, 173n49; and Susan Sontag's plagiarizing, 118–19; "The White Mulberry Tree," 85; and W. T. Benda, 176n23; on Yone Noguchi's poetry, 93, 99

Catholicism: and Quebec's population, 50; and Spanish law, 43

cattle, 51, 53, 55–58

*Cattle Brands* (Adams), 56

*cedulas*, 36

Central Europeans, 78. *See also* Bohemians/bohemians

Certeau, Michel de, 160n28

certifications, 40

Chandler, Raymond, 18

Chaplowski, Karol, 108

"Characteristic Ruin of the Pueblo San Juan, New Mexico, 1874" (O'Sullivan), 28

Cherokee tribe, 63–66

Chicago Columbian Exposition, 120–21

Chief Buffalo Child Long Lance. *See* Long, Sylvester

*Chief Buffalo Long Lance* (Long), 66–74

Chief Chauncey Yellow Robe, 70–71

children's literature, 49

Christianity, 23–24, 83, 104, 143

*Chronicle* (newspaper), 112

cities, 50, 84. *See also* San Francisco CA

civilization and savagery, 22, 144

Civil War, 34, 35, 165n30

Clappe, Louise, 3

"Clarence King on Rope, Uinta Mountains, Utah, 1869" (Russell), 24

Clark, William, 2

class, 22–23, 27, 30, 42, 47, 151–52

Clemens, Samuel. *See* Twain, Mark

Cocteau, Jean, 152

code-switching, 52

collage technique, 150

collective consciousness, 7, 127

colloquial style, 18, 117

colonization, 6, 43, 91, 134–35

comedies, 135, 137

King, Clarence, 21–32; and Ada Copeland, 21–23, 26–27, 31–32, 164n4;
"Catastrophism and Evolution,"
25; death of, 30–32; early life of, 23;
and Fortieth Parallel, 21, 28–29;
and gentlemen's clubs, 21–22,
161n31; as geological surveyor,
22–25, 28–30; and Great Diamond
Hoax, 21–22; and James Addison
Reavis, 33; and mountain climbing,
24; *Mountaineering in the Sierra
Nevada*, 7, 21–25, 27, 29–30, 32; and
national park system, 27–28; and
New York City, 22, 27, 161n32; and
passage of time, 158; and passing, 22–23, 24–25, 27, 30, 31; and
posthumous exile, 31; and race
and geography, 29–30; reconciling
Darwinism with Christian faith,
22–23; *Systematic Geology*, 7, 25,
30–31; and Toni Morrison's study
of blackness, 32; visibility of, 30;
and women of color, 26–27, 31; and
Yone Noguchi, 100
Kraków, Poland, 108–9, 122

Laban, Rudolf, 144–45
Labanotation, 144, 180n33
land grant fraud. *See* Reavis, James
Addison
*The Land of Little Rain* (Austin), 20
landowners, 39, 42–43
language, 51–52, 56, 57–58, 61, 71–73,
75, 88
La Réunion TX, 110
*Lark* (magazine), 98
Lawrence, D. H., 129
"Lectures on the Philosophy of World
History" (Hegel), 129
Lee, Ellen, 118

Lewis, Edith, 84
Lewis, Meriwether, 2
*Library* (journal), 80
Libuša, legend of, 171n8
*Life Amongst the Modocs* (Miller), 98
*The Life and Adventures of James P.
Beckwourth* (Beckwourth and
Bonner), 4
*Life on the Modjeska Ranch in the Gay
Nineties* (Payne), 114
"Limestone, near Ruby Valley, East
Humboldt Mountains, Nevada,
1868" (O'Sullivan), 28
Lindeman, Marilee, 79, 171n9
literary modernism, 18–20, 148
literary realism, 6–10, 49
literature, 18–19, 20, 26, 32, 130–31, 136
livestock associations, 56
*Lone Cowboy* (James), 49, 51–61
Long, Sylvester, 63–76; in Alberta, 66;
autobiography, 66–74; in British
Columbia, 66–67; at Carlisle
school, 64–66; *Chief Buffalo Long
Lance*, 66–74; as Chief Buffalo
Long Lance, 66–70, 72–74; and
criticism of Blackfoot tribe, 73–74;
death of, 76; early life of, 63, 77;
and Frederick Jackson Turner, 63–
64; *How to Talk in the Indian Sign
Language*, 73; physicality of, 74–75;
and sign language, 73; in *The Silent
Enemy*, 70–71, 74–76; Stanley Ves-
tal on, 75; "The Story of Carlisle
Indian Military School," 65; and
success as a performer, 71–72
Los Angeles CA, 60–61, 122
Los Angeles County Poor Farm, 47
Louisiana Purchase, 2
Louis XII (King), 50
"The Luck of Roaring Camp" (Harte), 8

and Five Civilized Tribes, 29; as
immigrants to the West, 43; and
notion of stereotypical Indian, 71–
76; and rapid development of U.S.
frontier, 77; and westerns, 128; and
women of color, 22
Wilde, Oscar, 79
wilderness, 125–28, 132, 140, 164n7
Wild West shows, 63–64, 168–69n2
Williams, Kenneth, 74
Willing, George, 35–36, 166n10
*Winnetou* (May), 127–29, 131–32, 134,
  136–37, 177n7, 179n50
*The Winning of the West* (Roosevelt), 8,
  160n18
*A Winter's Tale* (Shakespeare), 81
"Witches' Rock, Echo Canyon, Utah,
  1869" (O'Sullivan), 28

women: of color, 22, 24–27, 31; in Jap-
  anese theater, 103; and romantic
  melodramas, 136; and stereotypes
  of Japanese, 102; in Willa Cather's
  fiction, 78, 87–88
*World's End* (Sinclair), 148
World War I, 54, 91
World War II, 133–34, 137–38
writers, 2–8, 18–20, 26, 147–48. *See also*
  Cather, Willa; James, Will; King,
  Clarence; May, Karl; Noguchi,
  Yone

Yagoda, Ben, 162n48
Yarō Kabuki, 103
Yosemite, 100
Young Men's Christian Association
  (YMCA), 143